BLACK FAMILIES IN CRISIS
The Middle Class

Edited by

Alice F. Coner-Edwards, D.S.W.

and

Jeanne Spurlock, M.D.

BRUNNER/MAZEL, *Publishers* • New York

Library of Congress Cataloging-in-Publication Data

Black families in crisis : the middle class / edited by Alice F. Coner-
Edwards and Jeanne Spurlock.
   p.   cm.
  Includes bibliographies and index.
  ISBN 0-87630-524-9
  1. Afro-American families. 2. Afro-Americans—Social
conditions—1975- 3. United States—Social conditions—1980-
4. Middle classes—United States. I. Coner-Edwards, Alice F.
II. Spurlock, Jeanne.
  [DNLM: 1. Blacks. 2. Family. 3. Mental Health. 4. Social Class.
WA 305 B627]
E185.86.B5254 1988
305.8'96073—dc19
DNLM/DLC
for Library of Congress   88–14642
                                          CIP

Copyright © 1988 by Alice F. Coner-Edwards and Jeanne Spurlock

Published by
BRUNNER/MAZEL, INC.
19 Union Square
New York, New York 10003

MANUFACTURED IN THE UNITED STATES OF AMERICA

10 9 8 7 6 5 4 3 2

Foreword

Black people share some genetic relationship to ancestors in Africa, but diverse mixtures of racial and cultural characteristics from other sources also occur among them. After humanity spread around the earth and differentiated into various racial and cultural groups, Blacks in Africa were left with hundreds of different cultures and languages. Migration, trading, colonization, the slave trade, and population expansion left African Blacks interacting with the diverse cultures and races of many non-African people around the earth. Well over 100 million people of African descent now live in the Americas, and only 27% of these are in the United States.

Historically, the most severely stigmatized people within the United States have been enslaved Blacks and their descendants, who were stripped of prior cultures and pressed to develop only those cultural characteristics that fitted the derogatory stereotypes applied by Whites to Blacks.

During the slavery experience of Blacks in the United States, approximately 10% of Blacks had free status and were less oppressed and less stigmatized. For many generations, opportunity for higher status among enslaved and segregated Blacks in the United States depended on proximity to Whites and opportunities for some mutual identification. In some instances better status and opportunity were linked to similarities to Whites in appearance, education, occupation, or lifestyle. Different ideologies and political philosophies commonly have been represented in Black middle-class America, depending on their identification and on forces influencing them.

In the 19th and 20th centuries, gradual, ongoing improvements in opportunities for Blacks in the United States were accelerated by a series of historical events. Emancipation from slavery and a succession of wars in American, European, Pacific, Korean, and Vietnamese theaters provided American Blacks with some expansion of roles and some increase in benefits and respect. Through successive waves of migration from the South to the North and West and from rural to

iii

urban settings, more dynamic interactions between Black and White people became possible in areas of increased opportunity.

Following Civil Rights movements between 1954 and 1972, a dramatic increase occurred in opportunities for more sociopolitical activity, more education, better jobs, and better housing. Jobs in professions, in government, in educational systems, in industries, and in businesses large and small, and opportunities for artists, writers, and musicians and for ownership of small businesses and property, also dramatically increased. A wave of Blacks entered educational, occupational, political, and social systems from which they had been excluded. Doors that opened for previously excluded Blacks became the doors through which all excluded minorities competitively squeezed. Additional waves of Black people from Caribbean and Central and South American countries entered the United States to compete for the additional opportunities.

Black students in colleges and universities increased 30- to 40-fold. The number of Black mayors of cities increased from two to more than 200. Black homeowners, professionals, government workers, artists, writers, and musicians, and higher-income Blacks in industry, business, trades, and professional athletics, also escalated in number.

The lot and lifestyle of many more Black families shifted toward middle-class status during the 1970s and 1980s. This book focuses on some of the characteristics, experiences, dynamics, accomplishments, and problems of Black families in the expanded Black middle class. While focusing on this significant influential segment of Black people in the United States, it does not lose sight of that larger segment of Blacks who are still trapped in poverty and oppression.

In fact, long-standing oppression, poverty, and deprivation continue to affect the psychology, role relationships, and behavior of many Blacks who achieve middle-class status. These effects may be deeply embedded, outside of awareness, and unknowingly transmitted behaviorally from generation to generation and via interactions with peers. Negative self-images, serious role conflicts, and self-defeating behaviors often have such roots. Large numbers of middle-class Blacks unknowingly carry around these effects of oppression as an internalized source of stress experienced more frequently and more intensely by Blacks than by non-Blacks in this country. These internalized negative effects of oppression tend to be more serious in Black descendants of slaves in the United States than in Blacks from the Caribbean and from Central and South America. Several chapters in this book deal with unique biological, psychological, sociocultural, and historical factors that influence stress and crises in Black middle-class families in ways quite different from the experiences of other groups.

Readers are advised to be vigilant in several ways. There is neither a single meaning nor homogeneity to what is embraced by the term *Black middle-class.* Certainly income, occupation, education, lifestyle, value orientation, family history and other criteria may be used to define subgroups among Black middle-class families. Each Black middle-class family has multiple sources, and each represents a unique mixture of racial, historical, and cultural heritages. Multiple authors provide balance and a variety in perspectives. Keep in mind that no family exists in a static state and that family stability can exist only for relatively brief periods as each family constantly evolves through the dynamic interaction of influences and events within and outside the family.

All too often images and thoughts of middle-class Blacks are omitted from discussions of "Blacks," "the Black community," and "inner-city Blacks" despite the fact that many middle-class Blacks exist among all three. This book makes a contribution toward a more diversified and less stereotypical view.

This foreword would be incomplete without reference to the late Walter Bradshaw, M.D., the remarkable man to whom the book is dedicated. I had the privilege of working on several projects under his inspiring, clear-thinking, effective, soft-spoken, and calming leadership. Whether he was developing a cross-cultural psychiatry training curriculum, organizing a large conference, conducting an American Psychiatric Association course on mental health services to Black populations, or directing attention of American and South African psychiatrists to serious problems in South Africa's mental health services to Black patients, his clear understanding and his vision of what needed to be done were anchored in integrity, principles, and actions that were greatly enriched by Walter as he practiced medicine and psychiatry with the concerns and values of a minister.

Walter Bradshaw would have been a high-class person in any of the world's societies. Here he was classified as a middle-class Black American.

Charles A. Pinderhughes, M.D.
Boston University School of Medicine

Contents

Contents

Acknowledgments

We would like to acknowledge the many individuals whose genuine support, encouragement, and dedicated work made this volume a reality.

Grateful acknowledgment is offered to Rabiah and Kahlil Abdullah, whose objective and detailed reading of each page of the manuscripts helped to achieve clarity in each contribution to this volume.

We also thank the staff of the Office of Minority/National Affairs of the American Psychiatric Association. Special thanks are extended to Linda Roll, Janice Taylor, Rosely Stanich, and Nora Vasquez for their able assistance and untiring support. We acknowledge the support of Donna Green of Family and Medical Counseling Service, and thank her for her many efforts. We wish to recognize and thank librarians Zing Jung and Susan Heffner, from the American Psychiatric Association, for their patience and assistance in helping us locate and substantiate many references. Kenyetta Coner deserves special thanks for her patience throughout the development of this volume.

Both of us are deeply indebted to our respective mentors and teachers, who are too numerous to mention in this limited space. We have been inspired by their works, teaching, encouragement, and caring during the course of many years. To them, we will always be grateful.

Finally, we must acknowledge all members of the study group, of which Walter Bradshaw was a charter member. Marilyn Benoit, Martin Booth, Henry Edwards, Frances Rankin, Joan Sealy, and Inez White have been of considerable help in reading manuscripts and providing initial editorial assistance, and in providing material for this volume. In addition, each has made significant contributions to the work during the monthly meetings of the study group, since its inception in 1979.

This acknowledgment would be incomplete without a specific reference to the late Walter Bradshaw, to whom we pay tribute with the development of this volume. Knowing and working with Walter was inspiring for both of us; our continued love and respect for him has ushered us on to the completion of this work.

Alice F. Coner-Edwards
Jeanne Spurlock

Contributors

MARILYN B. BENOIT, M.D., Vice-Chairperson, Department of Psychiatry, Children's Hospital National Medical Center; Assistant Professor, Psychiatry, George Washington University School of Medicine; Clinical Assistant Professor, Psychiatry, Georgetown University School of Medicine

MARTIN B. BOOTH, M.D., Assistant Professor, Psychiatry, Howard University College of Medicine; Director, Child and Adolescent Psychiatry, Liberty Community Mental Health Center, Baltimore, Maryland

ALICE F. CONER-EDWARDS, D.S.W., Private Practice; Vice-President, Kids First, Inc., Washington, D.C.; Assistant Professor, School of Social Work, Virginia Commonwealth University, Richmond, Virginia

WAYMAN B. CUNNINGHAM, M.S., Assistant Professor, Psychiatry, Howard University College of Medicine

RICHARD G. DUDLEY, JR., M.D., Assistant Professor, Psychiatry, New York Medical College; Visiting Professor, Medicine, and Director, Behavioral Science, City University of New York, Medical School at City College

HENRY E. EDWARDS, M.D., Assistant Professor, Psychiatry, Howard University College of Medicine; Associate Member, Baltimore/Washington Institute for Psychoanalysis; Psychiatrist, Bureau of Forensic Psychiatry, D.C. Department of Human Resources

M. JEANETTE ESPY, M.D., Clinical Instructor, Obstetrics-Gynecology, Wayne State University School of Medicine

ADELBERT H. JENKINS, Ph.D., Associate Professor, Psychology, Faculty of Arts & Sciences, New York University

RENEE R. JENKINS, M.D., Associate Professor, Pediatrics & Child Health, Howard University College of Medicine

AUDREYE E. JOHNSON, Ph.D., Associate Professor, School of Social Work, University of North Carolina at Chapel Hill

CLARION E. JOHNSON, M.D., Research and Medical Officer, Evaluation Research Corporation International, Fairfax, Virginia; Assistant Professor, Medicine, Uniformed Services University, E. Edward Herbert School of Medicine

RONALD B. LONESOME, M.D., Director, Bronx Alcoholism Treatment Center; Dean, Black Alcoholism Institute, Howard University School of Social Work

LAURA G. PHILLIPS, B.S., Senior Medical Student, University of South Carolina School of Medicine

CHESTER M. PIERCE, M.D., Professor, Education and Psychiatry in the Faculty of Medicine, Graduate School of Education and Faculty of Public Health, Harvard University

ELAINE B. PINDERHUGHES, M.S.W., Associate Professor, School of Social Work, Boston College

FRANCES E. RANKIN, M.D., Assistant Professor, Psychiatry, Howard University College of Medicine

JEAN WHEELER SMITH, M.D., Private Practice, Clinton, Maryland; Clinical Assistant Professor, Psychiatry, Howard University College of Medicine

RICHARD E. SMITH, M.D., F.A.C.O.G., Director, Adolescent Clinic, Henry Ford Hospital, Detroit; Clinical Assistant Professor, Obstetrics-Gynecology, The University of Michigan Medical School

JEANNE SPURLOCK, M.D., Deputy Medical Director, American Psychiatric Association; Clinical Professor, Psychiatry, George Washington University School of Medicine; Clinical Professor, Psychiatry, Howard University College of Medicine

HARRY H. WRIGHT, M.D., M.B.A., Associate Professor, Psychiatry, University of South Carolina School of Medicine

Preface

The idea for this volume grew out of discussions held by a group of Black psychiatrists based in Washington, D.C., and the responses of a number of colleagues who attended a symposium, Black Families in Crisis, at Howard University Medical Center in November 1985. The symposium was planned by members of the study group (Marilyn Benoit, Martin Booth, Henry Edwards, Frances Rankin, Joan Sealy, Inez White, and the writer) as a tribute to our friend and colleague, the late Walter H. Bradshaw, Jr., who died at the age of 46 on Christmas Eve, 1984.

Walt was an original and central member of the study group, which was organized (in 1979) for the purpose of discussing particular issues that negatively affect the mental health of Black Americans, and helpful therapeutic interventions. Walt consistently inspired and challenged us to think clearly, to search for answers, to examine ourselves, and to share our understanding and findings with others.

Walt was a respected member of a broad psychiatric and psychoanalytic community. His colleagues knew him to be an able administrator (having served as Acting Chairperson of the Department of Psychiatry, Howard University College of Medicine, 1973 to 1974), a skilled clinician, and an able teacher. His stimulating ideas, well-thought-out publications, and demand to search for excellence are a legacy for all of us. The symposium was but one tangible manifestation of that legacy and an expression of our love and a tribute to Walt.

During our monthly meetings we often made reference to the fact that there is so little written about the emotional problems of the Black middle class, and reflected on the notions about the inverse relationship between economic stability and emotional disorders. But our clinical experiences did not support this idea, although it is held by many—professional and lay people alike. In keeping with Walt Bradshaw's plan of action, we developed the symposium as a format to share our ideas and findings with others. As our thoughts broadened to include the concept of a book, we invited other colleagues to join us in this venture.

As we did with our colleagues who attended the symposium, we share our understanding of certain concepts, as givens, with the readers. The Black middle class is not a homogeneous group. Although we view formal educational achievement and professional/occupational standing as criteria for middle-class status, we also point to reasonable economic stability as an important factor in defining middle-class status for Black Americans. Although our focus is on the Black middle class, we are not implying that the mental health problems discussed throughout this volume do not exist in families at each rung of the socioeconomic ladder. Mental health problems of Afro-Americans are not necessarily related to our racial identity. Many of the clinical examples presented in this volume, however, point to a connection—direct or indirect—with issues related to racial prejudices.

We view stress to be a physical or psychological stimulus that, when impinging upon an individual, produces strain or disequilibrium. Some of us weather the stresses without any untoward or overt disorder, but at some psychological cost. Others experience impairment, be it mild, moderate, or severe. Thus, the absence of stresses that are generated by poverty and poor educational opportunities do not necessarily make for immunity to mental illness in the middle class.

We have long been committed to the idea that psychiatric services must be available to Black Americans of all socioeconomic classes. We are concerned that mental health services are underutilized by Black Americans in many segments of our communities. Sometimes, underutilization comes about because the possible referral agent has some blind spots about psychiatric care. Often a clinician—whether an internist or pediatrician or surgeon—colludes with the family of the identified patient and minimizes the symptoms because of a belief that a psychiatric diagnosis will negatively affect the patient's future: thus, early and proper intervention is delayed. We hope that this volume will serve as a reminder that each one of us may be susceptible to impairment of our mental health. We trust that readers will find our suggestions about preventive measures to be of assistance in their helping roles—as parents, educators, physicians, or other service providers. Finally, we hope that references that pertain to therapeutic interventions will be of assistance to all clinicians who provide services for Black Americans.

Jeanne Spurlock

1

The Black Middle Class: Definition and Demographics

Alice F. Coner-Edwards and Henry E. Edwards

Although racial discrimination and economic isolation continue to be major sources of stress for most Black families, some nonetheless have been able to acquire the requisites for mobility, economic security, and a solid middle-class status (Billingsley, 1968; McAdoo, 1978, 1982). Families in this group have been able to emerge through the narrow "window of opportunity" that exposes them to education, advancement, success, and a sampling of the good life. These families have been able to develop particular maintenance functions or a culture-specific modus operandi for achieving solid middle-class status and for managing ongoing problems and stressors even after stability is achieved. This chapter addresses the specific stressors that confront Black middle-class families, as well as specific strengths, characteristics, or functions that have allowed these families to maintain their stability and status over time. Concepts stated in this chapter may prove useful in designing methodologically rigorous studies of Black middle-class families.

DEFINITION

The Black middle class is a varied and diverse group. The broad spectrum of income, occupations, and educational levels of lower-middle, middle, upper-middle, and elite middle-class Blacks fosters vastly different lifestyles, employment opportunities, work activities, and types of material acquisition among the middle class.

The most recent Census Bureau data (1980), although dated, amply substantiate the diversity among Black middle-class family income levels. Of 135,569 families assessed in the District of Columbia in 1980, 102,415 were Black. Four percent of these Black families reported income of $50,000 or above. Ten percent reported income in the range of $35,000 to $50,000, and 15% reported in the range of $25,000 to $35,000. These families fall within the middle class based on income. The range in income from $25,000 to above $50,000, however, indicates a diversity in income levels that could tremendously alter lifestyles, material acquisitions, and the like.

The Black middle class is equally diverse in educational backgrounds, with some having completed high school, one to three years of college, four or more years of college, graduate, or professional school, and postdoctoral education. These differences could also affect the lifestyles and other characteristics among the Black middle class.

Diversity exists equally among occupational groups within the Black middle class. These individuals include higher level executives, administrators, and managers; college professors, teachers, and small business owners; and some in technical positions, trades, or skilled positions.

Hill (1982) notes that Congress classifies as middle class all taxpayers with incomes between $20,000 and $50,000. For others, middle-classdom means anyone who makes more than $20,000 per year and less than the "fifty families who own all the wealth in America." Some writers have identified the middle class as having an annual income of $45,000; at the same time, families within the same group have been described as living in neighborhoods with houses that cost more than $200,000. Others associate multimillionaire Blacks with middle-classdom.

Some authors have questioned the process of assigning class standing to Black families, particularly when the instrument utilized emphasizes occupation or income (McAdoo, 1978; McAdoo, 1982; Scanzoni and Scanzoni, 1976; Heiss, 1975). These authors argue that discrimination against Blacks has meant that employment status and income are determined more by race than by educational attainment. Therefore, Blacks are unable to gain employment commensurate with their education. Heiss (1975), in a nationwide study of Blacks and Whites with parity in number of years of education, found a disparity in incomes: Blacks earned less. In studying stress-absorbing systems among the Black middle class, McAdoo (1982) observed lower income for Blacks at all social levels regardless of education or occupation. Like Heiss, McAdoo suggests that this Black economic disparity relates to discrimination in the labor market.

Prompted by the methodological questions raised about class assignment, McAdoo (1982) revised the Hollingshead scale, the primary instrument utilized by social scientists, because of its emphasis on occupation rather than education. Through specific statistical application that gave greater weight to education, McAdoo was able to modify the scoring of socioeconomic status. This revision placed more Blacks in the higher status.

The revision of the process by which Blacks are assigned to the middle class has failed to abate the inconsistencies in explicating Black middle-class status. The concept of social class is value laden, with negative and positive ascriptions to varying statuses. Discrimination, guilt, and other negative reactions can occur in response to this issue. Perhaps the continued debate around the definition of middle-classdom is rooted in guilt and dishonesty among those "elite" Blacks who are writing about the subject. One who defines oneself as upper class may be perceived as eccentric, egotistical, or condescending. Therefore, it is easier to define everyone as middle class—especially the "elite" Black professional who happens to be writing on the subject. Black middle- and upper-class scholars who can transcend the fears, guilt, and dishonesty around who they are can lead the way to more accurate definition.

The revision of the process of assigning class to Black families, does, however, increase the numbers of occupational categories assigned to the middle class to allow for higher-educated Blacks who remain in lower-level positions because of racial discrimination. This assignment process also expands the diversity of the Black middle class.

The restricted definition of middle-classdom does not account for the diversity found among Black middle-class families; rather, it highlights certain common attributes among the families. Specific characteristics appear to be common in all middle-class families regardless of education, occupation, or income. Moreover, the middle class appears to include two broad categories of families. Rather than focus on the diversity within Black middle-class families, the next section focuses on the common attributes of the two major groups of families.

THE NOUVEAU AND
ESTABLISHED BLACK MIDDLE CLASS

Observing numerous Black middle-class families during the past decade, the authors have identified two primary categories in which these families fall. The first group of families, considered by some scholars as the "nouveau Black middle class," have ascended into the middle class from families of lower socioeconomic status. Usually first- or second-generation middle class, these families have emerged through the window of opportunity to sample the "good life" by their own efforts or the efforts of their families. The nouveau Black middle class often perceive their status to be tenuous and temporary. They generally lack a solid sense of belonging to "middle-classdom" and worry about loss of status or stability.

The second category includes descendants of prominent families with their ascendancy originating at one of two points. The "established Black middle class" includes: (a) descendants of established, prominent Black families whose histories or ties can be traced back several or more generations, often with connections that can be traced to families who were free before the Civil War or were freed during the war; and (b) descendants with connections or blood ties to White families who allowed or even provided special privileges to them. Established Black middle-class families appear to have a solid sense of belonging. They have a deep sense of "having" and a sense of "place" which permit them to be free of worry that they will lose their middle-class status.

NOUVEAU BLACK
ASCENDANCY INTO THE MIDDLE CLASS

Nouveau Black middle-class families have generally placed their "racial status" second to the broader context of their lives. These families develop within a wider spectrum, having reduced the restrictions that would otherwise be placed upon their activities. They accept and buy into many aspects of the cultural activities of the dominant society. There are four primary ways in which these families handle their racial status within the broader context of their lives.

First, many Black families have been unconscious of or have disregarded the vicissitudes and consequences of racial issues as they emerge through the window of opportunity. The resulting setting aside of a primary focus on racial issues has permitted them the education, advancement, success, and advantages of the dominant culture.

It is not uncommon to observe nouveau middle-class Black adults who, for the first time, overtly acknowledge the fact of racial discrimination and the resulting social ills. When racial issues have been set aside temporarily, these Blacks move on to share in those experiences that are not common to the greater numbers of Black Americans. Many who set aside racial issues at one point, however, redirect their interest and energies to racial issues for the reworking process and a movement toward a "positive racial/ethnic identity" (Helm, 1987).

Many Black middle-class families remain acutely aware of the social ills of racial discrimination in society. Most have been the brunt of personal attacks or have suffered the effects of institutional racism, and they are quite angry about these experiences. However, they channel, or sublimate, the angry aggressive feelings into achieving energies. Thus, those Black middle-class families who are aware of and angry about the racial issues but can sublimate those feelings can emerge through the window of educational, advancement, and success opportunities.

The third group of Black families are acutely aware of racial issues and display tremendous anger, with a focus on their minority standing in society. Enormous energy is used in a defiant stance to achieve middle-classdom. These families are determined to emerge through the window of opportunity despite racial issues and they proceed with boldness, as well as contempt for the dominant society.

Other Blacks have emerged into middle-classdom on the shoulders of their families. Very often these are second-generation middle-class individuals who are supported and pushed along by the consistent strength and drive of a proud family. Without resistance, these individuals moved along quietly at the guidance and encouragement of their family, who responded that each generation must work harder to emerge. Unlike the first three types of emerging families, who respond to an inner locus of control, these individuals emerge passively without much commitment or determination.

CORE CHARACTERISTICS

Common characteristics have been found among the four groups of families who emerge into the middle class. The first characteristic is the *implicit or explicit embracing of the dominant culture*. Some families who at first glance appear detached, defiant, or exclusive of the dominant society under closer scrutiny can be observed as adopting the values and activities of the dominant culture. Other families are more open and direct in embracing the features ascribed to the dominant society. Whether implicit or explicit, all middle-class families have adopted some distinctive characteristics of the dominant society.

A second characteristic common to all Black middle-class families is *belief in the work ethic.* Families believe strongly that one can have the advantages afforded by the society. Middle-class Black families believe that they must work hard to achieve this status, and they are willing to work harder to maintain it. These families shun getting by, or laziness. They emerge through the window of opportunity because of their own efforts or those of their families.

Delay of gratification is a third core characteristic. Building on characteristics which allowed them to delay gratification earlier in pursuit of education and career, Black middle-class families continue to place importance on long-range planning (to build an estate, or an investment portfolio, or to buy their dream house or travel around the world). At the same time, they are enjoying the benefits of their attainments at the moment.

A fourth characteristic is a *strong sense of self and empowerment.* Emergence through the window of opportunity despite great odds is proof of the solidarity of the Black middle-class family. Having proved themselves, these families demonstrate more pride, self-esteem, and generally a "have" rather than a "have-not" mentality. Their minority status takes a relative, rather than a pervasive, position in their lives. Middle-class families have consistently demonstrated that they have what it takes to get what they want. This basic "having" what it takes, not the material "having," translates into empowerment and a strong sense of self.

A fifth common characteristic is a *sense of importance in the fact of their Blackness.* Contrary to the opinions of those who accuse middle-class Blacks of denying their heritage, these families tend to embrace their heritage and to show a strong sense of pride in themselves. This pride results, in part, from the fact of their Blackness. Composed of very special individuals within the wider society, Black middle-class families have been able to attain comparable, sometimes higher, levels relative to other groups. Against great odds, these families have been able to emerge through the window of opportunity relatively unscarred.

Another characteristic that has been found to be present in Black middle-class families is the *quality of life pursuits.* Every middle-class family has been able to advance beyond Maslow's (1954) basic survival needs and is involved in pursuits that will enhance the quality of life. The family members are engaged in a broader range of activities, all of which are directed toward improving the quality of life.

PSYCHOLOGICAL CONSEQUENCES
OF BLACK MIDDLE-CLASS STATUS

There can be major psychological consequences generated by the achievement of solid middle-class status. *Identity confusion* is not uncommon. As they partake of the activities of the dominant culture, Black middle-class families also desire acceptance by Blacks who have not achieved such status. Some Blacks are never able to become completely comfortable in either world. Others find themselves less involved in activities in the Black communities as they become more affiliated with the dominant society. All Black middle-class families must reconcile this issue or be tormented forever by feelings of abandonment, guilt, and rejection. The duality of worlds, when synthesized well, can enrich the lives of the middle-class Black families.

A second consequence of having achieved middle-class status is *guilt*. Many Black middle-class families have left behind family members who remain in lower-class status or even poverty. They are viewed as the "haves" while families of origin are "have nots." This discontinuity can engender a tremendous sense of guilt. Many such middle-class Blacks refuse to take a vacation outside of their regular trips home. In an effort to assuage the guilt, many go home for visits with gifts, money, and offers to help out. Out of a fear of appearing hedonistic or overindulgent, some save most of their earnings or dress less well than they could afford. Some become absorbed in their work and refrain from involvement in recreational activities. These families must resolve the guilt at the risk of losing ties or feeling rejected by their families, or they may never be able to enjoy their attainments.

A third psychological consequence of having achieved middle-class status relates to the strong sense of the *work ethic*. Many Black middle-class families fail to achieve balanced lives, feeling that they must work all the time. These families believe strongly that they have achieved their status through hard work and that they must work even harder to keep it. These families rarely take a vacation for pure pleasure. Any time off is faced with strong feelings of guilt. These families must resolve or mediate this issue so that they can work and enjoy life simultaneously.

A fourth psychological consequence for Blacks who have achieved middle-class status is a continuous feeling of *anxiety and insecurity* about their status. Some view their accomplishments as a result of luck, and they fear that bad luck may set in. Many are plagued with doubts as to whether they will be able to keep what they have attained. They quickly forget the hard work that went into the process of their becoming, and begin to see it as "easy come, easy go."

The last consequence identified for Blacks who have achieved middle-class status is a *lack of nurturance*. Many middle-class Black families, particularly in large urban settings, are isolated and starving for affection, acceptance, caring, and connectedness. They tend to live "on the edge," to be busy too much of the time with little communication outside the workplace. This lack of nurturance accounts in large measure for many families' frequent trips back home. Blacks who are starving "up north" go "down south" to get off the edge, to "get down" with the home folks, to recapture the early sense of family, connectedness, or community.

SUMMARY

For many Blacks the emergence into the middle class can be defined as an external and internal struggle against tremendous societal oppression and psychological conflict. It can also be viewed as a growth process, and is in keeping with a need to set goals and work toward their attainment.

The avenues that are available for the next generation to realize their potential may be different from those available presently; the number of possible routes may also be changed significantly. Furthermore, the growing number of second- and third-generation middle-class Blacks may have very different psychological responses to their position. Certainly, middle-class status is not static. To some degree the nature and direction of each of these shifts will depend on what transpires in the broader society.

REFERENCES

Billingsley, A. (1968). *Black families in White America.* Englewood Cliffs, NJ: Prentice Hall.
Heiss, J. (1975). *The case of the Black family.* New York: Columbia University Press.

Helm, J. (1987). *Development of a racial identity research.* Paper presented at the Columbia University Cross Cultural Roundtable.

Hill, R. B. (1987). The Black middle class defined. *Ebony, 40*(10), 30–32.

Maslow, A. (1954). *Motivation and personality.* New York: Harper & Row.

McAdoo, H. (1978). Factors related to stability in upwardly mobile Black families. *Journal of Marriage and the Family, 40*(4).

McAdoo, H. (1982). Stress absorbing systems in Black families. *Family Relations, 31.*

Scanzoni, L., and J. Scanzoni (1976). *Men, women and change: A sociology of marriage and family.* New York: McGraw-Hill.

U.S. Bureau of the Census (1980). Income by race statistics: Vol. I, Ch. D, Part IV, Table 222. Washington, D.C.: U.S. Government Printing Office.

Introduction to Part I

THE WORLD OF WORK

Jeanne Spurlock

More often than not, Black Americans of achievement experience multiple stresses. Many stressors are race related and rooted in the prejudices of individuals, as well as in institutionalized racism. Middle-class Blacks often find themselves straddling two worlds—the world of their origin, and the world of the dominant society, which continues to support discriminatory practices. Journalist Leanita McClain described this dilemma most poignantly in her column, "The Middle-Class Black's Burden."*

> I run a gauntlet between two worlds, and I am cursed and blessed by both. I travel, observe and take part in both; I can also be used by both. I am a rope in a tug of war. If I am a token in my downtown office, so am I at my cousin's tea. I assuage white guilt. . . .
> I have a foot in each world, but I cannot fool myself about either. . . .
> Whites won't believe I remain culturally different; blacks won't believe I remain culturally the same.

In the chapters that follow, Dudley points to the conflict described by McClain, in his reference to the opposing expectations that people (both Black and White) have of Blacks in policy-making positions. An additional stress for these Blacks of achievement is the constant scrutiny to which they are subjected. Four common problems are

---

* Page, Clarence (Ed.) (1980). *A foot in each world: Essays and articles by Leanita McClain.* Evanston, IL: Northwestern University Press, p. 14.

11

identified: (1) post-hiring restriction of policy-making authority; (2) constant questioning of competence; (3) questioning about motives underlying the development of policies; and (4) racial harassment.

Dudley alerts the reader to the fact that some Blacks use race to defend against exploration of personal shortcomings. In his discussion of management, he calls attention to preventive approaches (such as teaching one's children about the existence of racism so that they do not come to believe in their immunity to the fall-out of racism). He also provides techniques for handling the stresses of the here and now.

Pierce, using a theoretical approach, discusses the stress engendered by the racist atmosphere of the workplace and the unspoken policy that people of color can/should/will be placed at a disadvantage in any negotiation. He advocates the development of a theory of racism that could be useful in modifying traditions that have been damaging to Blacks. Three factors are considered essential for study in the development of such a theory: (1) the betrayal of Blacks by Blacks who curry favor with the dominant group; (2) the rarity of Blacks in controlling significant segments of the economy; and (3) the continuing vacillation of Blacks in regard to the avenue to be used in directing vocational efforts—integration or the development of collateral, independent Black-centered systems. Suggestions are advanced for other specific measures for immediate and long-range remediation.

The editors anticipate that many readers will view this section as overly focused on racism and as minimizing the difficulties experienced as individual responses to the various sequelae of upward mobility. Yet our collective personal and professional experiences have demonstrated that the institutionalization of racism provides a firm foundation for many of the stresses that middle-class Black Americans experience in the broader society, including places of work. This is not to discount the need for exploring individual conflicts and responses to work-related situations. As Dudley and Pierce have implied, different people may respond to a similar situation in different ways. We would add that each of us brings her or his own "set of baggage" from the past to the present.

We are also moved to raise a question about Pierce's conclusion that "Black females compared to Black males probably are found in much more favored numbers in such 'middle-class' occupations as executive management, tenured professorships, and membership in the learned professions." Although this statement has been circulated widely, we have found no data to support it. In fact, our suspicion is that advancements by nonminority women in the workplace have slowed the rate of increase of both male and female Black professionals. Should this prove to be true, it would follow that Black male professionals still remain numerically dominant over Black females.

2

Blacks in
Policy-Making Positions

Richard G. Dudley, Jr.

Policy-making positions couple authority and, sometimes, awesome responsibility with numerous personal and professional rewards and opportunities. Often, however, stress is associated with the authority and responsibility that are acquired. Blacks in policy-making positions must deal also with the stresses generated by racism. Despite all protestations to the contrary, it is clear that today, in the United States, racism against Black people continues to exist in its institutionalized form, as well as in the psyches of the vast majority of White Americans. It is also clear that even "highly educated," "middle-class," or "successful" professional Blacks do not, and cannot, escape the ravages of racism. Because most Black professionals work in or around predominant White institutions, they are required to spend a considerable amount of their time on the Black/White interface. As a result, they are forced to cope not only with the institutionalized forms of racism, but also with heavy exposure to the more insidious, day-to-day, personal insults that are consciously or unconsciously directed at them by White people.

This chapter will explore the experiences of a small subgroup of Black professionals: Blacks who are at the very top of their professions and hold significant policy-making positions. It will examine the unique stresses experienced by this subgroup and identify approaches for minimizing or managing these stresses.

The author wishes to express his appreciation to Fred Sabido, a third-year student at the New York University School of Medicine, for his assistance in the development of this chapter.

Policy is a "definite course or method of action selected from among alternatives and, in light of given conditions, [used] to guide and determine present and future decisions" (Webster's Seventh New Collegiate Dictionary, 1965). Policy makers are the persons who determine where and how human energies and financial resources will be spent. They are an extremely small but enormously powerful group of individuals.

We have little, if any, knowledge concerning Blacks who occupy these positions of power. My review of the literature disclosed no studies of or discussions about Black policy makers. More general studies of persons in policy-making positions failed even to include the race of the policy maker as a variable.

I initiated a small pilot study of Black policy makers, with the goal of generating a more formalized interview format for a larger study of the subgroup. In this pilot study, Black policy makers were asked if racism had a significant impact on their functioning as policy makers and, if so, how the racism was manifested, how it affected them, and how they managed it. They were also asked if they had intimate knowledge about the experiences of other Black policy makers; if they did, they were asked to share these experiences. The interviews were informal; other than the questions just noted, they were un-structured. Information was gathered on a total of twenty-five Black policy makers.

A few individuals believed that racism did not affect them, and a couple believed that racism accounted for the vast majority of their experiences; most respondents stated that race-related difficulties added significantly to the normal stress associated with their work. The most meaningful data gathered from the pilot study, however, were the narrative descriptions of the experiences of the individuals surveyed. These narratives were so compelling that I have chosen to use them as the basis for this chapter. I have attempted to distill the accounts of these difficulties, augmenting them with impressions drawn from personal experiences and the experiences of friends in policy-making positions. I have altered the experiences when required to protect privacy, while attempting to maintain their essence. In addition, where relevant, I have incorporated thoughts stimulated by the lectures and writings of other Black social/behavioral scientists.

OBSERVATIONS: THE
EXPERIENCES OF BLACK POLICY MAKERS

Most policy makers experience considerable stress in assuming the responsibility for so many lives and so much in the way of material resources. The more visible the policy maker and the decision-making process, the more easily critiqued the decisions. This constant and public assessment of one's work tends to make the policy maker's task even more stressful. Furthermore, there are always other men and women waiting to capture the power held by the policy maker, and if the position is not absolutely secure, the stress caused by knowing that any mistake could be one's last can be almost unbearable.

Black and non-Black policy makers must find ways to cope with these stresses. However, the Black policy-maker may face additional race-related difficulties that can make the work even more stressful. Although the precise manifestations of racism may vary with the setting or with the individuals involved, the four problems I will describe appear to be among the most common.

Restriction of Authority

Once they have accepted a new position, Black policy makers often find that their policy-making authority is much more restricted than they had expected it to be (Davis and Watson, 1985). Some discover that non-Black superiors are reluctant to release control and, as a result, the breadth of their responsibilities is reduced and their decision-making alternatives are much more limited than those of non-Blacks in comparable positions. Others have found that they were never intended to have real policy-making authority but, rather, were hired or promoted simply to serve as "window dressing." In addition, there are situations in which "political pressures" (i.e., anxieties about the new Black policy maker) are so great that they impede the development of new or revised policy initiatives, and Black policy makers find themselves limited to perpetuating the status quo. In each case, the Black policy maker lacks the authority to generate what he or she believes to be credible policy.

One interviewee noted that when he was promoted to the position of regional sales manager in a large corporation, it occurred to him that it might have been because the company was under pressure to identify Black upper-level managers. However, he had come up through the sales ranks like the other regional managers, and knew that he was certainly among the most qualified. The other regional managers even seemed to expect that he would be appointed. Furthermore, he knew that regional managers established policy for their regions, and since he had a clear understanding of the problems and opportunities in his region, he was sure that he would quickly be able to demonstrate his ability to do the job.

However, he was soon discouraged when he found that the White general sales manager took an unprecedented interest in his region, and dictated that the regional policy remain unchanged. He was further discouraged, frustrated, angry, and hurt when he found that he was forced to assume the bulk of the responsibility for the lack of growth in his region, and his adherence to an antiquated sales policy.

Black policy makers may also find that when they finally obtain policy-making authority, insufficient resources or other major underlying problems severely limit their alternatives. There are times when Blacks are given these almost impossible tasks because no one else wants them. There are times when Blacks are placed in these positions with the expectation that they will fail, and thereby prove their unworthiness. However, these extremely difficult policy-making positions frequently involve the making of policy that predominantly affects the lives of Black people. In these instances, Black policy makers often believe that they must accept these positions, and they do so with the hope that they will be able to make a positive difference despite obvious pitfalls. Yet Blacks who are faced with extraordinary challenges tend to be evaluated against standard norms and therefore, even if they "do the impossible," they may be perceived as only average.

The most dramatic examples of this type of difficulty are drawn from the experiences of Black elected or appointed government officials. Unfortunately, it is difficult to describe their experiences without revealing identifying details. However, the report of a marketing executive also demonstrates this point. She noted that when she was first promoted to a position of authority, she, like other newcomers, was given failing products. With enormous effort, she outperformed her colleagues, stopping the decline in sales for some of the products and actually restoring growth to others. Despite her successes, the expected transfer to the "big-ticket items" did not occur. While others moved on, she remained with her original assignment because, as she was told, "someone has to manage the smaller products."

Questioning of Competence

Black policy makers report that their competence is constantly questioned. This questioning can come in the form of full-scale attacks or via frequent but more subtle comments about their capabilities. In addition, the successes of these Black policy makers are frequently minimized, trivialized, or simply ignored by their non-Black colleagues (Watson and Williams, 1977). Many Blacks have noted that non-

Blacks commonly attack the competency of Blacks in an effort to manage disagreements about policy. One interviewee went so far as to say that he always knows that he is about to win a policy debate when his White opponents stop addressing substance and resort to disparaging innuendos about his intelligence, his knowledge, or his skills. Although "all's fair in war," the shared belief of Whites in the incompetence of Blacks makes these attacks particularly potent. Another interviewee shared an example of a more subtle attack. He noted that he and a similarly placed White colleague had each established a record of successes. Although the successes of each were acknowledged by their peers, there was a subtle but significant difference in the way in which they were acknowledged. When his colleague performed well, the response was "As we expected, you did it again." However, when he performed well, the response was "We're always surprised at how well you pull these things off."

As other authors have suggested, this sense of White entitlement can be observed almost anywhere that Blacks and Whites come into contact with each other. It can be found in the policy-making arena where the young, inexperienced White policy maker presumes that he will have something more significant to say than the seasoned Black policy maker. When the tables are turned and Whites are in the minority (for example, in a Black institution), the White participants' sense of entitlement often becomes even more pronounced.

Blacks also have found that Whites may challenge the competence of Black managers in an effort to maintain their sense of superiority. They have noted that many Whites simply find it difficult to accept the fact that a Black person is in a higher position or even in a position comparable to theirs. For some Whites, this reality is so painfully disturbing that they feel compelled to attack the Black policy maker in order to elevate themselves. This approach to the maintenance of self-esteem is effective for Whites because it is based on the shared system of beliefs which are core to racism.

Charges of Questionable Motives in Decision Making

Many Black policy makers indicate that they are distressed by the implication, and at times clearly stated accusation, that there are "questionable, underlying" motives behind most, if not all, of their policy decisions (Slocum and Strawser, 1972). The most common suspicion is that their decisions are completely and inappropriately motivated by racial considerations. Non-Blacks frequently suspect that decisions are based solely on the policy maker's concern about or overidentification with Blacks, and total lack of concern for others. Ironically, other Blacks often feel that the same policy maker is concerned only about non-Blacks and is unresponsive to their interests.

I am reminded of statements made by several young, White attorneys involved in juvenile justice matters. They described White judges who tended to decide in favor of their Black clients as thoughtful, sensitive, intelligent, knowledgeable, and insightful. In contrast, they presumed that Black judges who tended to decide in favor of their Black clients did so simply because they were Black, even though there were other Black judges who were quite harsh. A judge who was interviewed as part of the pilot study stated that this differential perception of Black and White judges is also held by her White judicial colleagues. She noted that White judges often presumed that she (as well as other Black judges) had not actually thought through a matter but, rather, had simply made her decision based on strong emotional ties to Black persons involved. A White judge who made a similar decision, with a similar stated basis for it, was perceived as thoughtful and wise.

Black policy makers are also frequently perceived as overly hungry for power and money. As a result, some non-Blacks suspect that their decisions are based only on their concern for themselves. The system of racism allows Blacks to be perceived in only two ways: they are either docile, friendly, dumb, and fearful (in which case they would not occupy a policy-making position), or hostile, sly, and criminal. Therefore, many Whites assume that Blacks in authority could only have gained their positions through questionable means. Many Blacks have noted that despite efforts to be explicitly detailed about the basis for their decisions and painfully honest about their consideration of all people, they are still presumed to be dishonorable, unfair, or self-seeking.

High Expenditure of Energy

Black policy makers frequently find themselves diverting emotional and cognitive energy from their designated tasks to respond to racial harassment, correct racist misconceptions, or battle against racist policy (Markham, 1980). Old stereotypes about the sexual prowess of Black men and women, the psychopathic nature of Black men, the mothering instincts of Black women, and a host of other racist beliefs surface as purposeful insults. Other stereotypes about Blacks, believed by White policy makers, become incorporated into the decision-making process, resulting in policy that is harmful to or exclusionary of Blacks.

A communications executive reported that his work environment was such that White employees felt free to clearly and directly insult Blacks with racist slurs, without any concern about rebuff from the company's highest authorities. He found that distressed Black employees were almost constantly at his door to discuss their experiences, and that a significant percentage of their time and energy was expended in coping with situations that took the White offenders only seconds to create.

An academic dean stated that a large percentage of her time was given to fighting racist policy that would limit the academic opportunities for Black students. She also noted that even the policies and programs that were developed specifically to aid Black students were so frequently based on racist misconceptions that the policies ultimately would be of more harm than help.

There are White Americans who have done the psychological work required to minimize the impact of racism on their perception of Black people, and who have grown to appreciate the similarities and differences between Blacks and Whites. Some have also been able to dismantle some of their conscious and unconscious racial stereotypes. However, their numbers are so small that it is almost impossible to imagine a setting totally populated by such people and therefore devoid of the problems we have outlined. Black policy makers, in common with other Black people, continue to perceive among most White people an attitude that seems to bespeak a belief that simply being White makes one special and worthy of deference from all non-Whites.

THE HIGH PERSONAL COST

The problems I have described all constitute attacks on the self-esteem and sense of positive identity of Black policy makers. Such attacks appear to be almost constant. Whether they come as full-scale frontal attacks or smaller assaults to the flank, they are carefully aimed and hard-hitting. The factors that determine how an individual Black policy maker will respond are varied and complex. However, some general statements can be made about the response process, and these statements can be used as a basis for the development of coping strategies.

Black policy makers who insist that racism does not affect them will spend an enormous amount of energy maintaining that belief. Quite often the belief is maintained by a narcissistic psychological defense, which consists of a denial of the devalued status assigned to the Black policy maker by non-Blacks, and a replacement of it with a more grandiose view of the self. With this defense, individuals perceive themselves as very special; they may view themselves as belonging to a special subgroup of Blacks or even as being beyond racial categorization. This supposedly positive self-perception is supported by the belief that they have "done all the right things" (i.e., met the standards of middle- to upper-class White America), gained the "respect" of Whites, and obtained the important policy-making position.

The problem is that because these individuals deny that racism exists, they are likely to presume that all attacks are based on substance. As a result, they may be falsely led to believe that their policy-making capabilities are severely impaired. Eventually, the onslaught of racist attacks will become so great that they break through the defense, destroy the individual's positive self-perception, and leave the person devastated.

On the other hand, some Black policy makers believe that all conflicts are race-related and tend to use race as an excuse for not exploring personal shortcomings. They tend to deny any real substantive concerns that are raised, and therefore find it difficult to grow and develop in their work. In addition, their anger about the injustices they experience can become all-consuming, sapping the energy available for more positively gratifying emotions.

Even the most racist attack may contain some substantive and helpful criticism. However, in the barrage, it is often difficult for the Black policy maker to determine exactly which are the substantive issues. Most Black policy makers realize that they must spend the time and energy required to assess each attack in order to determine whether it is totally racially motivated, partially racially motivated, or legitimate. When racism is involved, Black policy makers must then determine if and, then, how they will respond to the racism, while also responding to any legitimate criticisms.

Because the amount of intellectual and emotional energy that humans can expend is finite, most Black policy makers find it almost impossible to respond to every racist confrontation. Furthermore, there are those racially motivated attacks that, for whatever reasons, cannot or should not be responded to. Therefore, Black policy makers must decide which situations warrant their response, how they will respond, what repercussions can be expected, and how these repercussions will be managed. Making such judgments can be quite difficult, especially when personal concerns, policy concerns, and the views of other Blacks conflict.

Even the Black policy maker who determines that it would be unwise to confront racism directly must find some way to manage the more personal, psychological impact of the experience. If this more personal aspect is ignored, the Black policy maker runs the risk that repeated insults will eventually begin to destroy his or her self-esteem and sense of competency. This battle against racism can consume an enormous amount of energy, and the Black policy maker must often call on family, friends, and colleagues for direction and emotional support.

In essence, Black policy makers must manage the stress related to the actual policy-making task at hand, the stress related to identifying and addressing racism, and the stress associated with the more personal toll that racism can exact (Alderfer, 1980). Although it is difficult to assign energy units to each of these stress management tasks, the reports of those surveyed in this pilot study would suggest that the personal cost is quite high. Finally, it is clear that Whites, by maintaining a racist society, not only cause direct harm to Blacks, but also control how a significant amount of their time and energy will be spent. This time and energy must come from somewhere, and generally speaking, it appears that it is taken from the more personal side of the ledger.

APPROACHES TO MANAGEMENT

If Black policy makers are to manage both the institutional racism and the individual racist insults that are a part of their daily lives, they must first acknowledge that racism exists, and become familiar with the various forms it can take. Blacks who were fortunate enough to have parents or others who taught them how to cope with racism have a distinct advantage. Black parents should be encouraged to give their developing children this type of advantage. Blacks who were led to believe that they were beyond the reach of racism will find their task more difficult, because accepting the reality totally redefines the rules, and possibly the game that they must play. These Black policy makers might identify a more experienced Black professional who can function as a mentor by pointing out the ways in which racism is employed in the policy-making arena.

Most Blacks have a strong emotional response to personal experiences with racism, as well as to reports from others about their experiences with racism. Because racially motivated attacks strike at the core of the Black person's identity, a strong emotional response is normal. In order to survive, all Black Americans must expect such feelings, recognize that they are normal, learn not to be frightened by them, and learn how to use them to their own best interest. Given the intensity of the racial attacks on Black policy makers, and the fact that they may have to put aside personal feelings in the interest of urgent policy matters, it is particularly important that Black policy makers learn how to manage their emotional responses to racism. A supportive system (formal or informal) that provides an avenue for expressing feelings and exploring alternatives for managing these feelings is valuable.

As well-functioning family and extended family support networks care for their members, they must include their children and adolescent members. These caring experiences help children and adolescents realize that giving and receiving support is not only acceptable, but important to the survival of Black people. They will also learn that the intense feelings stirred by racism can be managed, and Black people can develop healthy alternatives for functioning in an unhealthy situation.

Learning to distinguish between racially motivated and substantive criticisms requires sophistication about racism and an extraordinarily keen awareness of one's strengths and weaknesses. Both Black and non-Black policy makers should find an honest and in-depth analysis of their capabilities an extremely helpful step toward further growth and development, and an important factor in assessing reactions from their environment. However, the environment can be even more dangerous for the Black policy maker who is unable to separate real questions of ability from racist attacks.

Self-assessment is often quite difficult, and it may be particularly so for Black policy makers. Even Black policy makers who have a fairly sound grasp of the role of racism in their environment are unlikely to have totally avoided mistakenly incorporating some of the racist insults that they have experienced into their self-perception. Therefore, at some level, they may have lingering questions about their ability, and their self-assessment may be inappropriately harsh. On the other hand, they may have so defended themselves against these insults that they find it difficult to explore weaknesses.

The Black policy maker's family of colleagues can help him or her assess performance more objectively. This may indeed be one of the most important reasons for Black policy makers to "network" with each other, as well as the larger group of other Black professionals. This spirit of cooperation is very much a part of the Black heritage. Although it is not always supported in this competitive American culture, it must be nurtured and maintained.

Black policy makers have several alternatives for responding to racist insults. They may respond directly to the racism, respond indirectly, or offer no response at all. With each of these alternatives, there are numerous possible strategies, each with its associated cost and potential benefits. As I have noted, time and energy limitations make it impossible to respond to every discovery of racism. In addition, political and other realities can dictate the nature of the best response. Therefore, it is critical that careful consideration be given to which situations merit a response, and which response is the most appropriate.

When selecting particular strategy, Black policy makers should have a clear and reasonable goal in mind. The goal may be an ultimate change in policy. The goal may also be to help one's self and other Black people cope with the racism and maintain a positive sense of self. The Black policy maker must take care when the goals are more personal, so that rage and hurt do not take over and interfere with sound judgment. Personal insight and clarity of purpose will help focus the selection of realistic alternatives and strategies.

The selection of strategies will also depend on such factors as personal style, the policy maker's ability to manage stress (for example, the stress of confrontation), the policy maker's support network, the environment, and how much of a risk the policy maker is willing to take. Considerations such as these are important, legitimate concerns, and they should not be ignored.

SUMMARY AND CONCLUSIONS

Unfortunately, very little has been written about the stresses facing Black policy makers, or the rewards they obtain from their efforts.

The numbers involved in our survey are too small to suggest that our findings are representative of the experiences of all Black policy makers. However, the responses were so painfully consistent that Black professionals who are considering accepting policy-making positions should heed their warnings.

Although the management strategies employed by those surveyed did appear to help them cope with the racism-related difficulties they encountered, not one even suggested that he or she had been able to eliminate the impact of racism at work. One can infer that even Blacks who manage racism quite well will continue to experience the stress and continue to sacrifice considerable time and energy to the effort. Some Blacks will decide that the personal cost involved in battling against racism as a policy maker is too high; others will decide that it is all worth it. Both groups will continue to face the challenges of racism and will need the loyal support of family and friends.

REFERENCES

Alderfer, C. P. (1980). Diagnosing race relations in management. *Journal of Applied Behavioral Science,* April–June, pp. 26–30.

Davis, G., & Watson, G. (1985). *Black Life in Corporate America.* New York: Anchor Press.

Markham, W. T. (1980). Self-expression at work: a theory-based questionnaire instrument. *Journal of Applied Behavioral Science,* October–December, pp. 82–86.

Slocum, J., & Strawser, R. (1972). Racial differences in job attitudes. *Journal of Applied Psychology, 56,* 28.

Watson, J., & Williams, J. (1977). Relationship between managerial values and managerial success of Black and White managers. *Journal of Applied Psychology, 62*(2), 203–207.

Webster's Seventh New Collegiate Dictionary (1965). Springfield, MA: G. & C. Merriam.

3

Stress in the Workplace

Chester M. Pierce

Regardless of site or social variables, all Blacks in any workplace suffer special added stress as a result of threatened, perceived, and actual racism. Neither income level, educational attainment, occupational status, nor gender confers immunity against this stress. The basic rule in the United States is that non-White people will be made disadvantaged in all negotiations.

In the workplace as elsewhere in the United States the inflexibility and certainty of this basic rule leads to three major confusions by Blacks, which have stressful and enduring psychosocial sequelae: (1) Blacks are confused about whether they are being tolerated or being accepted. (2) Blacks are confused about the supportive effort of individual Whites versus the destructive action by Whites as a collective. (3) Blacks are confused about when, where, and how to resist oppression, versus when, where, and how to accommodate to it.

The basic rule is intensified by two factors which compound the stress for a Black worker, regardless of class or social attributes. The first corollary to the rule is that the collective majority constantly finds ways to minimize, trivialize, and attenuate Black males relative to Black females. For instance, compared to their majority group counterparts, Black females compared to Black males probably are found in much more favored numbers in such "middle-class" occupations as executive management, tenured professorships, and membership in the learned professions.

Another corollary is that the majority group collective constantly finds ways to promote interethnic and intraethnic rivalries among minority groups. Thus, a common commercial observation would be to see a Caucasian Hispanic in a supervisory or spokesperson position over colored Hispanics and Blacks.

Yet Blacks have advanced in the workplace in the past two decades, although this advancement has not been without psychological toll. For example, many argue that greater individual well-being has been accompanied by a lessening of group solidarity or at least a reduction in the focus of common group aspirations. Further, for our youth it is more difficult to defend one's dignity and limited accomplishment by appeal to the truism that "the Whites only let me go this far." Finally, role models in many instances have become more distant and remote. In the thirties, forties, and fifties, world-celebrated Black athletes, scholars, or entertainers could be talked to readily and frequently by the Black community in Black restaurants, hotels, bar-bershops, and churches.

BLACKS IN THE WORKPLACE:
THE LEGACY OF SLAVERY

Undoubtedly, most Blacks would prefer to be a vice president of marketing in a large corporation than a porter in a bus station. But there may be considerable overlap in psychosocial stressors in the workplace between these two persons. The search for such universals may be more important than trying to understand the differences and special problems that beset the vice president or the porter. In addition, privileged Blacks may regard their opportunities more mod-estly and their duties more urgently when such a search is undertaken.

From the beginning of Afro-American history every Black worker has had intense stress. This legacy of slavery persists in each workplace to which Blacks are admitted or not admitted in the present day.

To sustain the condition of slavery, laws were passed and enforced that, among other things, prevented Blacks from having more than a modicum of material comfort. In fact, any possibility that a Black would have more than a White caused extreme resentment. The Blacks' function in the workplace was to benefit the dominant group. Skills were taught to this end. The same skills were disregarded when it became advantageous to give them to the majority group. While the slave's work was required, punishments deemed necessary were designed *not* to remove him from the workplace, even though the penalties could be unspeakably cruel and severe.

Slaves could not be taught to read; they often were unable to assemble (even for purposes of religion or health). Their communi-cations were controlled. Likewise, they were not permitted to "stroll or be about," nor could they be "insolent" or possess weapons or dogs. Interaction with Whites in dancing, game playing, gambling, or sexual contact was regulated. A free, self-reliant Black lived in fear of being snatched back illegally into slavery. All these problems are detailed in two masterly volumes pertaining to the laws about American slavery (Olshausen, 1983a, 1983b).

It takes little imagination to make parallels between the way slaves were treated and the conscious fears and worries of Blacks today, in either a vice president's office or a porter's closet. No thinking Black should exclude the possibility of harsh, negative consequences from having too much material comfort or from believing a job will not be eliminated in the service of advantage to a White. Neither vice president nor porter is as free as a White counterpart to "stroll or be about," or to be "insolent," or to remain unconcerned about social interaction with any person of the dominant group, because such interaction could be construed as an outrageous affront to community standards.

These parallels become reinforced and more compelling when the post–Civil War psychosocial climate is considered. Here, the early phases of the Industrial Revolution combine with the societal turmoil that was part of the process of peace.

Slaves had been part of a "closed" system of being controlled, guided, and directed. They were thought to do best at routine tasks. It was virtually unthinkable that they could or should be creative or intellectual. In a paternalistic mode it was believed that slaves had to be ordered about and that both justice and communication came to them from the top, without any recourse or response on their part. These attributes were later assigned a general importance for many workers in the Industrial Revolution, but the Black worker was the best example of a worker suited for what would become known as a closed organizational structure. Compared to a counterpart of the majority group, the present-day Black vice president or porter is less likely to be operating in a more "open" organizational structure. It would be rash for either of them to be unaware that their superiors would be more likely and quicker to exert sanctions on them if they operated too flagrantly in the style of an "open" organizational structure.

The insistence that Blacks in the workplace be commanded in a militaristic, conservative, closed style continued from slavery into the postbellum years. It may have contributed to the inability of Blacks to gain a foothold in the developing labor union movement (Harris, 1929; Wesley, 1929).

Our purpose is not to emphasize the labor movement itself so much as to focus on one important consequence. In the early days of the movement there was much verbalizing and considerable behavior which indicated the possible actualization of the ideal of color-blind labor. Predictably, some segments of labor opposed this strategy. As a result, national labor organizations allowed their local units to decide whether or not Blacks could be admitted. The common reason for declining Black candidates was that individuals of the dominant group should have the right to work with whom they pleased. This notion contributed to the increasing view of segregation of the races in work, recreation, schooling, and housing.

One hundred years after these issues were aired by the unions, the vice president and porter, unlike their counterparts, continue to be influenced (stressed) by the interrelationship of vocational behavior opportunity and security in terms of where one lives, where one's children go to school, and how and with whom one has recreation. The cumulative and unremitting stress from these considerations may contribute to making the Black more vulnerable to "burnout" (especially that part of the definition of burnout which speaks to thwarted hopes) (Nagy and Davis, 1985). At the least, the need to keep these stressors uppermost in mind influences both Black and majority group behavior and expectation of behavior.

In sum, the straight line tradition, psychoculturally, for Blacks in the United States is that: (1) you must work — and you must work hard for less reward; (2) you may be displaced summarily if it inconveniences a person of the dominant group; and (3) nevertheless, when you do work, you must be appropriately curbed, inhibited, and grateful. It is the widespread applicability of these traditions that engenders the extra stress that all Blacks in the United States, regardless of class, know or should know. The challenge is to understand this tradition so well that it can be altered to become less pernicious. The ultimate goal is to establish new traditions that facilitate and expedite meaningful, gratifying contributions by Blacks.

THEORY OF RACISM

To meet this challenge, Blacks in the workplace need some theoretical stance. The theory also must account for the chastening reality that our history of struggles in the workplace and the political arena are weighted with numerous betrayals of Blacks by Blacks currying favor with majority group persons. Similarly, the theory must engage the withering observation that rarely have Blacks owned or controlled significant segments of the economy or been major entrepreneurs. Likewise, the theory must address the incessant vacillation Blacks have had about whether their chief vocational effort should be to integrate into the mainstream or to develop collateral, independent Black-centered systems.

Such community concerns and the dominant group's response to them shape the hopes and possibilities of any individual Black in the workforce. To this extent, then, no Black worker, of any class, can be free of the limitations placed on his career. The more restricted options the worker feels, whether working in an executive office or from a porter's closet, the greater the impact of the stress. Overall, a Black worker is stressed in direct proportion to the inhibition to control space, time, energy, and movement secondary to overt or covert racial barriers. The worker may or may not be aware of or appreciate the full panoply and complexity of these barriers, both because they are concealed and because of the operation of a denial system. Even so, heightened vulnerability develops because of the chronic need for hypersurveillance of one's environment and for preparation for the manifestations of whimsical, arbitrary prejudice. The person comes to be at greater risk for fractured pride and mistrust of the system of justice. The handicap of never being able to banish these risks probably cannot be understood by the dominant group. Supervisors of this group may not, even with great effort and the best intentions, appreciate the ongoing, cumulative racial stress or the anger, energy depletion, and uneasiness that result from the time spent preoccupied by color-related aspects of one's job.

At least three components of racism theory are relevant to the worker (Pierce, 1970, 1974, 1980). These components evolve from the fact that operationally Whites act to keep Blacks in the inferior, dependent, and helpless role. The most important maneuver to this end is the offensive mechanism, which is often delivered as a non-verbal, kinetic microaggression. The maneuver is most effective when simultaneously, with mathematical precision, it controls space, time, energy, and mobility of the Black, while producing feelings of degradation, and erosion of self-confidence and self-image. For instance, a Black in a company cafeteria is made to wait while the White cashier attends to a same-race customer who came after the Black. The cashier then, wordlessly, reaches out a hand for the money for the sale to the Black after having registered it on a digital display on the cash register. Once paid, the cashier then tosses the change contemptuously to the Black patron. The Black has been immobilized, detained, demeaned, and mobilized for defense even though no actual law has been broken or even a cross word exchanged. It is these cumulative, subtle, stunning, unrelenting microaggressions that characterize and populate the daily existence of Blacks in whatever workplace they occupy. The solution to offensive mechanisms is educative, so that they can be anticipated, recognized, and deflected by selective defensive thinking and counteroffensive behavior.

Another component of racism theory is that the dominant group collective reduces and diminishes support to the Black community. For example, that community would receive fewer services and be requested to account more strenuously for and be more content with any service received. Lack of support calls forth stress. Stress is relieved directly in proportion to the effectiveness and efficiency of support rendered. Blacks as a group and often Blacks as individuals in the workforce recognize their environment to be more extreme than that of the dominant group due to lack of support. Among other features and along with factors mentioned already, this can easily lead to group hatred. The solution for amelioration is the provision of hope, supplied ubiquitously by a sustaining community.

Finally, Black workers under stress are threatened by adaptational failure as their lives swing from actual or potential racially conditioned mini-disaster to mini-disaster. The threatened failure demonstrates itself by a near-habitual first appraisal of any situation in terms of what cannot be done. The importance of the mischief done to Blacks by this psychology can hardly be exaggerated. The solution overlaps with and reinforces the solutions in the two prior instances. Here, too, the individual and community Black effort must be to develop and strengthen options by such means as viable social networks.

Therefore, in theory, to function better at work Blacks must increase their education, with the goals of diluting racism and finding more channels to express hope and options. All these can be attained by becoming more consciously in command, whenever possible, of one's space, time, energy, and mobility.

CONCLUSION

It is argued that all Blacks suffer special stress in the workplace. This psychocultural stress represents forces generated by historical and sociological processes peculiar to the Black in the United States. Historically, our wonder should not be that we survived badly but, rather, that we survived at all. To reduce stress we must define our own aims and our own selves. We must be mindful too that no matter how helpful some Whites have been to us, progress as we define it has depended on Blacks pressing forth on their own behalf. Blacks must be more generous and more proud of their accomplishment in surviving despite far-flung monumental hatred or indifference.

We must accept that for the foreseeable future Blacks will continue to work harder and longer for less reward, recognition, or status. Nevertheless, as a vital part of the workforce we can minimize stress by calling for excellence, competition, and pro-intellectualism. These qualities will aid us in many ways, including prompting us to be more venturesome. In the workplace our problem is not that we are too active and bold, but that we are too passive and timid.

All Blacks must have a strong theoretical grasp of racism in order to dilute its crippling effects in the workplace. Here our concern must be to reduce mortality and morbidity which result from living for generations under unrelenting enmity and duress.

Black workers need to be educated in propaganda analysis in order to view themselves and their surroundings without erosion of self. Also, we need to dwell on group dynamics in order to instill hope, especially in our youth. Finally, every worker needs to elaborate multiple options in order to cope with the universal color-related job stressors.

REFERENCES

Harris, A. L. (1929). The Negro and the new economic life. In V. F. Calverton (Ed.), *Anthology of American Negro literature* (pp. 324–338). New York: Random House.

Nagy, S., & Davis, L. (1985). Burnout: A comparative analysis of personality and environmental variables. *Psychological Reports, 57,* 1319.

Olshausen, G. (1983a). *American slavery and after.* San Francisco: Olema Press.

Olshausen, G. (1983b). *Case book for American slavery and after.* San Francisco: Olema Press.

Pierce, C. M. (1970). Offensive mechanisms. In F. Barbour (Ed.), *The Black seventies* (pp. 265–282). Boston: Porter Sargent.

Pierce, C. M. (1974). Psychiatric problems of the Black minority. In

S. Arieti and G. Kaplan (Eds.), *American handbook of psychiatry,
Vol. II* (pp. 512–523). New York: Basic Books.

Pierce, C. M. (1980). Social trace contaminants: Subtle indicators of
racism. In S. Withey and R. Abeles (Eds.), *Television and social
behavior: Beyond violence and children* (pp. 249–257). Hillsdale,
N.J.: Lawrence Erlbaum.

Wesley, C. (1929). Organized labor and the Negro. In V. F. Calverton
(Ed.), *Anthology of American Negro literature* (pp. 339–362).
New York: Random House.

Introduction to Part II

MALE-FEMALE RELATIONSHIPS

Jeanne Spurlock

The literature is studded with references to male-female relationships, both harmonious and those flooded with discord. The literature that focuses on Black male-female relationships is heavily weighted toward references to conflict. The problems that Black men have with the women in their lives and the problems that Black women experience with their men folk have also been the focal point of novelists, dramatists, and lyricists. The controversies that professional writers address in their creative works often spill over into heated debates among members of the various audiences, including couples involved in intimate relationships. This pattern has been vividly depicted by scores of individuals who saw and reacted to "For Colored Girls Who Have Considered Suicide/When the Rainbow is Enuf" and "The Color Purple." Black men, in particular, have been outraged. Black women have been offended by the put-downs of Black women in the writing of nationally known Black male behavioral and social scientists.

A number of these issues are addressed by each of the contributors to this section. Coner-Edwards focuses on the psychological domain of Black male-female relationships. She emphasizes the role of early socialization in the shaping of individuals for intimate adult relationships. Personality development and psychological needs are explored relative to the establishment and maintenance of relationships. Coner-Edwards suggests that middle-class Blacks who are able to develop the problem-solving tools necessary to endure the complexities found in all relationships can enjoy a life-long, rewarding, and satisfying relationship with an intimate partner.

The approaches of Edwards and Spurlock are more clinical. From his review of the concerns presented by 40 male patients, Edwards concludes that the basic difficulties in their relationships with women pertain to problems with intimacy and self-disclosure. During the course of the therapies Edwards determined there to be common factors that thwarted efforts to engage in positive intimate relationships. Suggestions for remediation are advanced.

Both Edwards and Spurlock emphasize the importance of the earliest relationship in the shaping and understanding of the relationships that adults have with the "significant others" in their lives. Using her clinical experiences as a data base, Spurlock notes that more than half of Black female patients identified problems in their relationships with the men in their lives, regardless of the stated reason for the referral. A typical response to a common charge of lack of support (primarily defined by middle-class women as emotional support) was anger, which was often only thinly veiled, or was turned inward and revealed as depression of varying degrees. Not infrequently, therapeutic intervention is indicated in order to help the patient terminate a relationship that is psychologically destructive.

4

Mate Selection and Psychological Need

Alice F. Coner-Edwards

Are Black male-female relationships in trouble? Several publications have reinforced the idea that the trouble is intense. The increasing divorce rate, the eschewing of matrimony, and the frequency with which problems in relationships prompt women and men to seek counseling are some of the supporting factors. The growing openness and acceptance of same gender preference, which decreases the pool of potential partners available to heterosexual women and men, is another factor to consider. Whereas one or more of these factors have been identified in troubled relationships, researchers have given very limited attention to issues such as mate selection, intimacy sharing, or relationship maintenance. Instead they have focused on surface issues such as economics or discrimination. It is suggested that solutions to many of the relationship problems confronting men and women are contained in the psychological aspects of the relationship. Thus, the psychological domain of relationships is the focal point of this chapter.

Exploration of the deeper relationship issues suggests such questions as: Why does A select B as a mate? What needs provide the driving force for the union? If we assume that A and B are living in a society that permits voluntary mate selection, does this imply that A anticipates more gratification of needs from a relationship with B than any other available potential mate? What causes A to feel lovable or special to B? Why do A and B get married and remain together? What are the unique factors within Black middle-class relationships, if any, that influence the mate selection and relationship process?

What are the implications of the mate selection and intimate relationship process for intervention and treatment?

The usual answers to such questions about Black male-female relationships, while generally offered within an economic or sociocultural context, are generally complex and elusive. Some of the answers may be contained within sociocultural, sociopolitical, economic, and perhaps other theoretical frameworks. However, because of the limited available understanding of the expressive realm of Black middle-class male-female relationships, this chapter examines relationship questions from a social-psychological perspective. The discussion focuses on early socialization, psychological need, and intimacy as factors in the establishment and maintenance of relationships in an attempt to depart from the economic or sociocultural perspectives and move toward understanding the essence of intimate relationships within the psychological realm.

HISTORICAL BACKGROUND AND RATIONALE

There is a need to broaden the focus of and expand the body of literature on Black male-female relationships. Many earlier studies have served to perpetuate negative myths and stereotypes about Black relationships that have been emphasized about Blacks in general within the literature. Whereas the body of knowledge on Black male-female relationships has expanded significantly since the 1960s, the trends and focus of the 1970s paralleled those of the earlier decade. Earlier studies generally focused on issues of marital happiness and satisfaction, decision making, and role enactment. Many works assessed female dominance in Black relationships and examined variables within a dominance or power theory perspective (Blood, 1955; Blood and Wolfe, 1960; Moynihan, 1965) wherein White and Black samples were compared. The results of these studies have often presented a negative or pathological view of Black relationships.

Recognizing the need for data based on the reality systems of Black male-female relationships, the inadequacy of comparative studies of Black and White samples, and the destructive myths that were being perpetuated about Blacks, some social scientists of the 1970s developed a new body of data (Billingsley, 1970; Scanzoni, 1971). Some scientists even attempted to test the theses of many critics or to clarify misconceptions within the literature (Scanzoni, 1971; Heiss, 1975).

There is a sizable body of literature on Black male-female relationships and such instrumental issues as economics, racism, and employment. Through Staples (1981a), Billingsley (1968), and others has come increased understanding of instrumental realm issues, including institutional racism as a dominant factor that affects the quality of Black relationships. Whereas the studies of the 1970s necessarily presented a more realistic picture of Black men and women, and researchers of the 1980s have begun to explore the expressive realm, limited and inconsistent attention has been given to the expressive issues, particularly as related to interpersonal intimacy.

Some authors have attempted to explain this omission, suggesting that the study of psychological aspects of interpersonal relationships presents more difficult methodological problems for empirical investigators. Rodgers-Rose (1980) stated: "Sociologists have in many cases failed to study the depths of interpersonal relationships between the groups of people they analyze. They have, instead, tended to study the surface areas — those aspects which can be easily defined, codified, and discussed" (p. 235). Historically, the absence of attempts to understand the intimate psychological or expressive dynamics of Black male-female relationships has been pervasive despite implications of the importance of these issues (Staples, 1981a).

Research of the eighties has advanced our conceptual understanding of practical issues that challenge the relationships of Black middle-class men and women (Leggon, 1980; Engram, 1980; Rodgers-Rose, 1980; Staples, 1981a, 1981b; Coner, 1983; Coner and McAdoo, 1985). A major research focus of the eighties is the conflict associated with the enactment of multiple roles by men and women (Leggon, 1980; Engram, 1980; Keith and Schafer, 1980). When individuals carry out multiple roles, relationship needs for intimacy and other affective qualities must sometimes give way to parenting, career, and other concerns. When this occurs, the relationship is potentially vulnerable to stress, particularly for Black middle-class women, who desire the affective qualities as much as, if not more than, other aspects of the relationship (Rodgers-Rose, 1980; Coner and McAdoo, 1985). Research of the eighties has also found women to be more dissatisfied with their relationships than men (Coner, 1983; Keith and Schafer, 1980). Many Black women are eschewing or delaying matrimony, and some are choosing to go it alone (Ball, 1982). Relationship alternatives to the monogamous marriage have also been elected by both men and women of the eighties. Some authors argue that it is the enactment of dual roles that causes the dissatisfaction and subsequent exit from relationships by some individuals, that the demands of the multiple roles do not permit adequate development and maintenance of intimacy and other affective qualities of the relationship that appear to be particularly important to women. Perhaps more important is the need for both men and women to acquire greater understanding of intimacy and the origins of the need for it in relationships.

EARLY SOCIALIZATION
AND PSYCHOLOGICAL NEED

Need, as defined by the Oxford English Dictionary (1982), is a condition marked by the lack of something required. For purposes of this discussion, the concept is limited to expressive and instrumental needs. *Expressive need* has been defined as the psychological or innermost strivings for fulfillment of intrapersonal requirements for love, companionship, emotional support, sharing, or affiliation (Freud, 1925; Sullivan, 1953; Winch, 1955; Centers, 1975; Haspel, 1976; & Heiss, 1981). *Instrumental needs* are those security strivings for survival or assumption of responsibility, economic sufficiency, food, clothing, shelter, protection, and social interaction (Sullivan, 1953; Maslow, 1954; Parsons and Bales, 1955; Heiss, 1981).

Maslow's (1954) hierarchy of needs illustrates a life-death association with need fulfillment. Maslow's five levels of need include physiological, security, affiliation, esteem, and self-actualization. As one's basic food, clothing, shelter, and security needs are completely ignored, the individual approaches physical death. When such needs are completely fulfilled and one moves toward affiliation, personal or psychological growth can occur, and without such fulfillment, psychological death can occur. Expressive needs are met and psychological growth occurs optimally through intimacy or a close shared relationship (Jourard, 1959). As both instrumental and expressive needs are fulfilled, one moves toward self-actualization and life fulfillment. Thus, relationships are formed out of the context of one's life experience in relations with self and others, with expressive and instrumental need fulfillment at the core of such interactions.

The process of relationship formation begins at birth or shortly thereafter. Each individual becomes a social being who, throughout life, lives in a complex dynamic series of intra/interpersonal situations. This process is characterized by the continuous surfacing of instrumental and expressive needs. Early Freudian thinkers (Freud, 1925) who examined personality development focused on the formative years (ages 1 to 5), emphasizing intrapersonal needs or psychosexual development. These theorists were concerned with the infant's ability to learn to discriminate and organize experiences in relation to inner needs. They emphasized the lasting influence of the appearances, attitudes, and behavior patterns of early significant others who satisfied those needs.

From a cultural psychoanalytic perspective, some authors (Sullivan, 1953; Erikson, 1959) focused on the extended developmental period and the elaboration and modification of the individual's social relations in response to needs or demands, limitations, and opportunities of the environment. Emphasis was placed on the other person required for the fulfillment of needs. While the Freudian and Sullivanian perspectives differ in terms of focus, both assert that the results of having both levels of needs met through significant others include growth, a sense of well-being or life fulfillment.

Early socialization of individuals in order to have needs met at the expressive and instrumental levels shapes the individual for adult relationships. Sullivan (1975) suggested that as a result, there is built into the human organism a striving for goal-directed process aimed at well-being through the fulfillment of needs. Sullivan stated: "Food and water, the approval of significant others, a worthwhile interesting job that one is capable of performing do provide euphoria. Physical, psychological, and socio-cultural conditions pertain to objective states of affairs, and it is the interaction of these with the requirements of the person that provide euphoria" (p. 601). In this instance, Sullivan is emphasizing the importance of instrumental and expressive need fulfillment.

The preceding discussion might offer some answers to the question "Why does A select B as a mate?" If the assumptions are that A and B are living in a society permitting voluntary mate selection, and that motives and needs, conscious and unconscious, are the reasons underlying most behavior, then we can conclude that A anticipates more gratification from the relationship with B than with any other available potential mate. Moreover, the implication is that the behaviors of A and B in the interactional process of courtship, relationship formation, and the subsequent relationship process are motivated to a great extent by various needs of A and B.

Expressive Needs

Conceptualizations of personality development and expressive needs in interpersonal relationships (Freud, 1925; Sullivan, 1953; and Erikson, 1959) suggest that expressive need fulfillment would be the most desired within interpersonal relationships and is most important to personal growth, development, and actualization.

Expressive need fulfillment meshes men and women in successful intimate relationships. One feels more ill at ease when expressive needs are unmet than at any other time. Such needs surface in feelings of wanting to be with or near the intimate other, or to share special moments, or in wanting not to be lonely. Expressive needs are also reflected in the characteristics identified in one's mate that make one feel comfortable or uncomfortable. Descriptive statements such as "He is dominant or aggressive and can take care of my needs" or "She is submissive or quiet and can be responsive to my needs" are often expressions of deeper psychological needs such as needs to be dependent, accepted, or validated.

Expressive needs are the most difficult to describe and to meet. Haspel (1976), in analysis of couples, found that such needs are often hidden or go unnoticed by one or both partners. Haspel found expressive needs to be hidden behind defenses, social values, or the interaction in the relationship that involves more surface issues. These needs are often hidden by filtering factors such as dishonesty about real needs and may surface after a period of interaction when defenses are more relaxed.

Expressive need fulfillment is most critical to the sustaining of the relationship; however, such needs are unlikely to surface at the initial meeting between partners or in the selection of a partner soon after the first meeting. In an analysis of the preferred mate characteristics and perceived marital benefits of 318 Black women, Coner and McAdoo (1985) found the women to prefer in prospective partners instrumental characteristics such as security, economic support, and the sharing of responsibilities. These same women desired from a marriage expressive benefits such as love, intimacy sharing, and emotional support. Thus, these women might select a partner based on instrumental needs rather than expressive needs.

Whereas it is at the deepest emotional level that individuals may seek to relate, very often filtering factors (Kerckhoff and Davis, 1962) intervene and cause individuals to relate or select a mate based on instrumental factors. An example is the status-seeking woman's selection of a man who is friendly, outgoing, and upwardly mobile. However, this woman may not have her strong needs for intimacy and companionship met in the relationship because her partner, who fears intimacy, has a strong need to be out with friends, attending parties and making contacts. Although the woman may have been socialized to seek a mate who is upwardly mobile, aggressive, and outgoing, her innermost need is for intimacy and close companionship. Thus, the filtering factor status needs or social values interfere with the selection of a mate based on inner expressive needs.

Instrumental Needs

Instrumental needs are basic and necessary to sustain life. Sullivan (1953), Parsons and Bales (1955), Maslow (1954), and others have emphasized the importance of basic instrumental needs. For many within the lower socioeconomic strata, the fulfillment of such needs becomes a central life-long activity. Some have suggested that among this group, instrumental needs would be emphasized (Ladner, 1972; Heiss, 1981; Staples, 1981b). Whereas middle-class Black relationships are the focus of this analysis and middle-class Blacks would be concerned with these basic survival needs to a lesser extent, these needs appear relevant to our discussion. Coner and McAdoo (1985) found that class notwithstanding, instrumental need factors were emphasized in evaluating mate characteristics.

The Selection Process

Instrumental needs are more observable and easier to define than expressive needs. According to Haspel (1976), such needs are generally the first that one seeks to have met. Needs so basic as security, protection, and economic support can sometimes become the sole criteria for the relationship (Coner, 1983; Coner and McAdoo, 1982, 1985). Thus, in dating, the security-conscious working or middle-class woman who seeks economic support as an instrumental need striving may select a financially secure man who cannot meet her more basic expressive needs. Thus, satisfaction of innermost expressive needs is never actualized in the relationship with the financially secure man who has difficulty with intimacy or self-disclosure.

Another example of the selection process is the man who sacrifices close companionship for supported family income provided by a successful woman who travels nine months of the year. Whereas it was his instrumental need to have a successful woman who could contribute to family income, his expressive needs were for love and close companionship. When these needs remain unfulfilled, frustration, depression, and often troubled marriages develop (Haspel, 1976).

The preceding discussion suggests that very often, the characteristics that one seeks in a mate are not representative of innermost expressive needs. In such cases, individuals find themselves surviving at the instrumental level, perhaps with some degree of success at the affiliation or interpersonal level. However, the growth, actualization, or reaching of one's potential that results from the process of a relationship at the higher, more intimate expressive level is never realized.

INTIMACY IN MALE-FEMALE RELATIONSHIPS

Each partner in a relationship must be able to reveal to the other deeper psychological needs. This can occur only through the process of continuous intimacy sharing through self-disclosure. Intimacy is a vital need of the relationship system. Only when it is fulfilled adequately will the couple be able to move on successfully with parenting, status, jobs, and income issues to time spent in those activities that enhance the quality of life individually and as a couple.

Intimacy is a special type of communication process by which an individual discloses feelings, perceptions, fears, and doubts of the inner self to the other partner (Ginsberg & Vogelson, 1977; Guerney, 1977; and Miller et. al., 1975). Intimacy allows relatively private thoughts and personal information to surface in the relationship that normally would not be revealed in the course of day-to-day interaction.

Intimacy is a key factor in the development of fulfilling and stable relationships (Altman and Taylor, 1973). Couples who are able to share intimate thoughts are considered by many to be building a foundation for a strong relationship that can enhance each partner's satisfaction with the alliance. Further, intimacy sharing can promote more efficient and effective interpersonal problem solving. This, in turn, will result in a more stable and satisfying relationship (Karisson, 1963; Jourard, 1964; Derlega and Chalkin, 1975; Gilbert, 1976).

These points have theoretical import for the understanding of intimacy in Black male-female relationships. As intimacy tolerance increases, the couple shares increasingly more of their deeper selves with each other. Subsequently, a strong emotional bond is developed that is less likely to be eroded by external stressors, or by one or both of the couple seeking this ongoing intimate interpersonal relationship elsewhere. Once the couple has shared what is perceived to be the deepest, perhaps ugliest parts of themselves, and find that they continue to be accepted, admired, loved, and thought to be beautiful and good by the person most important to them, their individual anxieties and fears begin to diminish. The partner can allow the underlying conflict associated with the fear and anxiety about the intimate content to surface. Thus, defenses are relaxed and increased closeness with the intimate partner is achieved.

The middle-class Black couple, without the structural constraints of joblessness, low income, or impoverished conditions, can work toward developing a high level of intimacy and self-disclosure, maintaining love, respect, and admiration for each other. In a satisfying relationship that can often minimize life difficulties, the couple can move, with a great deal of freedom, in pursuit of quality of life activities. The couple who develops intimacy and a high level of self-disclosure can develop a peaceful and dream-like quality of life more richly rewarding than any other external or objective pursuits.

BLACK MIDDLE-CLASS MALE-FEMALE RELATIONSHIPS

Most middle-class individuals spend a good portion of their lives in pursuit of education, self-development, a career, success, and advancement. For many Black middle-class individuals, the search for someone with whom to share their deeper, more intimate self comes only after the attainment of these pursuits. These individuals have set aside a focus on heterosexual relationship development toward the goal of achieving a solid middle-class status.

In addition to the greater stability of marriages among older adults, there may be some practical advantages in the delaying or eschewing of serious relationships among young adults. Time is available for maturation sufficient to cope with marriage, children, and other responsibilities, or to develop one's own interests. The practical advantages of delaying marriage appear to be more related to instrumental functions such as reaching economic stability, obtaining education, or developing one's own interests; the development of the essential relationship ingredients can be equally difficult later in life.

For older adults whose major existence is already defined, attempts to form a close intimate relationship can be fraught with anxieties and struggles. Coner-Edwards and Edwards delineate elsewhere in this volume the complexities of relationships and the varied dynamic issues with which couples are plagued. They note that these older established individuals are often relegated to a subordinate, childlike status in troubled relationships. The often prideful self-acclaimed middle-class individual who attempts to establish a satisfying intimate relationship is confronted with a most difficult challenge: placing her or his most vulnerable self at risk for repeated rejecting, devaluing, and critical attacks by a partner who is often unconsciously motivated. The middle-class individual, with money and other middle-class appointments, is no less vulnerable than someone less well off to the stresses and challenge of making a relationship work. No amount of money, education, success, or accomplishments can assuage the effects of these personally perceived assaults. However, those Black middle-class individuals who can develop the necessary ingredients (Coner-Edwards and Edwards, this volume) to endure these inevitable assaults can, with time, enjoy a rewarding and satisfying relationship.

SUMMARY

In this chapter, the author has focused on select issues relating to the psychological domain of Black male-female relationships. Emphasis has been placed on the role of early socialization in the shaping of individuals for intimate adult heterosexual relationships. Personality development and psychological needs are explored as they affect the establishment and maintenance of relationships. Intimacy-sharing and self-disclosure are emphasized as important determinants in the degree of satisfaction derived from the relationship. Black middle-class individuals who are able to develop the necessary ingredients to endure the complex dynamic problems found in all relationships can enjoy a life-long rewarding and satisfying relationship with their intimate partner. Individuals who have achieved stable and rewarding relationships can enjoy quality of life pursuits that can give their lives as a couple an even deeper meaning.

REFERENCES

Altman, J., & Taylor, D. (1973). *Social penetration: The development of interpersonal relationships.* New York: Holt, Rinehart and Winston.

Argyle, M., and Dean, J. (1965). Eye contact, distance and affiliation. *Sociometry, 28,* 289–304.

Ball, R. (1982). Marriage: Conducive to greater life satisfaction for American Black Women. Paper presented at the Annual Meeting of the National Council on Family Relations, Washington, D.C.

Billingsley, A. (1968). *Black families in White America.* Englewood Cliffs, NJ: Prentice-Hall.

Billingsley, A. (1970). Black families and White social science. *Journal of Social Issues, 26,* 127–142.

Blood, R. (1955). Retest of Waller's rating complex. *Marriage and Family Living, 17,* 41–47.

Blood, R., & Wolfe, D. (1960). *Husbands and wives: The dynamics of married living.* New York: Free Press.

Bowerman, G. E., & Day, B. R. (1956). A test of the theory of complimentary needs. *American Sociological Review, 21,* 602–605.

Centers, R. (1975). *Sexual attraction and love. An instrumental theory.* Springfield, IL: Charles C Thomas.

Coner, A. (1983). *Length of marriage, SES and relationship satisfaction in intact Black couples.* Research presented at Howard University Research Colloquium, Washington, D.C.

Coner, A., & McAdoo, H. (1982). *Effects of Black women's level of employment on their perceptions of heterosexual relationship conflict.* Research presented at the Annual Meeting of the Southern Sociological Society, Atlanta.

Coner, A., & McAdoo, H. (1985). Perceived marital benefits and preferred characteristics in prospective marital partners by Black single women. Paper presented at the Annual Meeting of the National Council on Family Relations, San Francisco.

Derlega, V., & Chalkin, A. (1975). *Sharing intimacy: What we reveal to others and why.* Englewood Cliffs, NJ: Prentice-Hall.

Engram, L. (1980). Role transition in early adulthood: Orientations of young Black women. In L. Rodgers-Rose (Ed.), *The Black Woman.* Beverly Hills, CA: Sage Publications.

Erikson, E. (1959). Identity and the life cycle: Selected papers. *Psychological Issues, 1,* 1–171.

Exline, R., Gray, D., & Schutte, D. (1965). Visual behavior in a dyad as affected by interview content and sex of respondent. *Journal of Personality and Social Psychology, 1,* 201–209.

Freud, S. (1974). Inhibitions, symptoms and anxiety. In J. Strachey (Ed. and Trans.), *The standard edition of the complete psychological works of Sigmund Freud, 22,* 87–172. London: Hogarth Press. (Original work published 1925)

Freud, S. (1974). On narcissism: an introduction. In J. Strachey (Ed. and Trans.), *The standard edition of the complete psychological works of Sigmund Freud, 14,* 73–102. London: Hogarth Press. (Original work published 1914)

Gilbert, S. (1976). Empirical and theoretical extensions of self-disclosure. In G. R. Miller (Ed.), *Explorations in interpersonal communication.* Vol. 5. Sage Annual Review of Communication Research. Beverly Hills, CA: Sage Publications.

Ginsberg, B., & Vogelson, E. (1977). Premarital relationship improvement by maximizing empathy and self-disclosure. In B. R. Guerney (Ed.), *Relationship enhancement.* San Francisco: Jossey-Bass.

Glick, P. (1975). A demographer looks at American families. *Journal of Marriage and the Family, 37,* 15–26.

Glick, P. (1981). A demographic picture of Black families. In H. McAdoo (Ed.), *Black families.* Beverly Hills: Sage Publications.
Guerney, B. R. (1977). *Relationship enhancement.* San Francisco: Jossey-Bass.
Hartmann, H. (1973). *Ego psychology and the problem of adaptation.* New York: International Universities Press.
Haspel, E. C. (1976). *Marriage in trouble: A time of decision.* Chicago: Nelson-Hall.
Heiss, J. (1975). *The case of the Black family.* New York: Columbia University Press.
Heiss, J. (1981). Women's values regarding marriage and the family. In H. McAdoo (Ed.), *Black families.* Beverly Hills, CA: Sage Publications.
Hollingshead, A. B. (1974). Cultural factors in the selection of marriage mates. In R. F. Winch & G. B. Spanier (Eds.), *Selected studies in marriage and the family.* New York: Holt, Rinehart and Winston.
Jourard, S. M. (1959). Self-disclosure and other cathexis. *Journal of Abnormal and Social Psychology, 59,* 428–431.
Jourard, S. M. (1964). *The transparent self.* Princeton, NJ: Van Nostrand.
Jourard, S. M., & Friedman, R. (1970). Experimenter-subject "distance" and self-disclosure. *Journal of Personality and Social Psychology, 15,* 278–282.
Karp, E. S., Jackson, J. H., & Lester, D. (1970). Ideal-self fulfillment in mate selection: A corollary to the complementary need theory of mate selection. *Journal of Marriage and the Family, 2*(32), 269–272.
Karisson, G. (1963). *Adaptability and communication in marriage.* Englewood Cliffs, New Jersey: Bedminister Press.
Keith, P., & Schafer, R. (1980). Role strain and depression in two-job families. *Family Relations, 29,* 483–488.
Kerckhoff, A. D., & Davis, K. E. (1962). Value consensus and need complementarity in mate selection. *American Sociological Review, 27*(3), 295–303.
Ladner, J. (1972). *Tomorrow's tomorrow: The Black woman.* Garden City, NY: Anchor Press.
Leggon, C. B. (1980). Black female professionals: Dilemmas and contradictions of status. In L. Rodgers-Rose (Ed.), *The Black woman.* Beverly Hills, CA: Sage Publications.
Mahler, M. (1975). *The psychological birth of the human infant.* New York: Basic Books.
Maslow, A. (1954). *Motivation and personality.* New York: Harper & Row.
McAdoo, H. (1983). *Extended family support of single Black mothers.*

(Final Report No. 5 Ro1 MH32159.) Washington, D.C.: U.S. Dept. of Health, Education & Welfare, Office of Child Development.

Miller, S., Corrales, R., & Wackman, D. B. (1975). Recent progress in facilitating and understanding marital communication. *The Family Coordinator, 24,* 143–152.

Moynihan, D. P. (1965). *The Negro family: The case for national action.* Washington, D.C.: Office of Policy, Planning and Research, U.S. Dept. of Labor.

Murray, H. A. (1938). *Explorations into personality* (pp. 36–141). New York: Oxford University Press.

Parsons, T., & Bales, R. F. (1955). *Family socialization and interaction process.* Glencoe, IL: Free Press.

Rodgers-Rose, L. (1980). Dialectics of Black male-female relationships. In L. Rodgers-Rose (Ed.), *The Black woman.* Beverly Hills, CA: Sage Publications.

Scanzoni, J. H. (1971). *The Black family in modern society.* Boston: Allyn & Bacon.

Staples, R. (1981a). Race and marital status: An overview. In H. McAdoo (Ed.), *Black families.* Beverly Hills, CA: Sage Publications.

Staples, R. (1981b). *The world of Black singles.* Westport, CT: Greenwood Press.

Sullivan, H. (1975). Interpersonal relations. In A. M. Freedman, H. I. Kaplan, and B. J. Saddock (Eds.), *Comprehensive textbook of psychiatry,* 2d ed. Vol. 1. Baltimore: Williams & Wilkins.

Sullivan, H. (1953). *The interpersonal theory of psychiatry.* New York: Norton.

Winch, R. F. (1955). The theory of complementary needs in mate selection: A test of one kind of complementariness. *American Sociological Review, 20,* 52–56.

Winch, R. F. (1974). Complementary needs and related notions about voluntary mate-selection. In R. F. Winch & G. B. Spanier (Eds.), *Selected studies in marriage and the family.* New York: Holt, Rinehart and Winston.

5

Male-Female Relationships: The Woman's Perspective

Jeanne Spurlock

Black middle-class women hold a variety of views about male-female relationships. In part, the various perspectives stem from experiences during early psychosocial development and influences from the broader environment, as they affect the woman's family of origin and experiences during development. We will address these factors in a discussion of common experiences of middle-class Black women. Several examples from the literature and clinical vignettes illustrate these points.

WHO ARE BLACK MIDDLE-CLASS WOMEN?

Black middle-class women are as varied as the middle-class population in general. We are homemakers, educators, bankers, health service professionals, lawyers, elected government officials, engineers, and artists. Some of us own and operate businesses; others have partnerships in successful enterprises. Women who hold senior-grade government posts and managerial positions are among us. The younger set is working for undergraduate degrees; others are pursuing postgraduate training, and some of us have formally retired but are still actively involved in volunteer work, or even in a second career. Some of us are first-generation middle class; others come from families with a long history of middle-class status. We grew up in single-parent families (often made so by divorce) as well as two-parent households. For some of us, our childhood family life was troubled; others grew up in a relatively trouble-free environment. Obviously, we represent a wide age range, as well as a range of physical characteristics and a varied health history. We are married or single, divorced, or widowed. Some of us have positive relationships with the men in our lives; others of us are in relationships studded with conflicts and we ourselves question why we stay. Others among us are currently (or episodically) devoid of male companionship because of fate, happenstance, or choice.

NOTES FROM THE LITERATURE: BLACK FEMALE-MALE RELATIONSHIPS

Much that has been written about our relationships with men has been negative. Impairment of male-female relationships is reflected in the writings of Black dramatists, novelists, and other authors, as well as in the writings of behavioral scientists. The history of the recent Civil Rights movement also highlights some of the problems existing in our relationships with men; Giddings (1984) cites a number of situations that illustrate the "need for male affirmation" as a root for some of the problems. She notes that women with leadership abilities were called upon to make significant contributions but were then labeled as domineering or castrating of the men, who appeared driven to affirm their primacy. Giddings provides a number of illustrations; two have been singled out as representative. The highest-ranking woman on the staff of the Southern Christian Leadership Conference (SCLC), Dorothy Cotton, reported her observations of the male chauvinism that was present within the organization. However, she also called attention to the fact that it was a male member of the staff who insisted that she *had* to be involved in the deliberations and decision making; this stand was taken after Cotton had been excluded from several important sessions. Ella Baker, who also played a significant role in the creation of the SCLC, cited the male participants' restrictive definition of a woman's role as the reason for not seeking a leadership role herself. Angela Davis, who did have a leadership role in the Los Angeles chapter of the Student Nonviolent Coordinating Committee, made similar observations. Davis (1974) concluded that the steady influx of male supremacist attitudes provoked the men to oppose female leadership. Male chauvinism appeared to intensify with the decline of the Civil Rights movement (Giddings, 1984). Former Congresswoman Shirley Chisholm was a victim of this circumstance.

Grier and Cobbs (1968) suggest that the child-rearing practices of

Black women have earned the hostility of Black men. They charge us with curbing our sons' assertive and aggressive tendencies, thus depriving them of the necessary elements of manhood. Staples (1970) views the strength of Black women as a root cause for the disdain of Black men. He wrote of Black men's wide range of choices in mate selection and of their tendency to screen out strong Black women. However, in another context, Staples (1973) emphasized that "Black women had to be strong in order to ensure their family's survival." According to Staples, the label *matriarchs* has been misapplied to Black women. He noted that the dominant society has "ignored the fact that circumstances forced Black women to be strong and self-reliant in order to achieve the survival of the Black community." However, there is more than a hint that the myth of the Black matriarchy is kept alive, in part, by Black men.

Other investigators have reported positive responses to the strengths of Black women. Harrison (1977) noted that many people in the Black communities value Black women for traits that have been viewed as components of the stereotype of American masculinity: "strength, independence and resourcefulness." The differences in the concept of femininity — at least, that which is accepted and even applauded in some sections of the Black communities — from the traditional, stereotypic view of the dominant group may be a source of conflict for some Black women. Harrison also reported little or no fear of success among Black women, and concluded that this finding explained Black women's perception of competitively based accomplishments as compatible with femininity. However, Puryear and Mednick (1975) reported fear of success in Black women who were involved in the Black Power movement. They viewed the fear to be related to the premise that female independence is antithetical to Black survival.

In a study of perceptions of the female role by persons of both sexes, Steinmann and Fox (1970) determined that Black women perceived men as preferring women with a balance of self-achieving and familial orientations. Another significant finding was the common perception of Black females and Black males that the ideal Black woman paralleled that which the Black women subjects were, and wanted to be.

FOUNDATION OF RELATIONSHIP
BUILDING: THEORETICAL CONCEPTS

The child-rearing experiences of Blacks, like those of others, serve as a foundation for future relationships. The early interaction between

Black children and the primary caretaker (usually the mother) provides their first intimate relationship, as it does for others. However, other factors, such as stresses generated by economic instability, are likely to have a decided impact on the mother-child relationship. Davis (1968) noted there to be a decrease in a mother's capacity to provide emotional security for her child if she is unable to obtain the necessary physical, economic, and emotional support for herself in the mothering role. Likewise, a mother's (and father's) specific responses to experiences with racism may influence the shaping of this first intimate relationship. However, the influences of the political-social climate are not introduced here to diminish the importance of the differences in the personality development of females and males.

An early theory of personality development was constructed around the experiences of the male child (Freud, 1953). Later, efforts were directed toward understanding female development by utilizing the concept of male development as a reference point (Freud, 1961). Psychoanalysts Karen Horney (1926) and Clara Thompson (1942) were among the early challengers of these theories. More contemporary challenges parallel the resurgence of the feminist movement. Jean Baker Miller (1976) called attention to the different starting point of women's development, in that affiliation is likely to be more highly valued than self-enhancement (as compared to men). She noted that "women stay with, build on, and develop in a context of attachment and affiliation with others. . . . Women's sense of self becomes very much organized around being able to make, and then maintain, affiliations and relationships. . . . Eventually, for many women, the threat of disruption of an affiliation is perceived not just as a loss of a relationship but something closer to a total loss of self" (p. 83).

This same concept is emphasized by Chodorow (1974), who writes of gender differences as related to the universal pattern of women as the early child care providers. This early pattern serves as a foundation for later patterns of behavior observed in women: caring for and taking care of others. Gilligan (1982) also wrote of the differences in relationships as experienced by females and males. Separation (from mother) and individuation are critical steps in the development of masculinity. The process is in sharp contrast to the steps taken by females, who need not separate from the first love object, the mother, in the course of developing femininity. "Since masculinity is defined through separation while femininity is defined through attachment, male gender identity is threatened by intimacy while female gender identity is threatened by separation. Thus males tend to have difficulties with relationships, while females tend to have problems with individuation" (p. 8).

DESIRES AND EXPECTATIONS

What characteristics do Black women see as most desirable in the men in their lives? What do we expect? Staples (1973) points out that education has become increasingly important as a status requirement in the Black middle-class community. Those Black middle-class women who are reasonably financially secure are likely to put a greater emphasis on emotional gratification as a key factor in a male-female relationship (Staples, 1973; Coner-Edwards and McAdoo, 1985). Emotional support and gratification has been found to be a requirement among Black middle-class women who have consulted me.

Whether married or separated or divorced, most women expect financial support for their minor and college-age children; most hope for a healthy emotional father-child relationship. Some women expect a monogamous relationship, especially in a marriage. Others expect their husbands will be involved with other women, and "suffer" silently, or loudly. However, other women show no overt emotional response to their husbands' affairs. They view the marriage as an arrangement that provides a certain status that meets some of their needs (social standing, financial security).

In a survey using open-ended, unstructured questions to determine the qualities liked and disliked in intimate relationships between Black women and men, Rodgers-Rose (1980) found some striking similarities between men and women. For example, both listed honesty and understanding as desirable and key qualities in a partner. Women over 30 years of age stressed the importance of affective behavioral qualities (particularly, open communication); younger women viewed specific character traits, such as intelligence, stability, and positive self-concept, as most important to them.

POSITIVE RELATIONSHIPS

In the responses to the Essence Quality of Life Survey of 1980, over one-half (52%) of the 6,157 respondents disagreed with a statement that Black men are supportive of Black women. "I can't count on him to be supportive when I'm down" is a frequent lament of women referred to me. An additional and parallel complaint of women who have sought mental health services is the absence of psychological support for their efforts in "holding the family together." So it was for E. S., who made use of her accounting skills and set up a small consulting operation. The idea was discussed with her husband, who was in accord with the plan and goal, which was to supplement the family income. But his ongoing support was not to be.

Not all Black men, however, are alike. Over one-third (37%) of the respondents to the aforementioned survey indicated that Black men are supportive of Black women. J. E. would have agreed. Her husband had been extremely supportive of her wish and subsequent efforts to earn the highest degree in her field. Her husband volunteered to take on some of the housekeeping chores, and assumed more responsibilities in "overseeing" the children's homework so as to allow J. E. ample study time.

R. G. would have also been one of the respondents who indicated that husbands are supportive. Both she and her husband were health service providers; he was as supportive of her goals for career advancement as she was of his. They were truly equal partners in their marriage. They shared child-rearing responsibilities, and before they could afford household help they shared housekeeping tasks. They liked and respected each other, and, after 35 years of marriage, they continued to love each other. "Of course, it's a different kind of love; it's more mellow than exciting, but we still light fires."

The relationships that J. E. and R. G. have with their respective partners are not unusual among the Black middle class. However, many of their sisters do not fare so well.

Problems in Relationships with Men

The following findings were culled from a review of the psychotherapeutic work (mine and several colleagues) with fifty Black middle-class women. A wide age range was represented — 28 to 67. Some women were single; others were divorced or were widows. Some were in their second marriage, but the majority of the married women were in their first marriage. All had some college education; most had earned advanced degrees and several had earned the highest degree in their respective fields of work. Several were formally retired but were effective contributors to various civic activities. Most of the women were reasonably successful in their workplaces. Others were exceptional achievers, but a few were having difficulty maintaining adequate productivity (primarily because of depression).

Regardless of the reason for referral, the majority of the women identified problems in their relationships with the men in their lives. Although these relationships did not exist in isolation from other life experiences, the relationship issues have been singled out for emphasis in the following discussion.

Their complaints about the men in their lives focused primarily on the man's insensitivity to their emotional needs. The spin-off of this complaint included perceived neglect or unavailability on the part of the man. "He's seldom [or never] around when I need him [or when the children need him]"; "He may be home, but he's not psychologically available"; "He's more interested in the football game than he is in spending time with me." These are common statements offered by the women in this sample. Depression and overt or thinly veiled anger were common reactions of the women.

Another concern frequently expressed pertained to the man's negative reaction to the woman's achievements and success in the workplace. An elaboration of this point was made by a 35-year-old married senior-grade government employee. Her statement paralleled the descriptions provided by others in this sample group.

> Before our marriage we talked about our respective needs to succeed in our work, and the importance of work in terms of the financial rewards that would lend toward the making of a nest egg for our future. Our marriage was supposed to be a partnership. Things seemed to start going down hill when I got a two-step promotion, which allowed me to bring home a bigger pay check than his. I thought he'd be pleased. Oh, he said he was, but later, he made sarcastic remarks about my promotion. To add insult to injury, he began to make these comments in social settings.

Campbell (1987) writes of similar "case histories" in her book, *Successful Women, Angry Men: Backlash in the Two-Career Marriage.* Certainly, as Campbell notes, there are added stressors in dual-career marriages. But some couples handle the stress better than others. A number of women who have consulted me have identified their success and their husbands' career problems as key factors in their marital discord. For most of these women their successes meant that they spent more time in the workplace or at work-related meetings and were less available to their husbands. (This pattern has also been observed in situations involving a husband's career successes.) Several times it became apparent in joint sessions with a couple that the husband had difficulty in revealing any dependency needs (e.g., for sustained emotional support) and had covered these feelings with expressions of irritation, if not overt anger, toward his wife about minor issues.

"I'm being stifled in this relationship" is another complaint of more than a few women who have sought treatment, for whatever reason. The following vignettes are illustrative of many expressed concerns.

> Jim and I were discussing a current political situation. We didn't see it as a debate; we were just sharing our opinions about an issue that was being widely discussed in the community. I don't remember what it was that I said that prompted his comment, "That's your problem; you're too smart." I knew that there had been trouble brewing in our relationship, but I hadn't noted that he saw us as competitors. We both had earned the highest degree in our respective fields; I respected and admired his contributions to his field. Certainly, I was unprepared for his comment, which was followed by a sarcastic elaboration. I knew, then, that I would be stifled if I tried to hold on to this relationship. Even so, I feel a sense of loss, and am depressed about it.

> Forty-year-old Dolores K. had responded differently to a similar situation for the past fifteen years. Early in her marriage she had understood her husband to want and need her to be submissive. Since the maintenance of the relationship was of highest importance to her, she was willing to "take my place as he designed it." She had once verbalized her wish to pursue graduate study, but didn't press the subject; her husband had stated that she didn't need further education, and had wondered whether she doubted his ability to take care of her. Now her husband was critical of her insularity. In retrospect, she felt she had made a grave error in allowing herself to be smothered as an individual.

In therapeutic encounters with women with histories similar to that of Dolores, therapist and patient must be aware of the possibility that reaching the therapeutic goal of restoring the patient's positive sense of self may result in termination of the marriage. A successful therapeutic outcome can afford the patient an opportunity to leave a relationship that is psychologically destructive.

Like most of us, a sizable number of the women in this sample brought some of the "baggage" of past relationships into their current ones.

Thirty-year-old Ellen W. had had very limited contact with her father after her parents were divorced when she was about to enter junior high school. She recalled that her parents had had a stormy marriage, partly because of her father's drinking. So she had been relieved that she would not have to witness the results of his drinking sprees. However, she recalled that she also had been saddened by his leaving and had looked forward to his visits. The sadness soon gave way to disappointment, then anger, when he became less and less responsible about keeping his promises (e.g., about visiting, or shopping for school supplies or clothing). In the course of therapy it was determined that she looked for "positive fathering" in her later relationships with men, or she entered a relationship with an uneasy feeling about abandonment. It had been impossible for her to consider making a commitment because of her fear of being left. Her pattern of dealing with this concern was unconsciously to set up a situation that would lead to the termination of the relationship. The therapeutic work brought about considerable insight and an opportunity to work through her anger and disappointment with her father. She began to see men "through a different lens" and entered relationships from a healthier frame of reference.

SUMMARY

There are multiple roots in the development of Black female-male relationships, as well as in the stabilization or breakdown of the relationships. A cursory review of the literature reflects negativity as a primary focus. Different women have different expectations of the men in their lives, and expectations as well as needs may change during the course of a woman's life cycle. At a particular critical period in her life, a woman may determine that an ongoing relationship with the man in her life is not in her best interests, or that it is more important that she direct her primary efforts in other channels (e.g., her career).

Examples of positive and stable relationships, and those in turmoil, were presented. The impact of societal pressures, particularly racial issues, was addressed. The effectiveness of psychotherapy was emphasized as a means of eradicating "ghosts from the past" that interfere with the development of a positive relationship in the present.

REFERENCES

Campbell, B. M. (1987). *Successful Women, Angry Men: Backlash in the Two-Career Marriage.* New York: Random House.

Chodorow, N. (1974). Family structure and feminine personality. In M. Z. Rosaldo and L. Lamphere (Eds.), *Woman, culture and society.* Stanford, CA: Stanford University Press.

Coner-Edwards, A. F., and McAdoo, H. P. (1985). *Perceived marital benefits and preferred characteristics in prospective marital partners by Black single women.* Paper presented at the Annual Meeting of the National Council on Family Relations, San Francisco.

Davis, A. (1974). *Angela Davis: An autobiography.* New York: Random House.

Davis, E. B. (1968). The American Negro: Family membership to personal and social identity. *Journal of the National Medical Association, 60,* 92–99.

Freud, S. (1953). Infantile sexuality. In J. Strachey (Ed. and Trans.), *The standard edition of the complete psychological works of Sigmund Freud, 7,* 173–206. London: Hogarth Press. (Original work published 1905)

Freud, S. (1961). Female sexuality. In J. Strachey (Ed. and Trans.), *The standard edition of the complete psychological works of Sigmund Freud, 21,* 225–243. London: Hogarth Press. (Original work published 1931)

Giddings, P. (1984). *When and where I enter: The impact of Black women on race and sex in America.* New York: Bantam Books.

Gilligan, C. (1982). *In a different voice.* Cambridge, MA: Harvard University Press.

Grier, W. H., and Cobbs, P. M. (1968). *Black rage.* New York: Bantam Books.

Harrison, A. O. (1977). Black women. In V. E. O'Leary (Ed.), *Toward understanding women,* pp. 132–146. Monterey, CA: Brooks/Cole.

Horney, K. (1926). Flight from womanhood. *International Journal of Psychoanalysis, 7,* 324–339.

Miller, J. B. (1976). *Toward a new psychology of women.* Boston: Beacon Press.

Puryear, G. R., and Mednick, M. S. (1975). Black militancy, affective attachment, and fear of success in black college women. *Journal of Consulting and Clinical Psychology, 38,* 343–347.

Rodgers-Rose, L. (1980). Dialectics of Black male-female relationships. In L. Rodgers-Rose (Ed.), *The Black woman.* Beverly Hills, CA: Sage Publications.

Staples, R. (1970). The myth of the Black matriarchy. *Black Scholar, 1,* 8–16.

Staples, R. (1973). *The Black woman in America.* Chicago: Nelson-Hall.

Steinmann, A., and Fox, D. J. (1970). Attitudes toward women's family role among Black and White undergraduates. *The Family Coordinator, 19,* 363–368.

Thompson, C. (1942). Cultural pressures in the psychology of women. *Psychiatry, 5,* 331–339.

6

Male-Female Relationships: The Man's Perspective

Henry E. Edwards

This chapter will examine elements in the relationship between Black middle-class men and women from the male perspective. Information for this clinical study came from data collected in a literature review and analysis of observations made on a random sample of forty middle-class Black male patients in psychotherapy with the author.

BACKGROUND

Much has been written on the legacy of the historical experience of Blacks in this country and the negative impact that slavery, racism, and poverty have had on the self-esteem, identity, roles, and quality of relationships of Black men and women. Braithwaite (1981), for example, describes "the perspective of the basic slave social order which has sustained the Black man in a subservient and dependent role" (p. 83).

Despite the obvious daily impact of racial discrimination, such as the "microaggressions" described by Pierce (this volume), racial factors are seldom mentioned when Black middle-class men discuss the trouble they are having in their relationships with women. This observation was also made by Cazenave (1983) in his study of 155 middle-class Black men.

Relationships between Black middle-class men and women are not inherently different from those of other racial, ethnic, economic, or gender groups in this country. Culture and history affect the staging, goals, and activities of different groups, but certain basic issues, patterns of interaction, and conflicts are critical, recurrent, and found in most close, long-lasting relationships (Blumstein and Schwartz, 1983; Scarf, 1987).

Perhaps this commonality is related to similar features in the child-rearing process between parent and child. This earliest and most intimate interaction serves as the basic template for all future deep and romantic relationships. An intense drama is played out in infancy and childhood surrounding the feelings of love, intimacy, and sexuality. Much of the later struggle between men and women is, in effect, a blind attempt to reestablish or induce with the current partners the conditions of this earliest love relationship. Success or failure in a relationship is often measured by how well one "feels" one has accomplished this mostly unconscious task.

The process of identity formation also influences later relationships between men and women. This process, which, as Stoller (1964) and others point out, begins so early in life, unfolds in the context of ongoing relationships. It is thus not surprising to observe Black men struggling to confirm, protect, or finally crystallize their identities in the context of their current relationships with women.

As described in the last chapter, Gilligan (1982) presented ideas about male and female identity formation that have intriguing and provocative implications for understanding relationships. The mother, she points out, is the primary love object initially for both boys and girls. Girls are able to form their feminine identities while continuing this important relationship with their mother. On the other hand, for boys to define themselves as masculine, they must separate their mothers from themselves, thus curtailing their primary love and sense of empathic tie. "Male development entails a more emphatic individuation and a more defensive firming of experienced ego boundaries. . . . All of this has important . . . impact on later male-female relationships" (Gilligan, 1982, p. 8).

Another important factor in understanding Black male-female relationships is role definition and function within the American society. The degree of "masculinity" is measured in terms of the role the man assumes and how successful he is in the enactment of that role. Cazenave (1983) found that the most valued role for Black men was that of economic provider. The ability to provide is a key societal determinant of how successfully men are able to carry out their masculine role responsibilities and the degree of their emotional involvement in family life.

Lower-class Black males are often unable to be providers because they have limited access to resources, job opportunities, and education, and are therefore often unable to establish a masculine identity as provider for their family. They may find themselves forced into the "double bind" of attempting to prove their manhood while being denied access to the legitimate tool with which to do so (Cazenave, 1981). This situation may lead them to alternative lifestyles and modes of behavior that may serve to prove their masculinity or allow them to retreat from the effort, but may make it difficult, if not impossible, to establish and maintain a satisfying relationship.

The Black middle-class male, on the other hand, is more able to be a provider. He has job and status and does not face the same economical survival need. He is also more likely to have a wife who works, who may also be a professional, and who married him not for economic support as much as for emotional support and satisfaction of psychological needs. Thus, because he has more economic security (although he often experiences much stress and challenge in maintaining it), the Black middle-class man is able to think more about pursuing quality and satisfaction in his relationship. There are, however, difficulties in this pursuit, and that is the focus of the remainder of this chapter.

Black men, like Black women, are needy for and searching for love, nurturance, support, and a haven to which to retreat. Leland Hall (1981) points out that as the Black male grows older, his need for support becomes more sophisticated but no less important than when he was a child. The problem is that once he leaves the protection of his family of origin and his early subgroups it is often difficult to find a place to go for this support. He continues to search for but is unable to find a place to be intimate.

Maggie Scarf (1986) describes intimacy as "the ability to talk about who he is and to say what he wants and needs, and to be heard by the intimate partner, . . . being able to tell his mate about how rotten and defeated he happens to be feeling, rather than having always to pretend to be masterful and adequate. But, he has a fear of getting too close . . . so close that the mate will see and condemn his weakness and failings" (p. 49). Intimacy, then, can be said to exist when one is able to expose one's inner self *and* get a response of empathy. Black men often express the fear that they will get not empathy but, rather, criticism or attack if they "open up."

BLACK MAN'S BLUES

This section focuses attention, more specifically, on today's Black middle-class man's struggles within his intimate relationships with

Black women. Being a physician and not a sociologist, I will emphasize what is hurting, what is the "dis-ease" that has brought these men to my consultation room, rather than statistics or cultural or other sociological issues. Black men come to the psychiatrist's office in large numbers, in pain and genuinely seeking help. They have little or nothing to say about the statistics, myths, and other sociological pronouncements so often made about them. Rather, they come in talking about the depression, anxiety, frustration, fear, guilt, esteem issues, and anger that are most often related to the close, ongoing relationship with the important women in their lives. They are vague and unknowing about many things that bother them; however, they are very clear about their "bad" feelings in their intimate relationships.

SAMPLE DESCRIPTION

To provide some specific data for this chapter, I randomly selected and reviewed the charts of forty Black men who came to my office over the past five years. The forty initially came into treatment for marital or relationship difficulty, family conflict, identity confusion, fears of own impulses, and court- or other-related evaluations. These Black males were all residing in the Washington, D.C. metropolitan area.

The men in this sample ranged in age from 18 to 65. Sixty-five percent of the sample were married at the time they were seeking psychotherapy; 87% had been married at some time. Thirteen percent of the men were separated and 10% divorced.

The men were generally of the upper middle-class, engaged in managerial, professional, or higher-level executive positions. The most frequent complaint was marital conflict, and the men suffered anxiety and depression.

The data to follow come primarily from reviewing the charts of these men and listening to what they had to say about the women with whom they were currently sharing, or attempting to share, their lives. The data consist of their personal accounts of their lives, and analysis, in psychotherapy or psychoanalysis, of their wishes, fears, fantasies, and dreams. In using this type of material it is important to keep in mind Brenner's (1982) caution: "Everyone, without exception is at considerable pain to deceive himself or herself about his or her own motives, past experiences, and current plans or wishes for the future. It is for this reason that the data of introspection are so unreliable. They are invariably, systematically falsified, suppressed or both" (p. 3). Nonetheless, systematically collecting and analyzing this information over a period of time, matching it with its manifestations in the transference (to the therapist), and comparing it with information from other patients reveals reliable, consistent data that can be very helpful in understanding problems of Black men in their relationships and in helping them to recognize and deal with these problems in therapy.

TYPICAL PROFILE

The typical man in this sample was a well-educated, professional, married, upper-middle-class, Black man of approximately 35 years of age. He could be labeled an intelligent, "obsessive-depressive achiever." Although achievers in the world, the men tended to be depressed and felt like failures in their relationships, or more often, at least initially, that their relationships (or women) had failed them.

Despite racism and, for many, growing up in families of lower socioeconomic status, most of these men had grown up with a sense of importance, power, or status in their significant reference groups (home, church, school, etc.). They had a sense of being "somebody," the "apple of their mother's eye," the teacher's favorite, basketball hero, acolyte or junior deacon, president of the student council, or the like.

Many grew up unevenly — early in some ways, delayed in others — "little men" and "little boys" simultaneously. They tended not to be rebellious but, rather, to accept and carry out the directives of significant others to be "good," go to church, do well in school, get a job and help take care of their mothers, their siblings, and themselves. Many had their first regular job as early as age 9 or 10, delivering newspapers or cutting grass, and had worked constantly or gone to school since. In essence they tended to be "good," "nice boys," whose behavior was designed to please their elders, sometimes at the expense of the scorn of their siblings and peers. They were rewarded for this "goodness" by being considered "special."

Typically, these men saw their mothers as strong but needy. Their fathers most often were portrayed as either absent (early death, desertion, military, working two or more jobs, pullman porter, etc.) or weak (alcoholic, passive, uninvolved, unemotional, unemployed, etc.).

As young boys the men often had been substitute love objects for their mothers, many of whom were young themselves, with absent or unsatisfying husbands. Mother and son often spent a lot of time together talking, going places, working around the house, and day-dreaming. This situation was often overstimulating. A common view of the mother as unhappy and needy, materially and emotionally, often elicited a desire to rescue, protect, and take care of her. This was typically accompanied by conscious disparagement and anger at the father, and a determination to be better than the father and take better care of the mother. It became more clear in treatment that the men unconsciously were afraid of their fathers' retaliation, guilty over their anger and envious desire to replace the father and, indeed, ashamed of failing to replace the father and take care of the mother. (A resurgence of the oedipal complex in the prepubertal or early adolescent period.)

These men also, consciously or unconsciously, were often angry with their mothers. Although considered "special" and the "favorite," they were clearly not the "preferred." They would immediately be relegated to second place when the father or another adult male loved one returned. They were also angry with their mothers for "conditional love." It was as though the mothers were saying, "I will love you on the condition that you are good and obedient [or that you deliver high performance, or that you help around the house, etc.]."

As young boys they often feel emotionally isolated and alone with their feelings. Lacking opportunities to share or explore many of their feelings and thoughts, and driven by an intense desire to maintain their "good/special" image, they learned well how to control their feelings by suppression, acting out in fantasy, and especially by sublimation. For example, they often had much underlying, unex-pressed anger and hostility toward the father for his absence, weak-ness, inconsistency, punitiveness, or cruelty to family, and especially his apparent lack of love and acceptance of them. Very often this hidden anger was sublimated, used to fuel their own development. Maturation was derived from a defiant, "I'll show him" attitude. It was only in therapy that some of these men finally realized the strong yearning they had for closeness with their fathers and developed a sense of understanding and admiration for them.

To let strong feelings show was viewed as bad, dangerous, or a sign of weakness. It was "wrong" to say the "right" thing. Some patients reported being afraid to show weakness because it would show their vulnerability and others might hurt them, take advantage of them, try to control them, leave them, not love them, or make them feel castrated.

The basic fear of men is "castration fear" — i.e., fear that they will not be seen as strong, or that their strength will be taken away. At base this has to do with viewing the self vis-à-vis other men. The man constantly makes comparisons that lead to performance anxiety. These men tended to date later, to be more serious when they did, and to have a more controlled, repressed, and delayed sexual life. It was not uncommon to hear that conscious masturbation did not take place until college. Initially, they tended to prefer younger, innocent, virginal females with little experience so that they were less likely to fail the comparison test. Their attitudes and anxieties seem related to faulty education about sex. Such education was usually absent at home, and much misinformation was picked up in the streets or barber shop, or behind the school. These men, as boys, had heard a lot of lies, fantasies, and exaggerations about men's sexual performance that were taken literally. Many felt they could never measure up to "Loving Dan," who, according to the song, could "rock 'em — roll 'em — all night long." He was "a 60-minute man." So when they could only "rock" their women for 5 or 10 minutes, they felt like failures. This speaks to the emphasis men put on performance and the competitiveness, fears, and comparisons revolving around other, usually fantasied men.

Having failed at accomplishing the fantasied oedipal goals in their youth, this group of men seemed to have an especially intense need to succeed in doing for their wives what they were unable to do for their mothers — to finally be able to take care of the important woman in their lives, make her happy and provide for her as they wanted but couldn't as young boys. Unfortunately, for these men now seeking therapy, they see themselves as having failed once again. They yearn for closeness and the opportunity to be important but are frustrated in their efforts.

PRESENTING COMPLAINTS

These men had many complaints about the important women in their lives. These often highly criticized women could be categorized on the basis of these complaints as intimidating, castrating, neglecting, or frustrating.

Intimidating

There were more complaints in this category than in the other three. The complaints were of two types: (1) *wife as controlling* — "She wants to dominate"; "My wife hits me"; "She humiliates me"; "She's so rude to me"; "She treats me like a kid"; "She always has to be on top"; "She takes advantage of me because I'm nice"; and (2) *wife as more successful* — complaints here are related to the fact that wife makes more money, has more education, is more independent and "well rounded." "She and her family look down on me"; "I don't understand what she sees in me."

Castrating

Complaints in this category have to do with the man blaming his wife for making him feel "less than a man." This was often related to: (1) the woman's decreased interest in sex or (2) the woman's criticism of his sexual performance — he's told he's too old, it's not like it used to be, or he's chastised for being interested only in sex. Also very deflating were "cold" comments from the wife, after what the man felt was a pretty notable performance, like "Are you finished yet?" or "You can get off me now!"

Neglecting

Many married men felt neglected by their wives — "She never spends any time with me"; "She leaves me all the time"; "She doesn't do anything for me"; "She never shows she loves me." The wife is also often described as being unsupportive — "She doesn't show any interest in anything I do"; "I never get any respect for any of my ideas or anything I say"; "It's like not having a wife."

Frustrating

Here the women are described as impossible to please. "I don't know what she wants"; "I can't make her happy"; "She won't let me do anything for her"; "She doesn't seem to care about herself."

These complaints collectively and consciously reflect the underlying loss or chronic absence of intimacy between these men and the important women in their lives. They don't feel they are loved in the sense love is defined by the Oxford Dictionary (1971): "that disposition or state of feeling with regard to a person which . . . manifests itself in solicitude for the welfare of the object, and usually also in delight in his presence . . .; warm affection and attachment." As the complaints demonstrate, these men characteristically find no "solicitude" for their welfare, feel their wives have lost that sense of "delight in his presence" they seemed to have during courtship, and when together no longer experience that state of "warm affection and attachment." What, then, leads these men to sing, like the Righteous Brothers, that we've "lost that lovin' feeling"?

INTERFERENCE WITH INTIMACY

Observation of this group of Black middle-class men reveals that factors interfering with intimacy fall into two broadly defined and overlapping categories, intrapsychic/unconscious and interpersonal/conscious.

Intrapsychic/Unconscious Factors

These are critical factors within the psyche of the individual that affect his personal psychological functioning as well as his interactions with others. Interferences with intimacy are related to these underlying, largely unconscious, dynamic issues involving the individual's unconscious wishes, conflicts, fears, and defenses. According to psychoanalytic theory (Brenner, 1982), it is "unpleasure" that is responsible for defense and conflict in connection with infantile instinctual wishes. In 1926 Freud (1961) spoke of anxiety (unconscious fear) as being the "signal" that would cause the individual to use some defensive maneuver in self-protection from this unconscious fear — usually by distancing oneself in some way from the threatening idea, feeling, or situation. This defensive maneuver and distancing has a clear impact on intimacy. Brenner (1982) expanded on Freud's idea by stating that in addition to anxiety (unconscious fear) there is another form of unpleasurable affect that can also cause defensiveness (and result in pulling back or distancing in relationships): what Brenner calls "depressive affect." Whereas "anxiety" refers to the anticipation (fear) of some danger ahead, "depressive affect" deals with something that has already happened. These two similar mechanisms triggering the use of defenses and withdrawal can be characterized:

Anxiety as trigger. I won't be open and show you my true feelings because (1) you might leave me, (2) you might stop loving me, (3) you might attack/hurt/damage me, or (4) I might feel it was wrong and punish myself with guilt.

Depressive affect as trigger. I won't be open and show you my true feelings because one or more of the above has already happened and I am feeling depressed (and also anxious that it might happen again).

These defensive and distancing responses are automatic, largely unconscious, and related more to childhood wishes, fears, and conflicts than to the current relationship that activates them.

Interpersonal/Conscious Factors

Five common recurring themes were identified in this sample of Black middle-class men that interfered significantly with intimacy in their relationships: a tendency to use stereotypes; difficulty with anger; inability to appreciate the complexity of oneself and the other; failure to allow one's "child" self in the relationship; inability to fully exert one's "adult" self in the relationship.

These factors were generally unconscious and were easily discussed, but when examined in the treatment process were usually found to lead to the deeper-seated intrapsychic conflicts just mentioned. I will describe and illustrate each of these briefly.

Tendency to stereotype. "I can't be intimate with you because you don't see *me*, and I feel you don't want to know who *I* really am." These men feel prejudged and found guilty before committing a crime: "You don't have any feelings"; "Given half a chance you'll run around"; "I know you've been running around — all men do"; "Men are just little boys — irresponsible." These men often saw themselves as victims of statistics and the sexism of women.

Men also judge themselves by stereotypes. In order to "be a man," there are certain things he feels he should or should not do. He can't just "be himself." These stereotypes of both men and women are derived from their heritage, general cultural experiences, childhood learning and myths, fantasies, prejudices, projection, and transferences.

Difficulty with anger. "I can't or won't be intimate with you because I'm so angry with you." This is a central issue because of the quantity of anger these Black men have and the difficulty they have knowing what to do with it.

Why is the Black man so angry with the woman in his life? For several reasons:

- A lot of anger is displaced or brought home and taken out on the mate, i.e., scapegoating.
- A lot of anger is a substitute for other feelings — it is easier, or safer, to be or to act angry than to feel guilty or to act hurt or needy.
- A lot of anger is a reaction to the complaints listed earlier — intimidation, castration, neglect, and frustration.
- There is anger at being placed in a double bind — "If I act strong you say I'm trying to control you, have no feelings, etc. When I show needs and feelings, you tell me to grow up, stop being a baby, you're not my mama, etc."
- Anger toward their wives is resurrected or left over from the early relationship with their mothers, e.g., once again feeling the love they receive is conditional, based on implicit demand to deliver or perform.
- Basically these men are angry because of a sense of frustration or lack of gratification of basic wishes and needs, and because of what they feel is a lack of nurturance, acceptance, protection, and the opportunity to "be a man."

Having all this anger these men then face the challenge of doing something with it. It is the same problem they faced when younger when they learned to deal with it indirectly, through sublimation, or not at all. Without good problem-solving techniques, anger often became a major factor in their current relationships, manifesting itself in such behavior as withdrawal, staying away, extramarital relations, drinking, depression, increased involvement in careers at the expense of relationships, and psychosomatic illness.

Difficulty appreciating the complexity of oneself and the other. "I am unable to self-disclose and be intimate with you because you and I are unaware of or unable to accept our complexity." Men and women behave as if they are one-dimensional and generally show a lack of sophistication about their and others' complexity. However, if you live intensely and for some time with someone you love, your total self, or all your "selves" and all your needs, fears, conflicts, anxieties, coping and problem-solving behavior, idiosyncracies, and unsettled issues from the past, get activated and come into the picture. In other words, transference sets in. Transference was a concept originally described by Freud characterizing an important phenomenon occurring in psychoanalysis (1961). As detailed by Brenner (1982, p. 194) it is now clear that transference is a characteristic of every object relation, especially in every relation where another person is important in one's life: "Wishes for gratification, anxiety, depressive affect, defense and superego derivatives, all originating in early childhood, play major roles in every object relation of later childhood and adult life." Every object relation is therefore a new edition of the first, definitive attachments of childhood. Thus, transference can be understood as being derived from the libidinal and aggressive wishes of early childhood — wishes that have to do with the early relation with mother, father, siblings, and other important figures from the past.

"I don't know what happened, she used to be so nice and caring — life together seemed so simple." "We were having a ball." That was true, but once this change occurs, it's not simple anymore — it's no longer just the two together. Each becomes at various and the same time mother, father, sister, brother, previous loved and hated ones, and so forth, with all the old feelings, reactions, attitudes, and behaviors joining in the current interaction.

Once this sets in, and it inevitably does, it can't be wished or talked away or denied. It must be dealt with, but unfortunately most don't know how.

Failure to allow child in relationship. "I can't be intimate with you because it might reveal my child self, my little boy, and I have to be grown up." The curtain was pulled down and stayed down on the childhood core of many Black men. The part that loves, hates, fears, is bold, laughs, cries, gets excited, feels sad, is nothing but the child in us.

All too often in relationships this part cannot be lived out, shared, or respected. It must be hidden, and in the process a very significant part of the self is repressed. "Black men aren't in touch with feelings and emotions," the Black woman says. At the same time, the same Black woman is apt to be the first to accuse the Black man of being a childish, irresponsible, little boy who just wants to play or be taken care of. This did not start in adulthood. Many of the men in my group were not allowed to be children when they were boys. They had to be mature at an early age. They had to act like little adults in order to get approval or sometimes in order to get by. They never really learned how to play well as children. Many adults can't play. Erikson (1963) describes genuine adult play well: "When man plays he must intermingle with things and people in an uninvolved and light fashion. He must do something which he has chosen to do without being compelled by urgent interests or impelled by strong passion; he must feel entertained and free of any fear or hope of serious consequences. He is on vacation from social and economic reality — or as is most commonly emphasized: he 'does not work' " (p. 212). By this definition many Black men can "party" but they can't play. "Partying" is serious business.

Inability to reveal full adult. The opposite problem is also true — "I can't be truly intimate with you because I can't reveal my full adult self to you." The Black male, all too often, must be apologetic for, or deny, his success or strength, or risk the scorn, envy, and hostility of siblings, parents, or colleagues. To be a successful Black male usually means swimming upstream, against the tide not only of racism but of times and, more important, against the resentment and opposition of his own significant others — starting with his family of origin and very possibly continuing into his present life with his wife. It became familiar to hear, "You think you're better than us?" "You're acting white." "You're arrogant . . . stuck up . . . phony . . . seditty."

It's a problem when the Black man has to curb his enthusiasm or the extent of his involvement with his work when he is with his wife. I'm not talking about the so-called workaholic, for whom work is an addiction and is used, among other things, as a defense and way to avoid other critical issues in life — like one's marriage. Rather, I'm talking about the professional man or other man whose work is an essential part of the way he defines himself. If he can't or doesn't bring his enthusiasm and interest in his work home with him he is leaving a large part of himself out. Wives often see the work as competition: "You're more interested in your work than in me."

Most Black men are looking for "someplace to be somebody" — they would like that place to be with someone they love. One of the ways that they are somebody is through their work.

CONCLUSION

The aim of this chapter has been to focus attention on critical elements in the relationships between Black middle-class men and women from the male perspective. The basic failing in the relationships examined here is in achieving and maintaining intimacy, i.e., that state existing between two people in a close, ongoing relationship where each is able to make self-disclosures and receive a response of empathy. Interferences with intimacy in these relationships are based in intrapsychic fears and anxieties that lead to defensive withdrawal and distancing. More specifically, five commonly recurring issues were identified that lead to disturbances in intimacy: (1) a tendency to use stereotyping, (2) difficulty dealing with anger, (3) inability to appreciate and handle the complexity of each other, and failure to allow (4) one's "child" and (5) one's "adult" self fully into the relationship.

REFERENCES

Blumstein, P., & Schwartz, P. (1983). *American couples.* New York: William Morrow.

Braithwaite, R. L. (1981). Interpersonal relations between Black males and Black females. In L. Gary (Ed.), *Black men* (pp. 83–97). Beverly Hills, CA: Sage Publications.

Brenner, C. (1982). *The mind in conflict.* New York: International Universities Press.

Cazenave, N. A. (1981). Black men in America: The quest for manhood. In H. McAdoo (Ed)., *Black families.* Beverly Hills, CA: Sage Publications.

Cazenave, N. A. (1983). Black male-Black female relationships: The perceptions of 155 middle-class Black men. *Family Relations: Journal of Applied Family and Child Studies, 32,* 341–350.

Erikson, E. (1963). *Childhood and society* (p. 212). New York: W. W. Norton.

Freud, S. (1961). Fragment of an analysis of a case of hysteria. In J. Strachey (Ed. and Trans.), *The standard edition of the complete psychological works of Sigmund Freud, 7,* 1–122. London: Hogarth Press.

Freud, S. (1961). Inhibitions, symptoms and anxiety. In J. Strachey (Ed. and Trans.), *The standard edition of the complete psychological works of Sigmund Freud, 20,* 75–172. London: Hogarth Press.

Gilligan, C. (1982). *In a different voice.* Cambridge, MA: Harvard University Press.

Hall, L. (1981). Support systems and coping patterns. In L. Gary (Ed.), *Black men.* Beverly Hills, CA: Sage Publications.

Oxford English dictionary, compact edition (1971). Oxford: Oxford University Press.

Scarf, M. (1986, November). Intimate partners. *The Atlantic,* p. 49.

Scarf, M. (1987). *Intimate partners.* New York: Random House.

Stoller, R. (1964). A contribution to the study of gender identity. *International Journal of Psychoanalysis, 45,* 220–226.

Introduction to Part III

PARENTING

Jeanne Spurlock

The contributors to this section address the particular stresses that stem from the repercussions of racism. In the context of parenting in general, however, the authors call attention to a wide range of factors that may generate stress for the parent figure, as well as for the child, adolescent, or elderly parent who needs parenting.

Spurlock and Booth use composites, from their respective clinical experiences, as a reference point to discuss parenting in relation to the stresses generated by marital instability, problems in the workplace, identity confusion, and substance abuse. Attention is also directed to the complexities of the issues addressed, particularly the many ramifications of upward mobility; measures for ameliorating the problems are addressd.

Jenkins provides a comprehensive review of the current statistical trends pertaining to adolescent sexual behavior, and addresses issues that are of particular concern to Black middle-class families and the professionals who provide care for them. Significant recommendations, primarily directed toward reducing adolescent pregnancy, are offered.

Johnson discusses the problems of parenting one's elderly parents from a very broad reference base — social, physical, and mental problems of the individual elderly parent and the family, as well as the social and political climate of the wider society. The growing number of individuals living longer, the parallel increase in health issues that pertain to senility, and the high cost of care for the aged and infirm support Johnson's call for more attention to adequate planning for the elderly in our families. Her references to family and community support systems are of particular relevance to the themes of this volume.

Each of the contributors addresses the fact that parenting extends beyond the confines of the mother and father; the involvement of extended family members, health care providers, and teachers has been very beneficial in many instances.

7

Stresses in Parenting

Jeanne Spurlock and Martin B. Booth

Parenthood, like other phases of the life cycle, may be studded with periods of stress or may be relatively free of stress, and yield satisfying experiences throughout its various phases. For some, parenthood occurs early and is anxiety producing, especially if the parent is a single mother. For others, parenthood has been postponed or comes after a long series of medical interventions and efforts on the part of the would-be parents to reproduce. Any one, or several, factors may lead to positive parenting experiences; other factors, or similar factors for some parents, may contribute to stress-ridden situations. When parents are of a group which is viewed as "second class" by the broader society, stresses of parenting are likely to be compounded. All things considered, relative to the dominant population, Black Americans are exposed to stressful situations more frequently. Although some stresses may be negligible for the Black middle class, economic status does not guarantee immunity from stress in general and race-related stresses in particular. However, economic stability allows parents to seek professional help in the early stages of a stress-induced problem — their own or that of a child. Furthermore, they have the freedom to select the professional service of their choice. A range of examples is presented in the following composites from our clinical experiences. Stresses generated by marital instability, problems in the workplace, identity confusion, and substance abuse serve as reference points.

TROUBLED MARRIAGES

Marital instability is quite prevalent among the middle-class and is a common stressor in parenting. Stress often escalates with separation and divorce, frequently accompanied by parental guilt. So it was for W. W., a well-established professional and father of three. He handled his guilt about leaving the household by fostering prolonged dependency in his children, especially his eldest daughter, who was apparently his favorite. This behavioral pattern, while unconsciously determined, set the stage for his daughter's expectations that she, at age 28 and a parent herself, could count on him for financial help for nonessentials as well as essentials. It was as if she saw these contributions as a kind of allowance, not unlike that which she had received during her adolescence. It was clear that this young woman had come to feel that she was entitled, that her father "owed" her, and he obviously felt obligated to pay. Certainly, these attitudes put a strain on their relationship. The "paying" contributed to the daughter's prolonged dependency and thwarted her psychological growth. The "paying" continues with W. W.'s partial support.

When marriages fail, a sizable percentage of the fathers become unavailable as stable father figures. They like to see themselves as involved with their children, however, and tend to rationalize about why they are not involved. "I can't deal with my ex-wife," is a common reason given for limited involvement with children. Often, fathers walk away so as to protect the child from disputes between the parents or project the problem onto the ex-wife. This has been the case for a sizable number of middle-class Black fathers we have known. For several who have sought therapy, one of the root causes pertained to their own conflicts about parenting. As one stated, "I probably could be a better father if I had had a model; my father was in and out of our home and when he was there he wasn't really accessible — at least emotionally — to my brother and me." Of course, the unavailability of one parent usually puts more pressure on the custodial parent and often leads to parents using the children to "fight" each other.

For most families, separation or divorce stirs up, or reinforces, problems pertaining to finances. Most middle-class families live comfortably only because there are two incomes. Black families are no exception. In fact, it is more likely that two incomes are essential for comfortable living for Black families, because the income of Blacks is generally less than that of the dominant group, even for a like job and performance. We have known more than a few middle-class Black men who have shouldered their child support responsibilities for only a brief period following the break-up of their marriage. The often-stated reason is their inability to afford the total payments. Yet these same fathers are not prepared to experience any changes in lifestyle.

They need to maintain the "right" apartment in the "right" location for entertainment of business clients, as well as for the children's visits. Of course, estranged and divorced wives are not immune to the "reluctance to change my lifestyle" syndrome, nor are the children. Perhaps neither parent wishes to uproot the children, especially if the move to another community relates adversely to their educational opportunities. Money, or the lack of money, generates stress and anxiety for both parents that spill over onto the children.

IMPACT OF WORK-RELATED STRESS ON CHILDREN

Many parents who have consulted us about problems with their children, as well as those adults who seek help for themselves, refer to work-related stress. These kinds of experiences have been addressed in other publications (Ford, 1978; Davis and Watson, 1982; Pierce, this volume). Several commonplace work-related stresses and sequelae are noted in the following case composite.

S. M. had earned the highest academic degree in her field and had received several awards, which attested to her significant contributions to her profession and respect from her peers. She was pleased to accept an appointment to a committee that had been mandated by the state legislature. The committee was charged to review high school and college curricula, to identify deficiencies, and to recommend modifications and steps for improvement. Because of her experiences in the vineyards of secondary and college education, as well as her reputable standing in her field, she felt strongly that she could make a significant contribution to the group. However, she perceived early on that this would not be without considerable struggle and frustration on her part.

Although she thought she was prepared for possible racial discrimination, she hadn't anticipated that it would be continuous or so blatant. Or was it that the slights and put-downs were rooted in the sexist attitudes of the men, who were 90 percent of the committee membership? For the most part, her comments were ignored; that is, there was no follow-up to the points she made. Yet there were times that the core of the idea that she had expressed was advanced, with different phrasing, by a man and was accepted as a capital suggestion. Depending on her frustration tolerance on that particular day, S. M. reacted by either (1) suppressing intense anger and withdrawing or (2) noting the similarity with her earlier suggestion and, therefore, supporting the slightly modified version.

The psychological distress provoked by such experiences is not dissipated when an individual leaves the office. The sequelae are likely to be especially troublesome for parents who have legitimate demands made of them when they arrived home. The conflicts engendered by the apparent racist atmosphere of the work environment are compounded when 8-year-old Jamal reports, "My teacher says Black people can't follow instructions. That's why I didn't do the right assignment," or 16-year-old Judy pleads for permission to live with an aunt and go to school in the city. Her voice escalates as she complains that the Black boys aren't interested in dating the Black girls at her school. Judy's anger is redirected toward her parents; she suggests that they made a bad decision; their decision to move to suburbia so that she and her brother could have a better education had "backfired" — at least for her. She was so miserable that she was unable to direct her full attention to her studies.

RESPONSES TO RACE-RELATED
PROBLEMS, AS VIEWED BY CHILDREN

How are such situations best handled by Black parents? We agree with the advice offered by Comer and Poussaint (1975) in their book, *Black Child Care*. Preferably, parents should not react by lumping all non-Blacks in one category, even though it is a likely association if mother or father has experienced blatant racism in the workplace the very day of a child's similar experience. However, such a reaction is unlikely to be of help to the child in the long run. We applauded Jamal's parents' handling of the problem with which he confronted them. Mother, who had arrived home earlier than the father, recalled feeling intense anger, as well as a need to "cool off" before responding to her son. She suggested they talk about the matter as soon as she changed clothes and started dinner (knowing this interval would give her time to "cool off"). However, initially she told Jamal that she was angry about the teacher's comment, as he had reported it, and added that he seemed angry also. She also referred to the fact that people often say things they don't mean when they are angry. In subsequent discussion, first with mother and then with both parents, attention was directed to the fact that Jamal had done the wrong assignment, but one's racial identity was irrelevant to whether or not one could follow directions. Both parents underscored their plan to discuss the matter with Jamal's teacher and, at the same time, recalled the many times Jamal has followed directions very well — but there had been times when he had not. All three agreed that they would discuss the matter further when Jamal asked, for the third time, "What time is dinner?" Later, both parents emphasized that not every problem they (including Jamal) had or would experience was rooted in racial bias.

Judy's problem was more difficult to deal with. Ideally, the parents should have done more preventive work. But they thought they had done enough by continuing their affiliation with the church in their old neighborhood and arranging for Judy and her friends in the old neighborhood to have occasional weekend visits together. The parents had been very much aware of the losses that Judy had experienced because of the move to suburbia, and expressed some guilt that their work-related pressures had deterred them from being fully cognizant of Judy's emotional turmoil. They wondered if they were rationalizing as they reflected on the possibility that Judy's outburst was related to matters other than the move itself. After all, there were other Black families in the area and Judy had developed what appeared to be a good relationship with a number of her peers, some of whom were from the dominant group. During their exchange with Judy they indicated their recognition of her distress, empathized with her, but stressed (as they had before the move) the importance of family togetherness, and their support in helping her overcome the difficulties she was experiencing. For the moment, it seemed enough for her to have them listen to her. However, the matter was not settled for the parents. They were aware of the interracial dating among the students at Judy's school, and wondered about their reactions (and the responses of the extended family) should one of their children choose to marry across racial lines. They decided to seek professional guidance about Judy's immediate concerns.

The need for Black parents to teach their children that race is not the only reason for everything that happens to them has been addressed by Comer and Pouissant (1975) in several sections of *Black Child Care*. On the other hand, the tendency for many Black middle-class youth to deny the existence of racism is of concern to their parents. An illustration of this dilemma (Morgan, 1985) was presented by a 15-year-old boy. He was reported to have complained to his family that older folks talked too much about discrimination. He had apparently seen nothing untoward about an experience pertaining to a school production of the Wizard of Oz, in which none of the Black students had major roles. However, they were given parts as monkeys. The only non-Black student who played a monkey was given a mask; the Blacks had none.

It is likely that the reality of the situation was too painful for this lad, who, like many of us who have been confronted with an especially distressing circumstance, used the defense of denial. The denial provided a refuge, at least temporarily. Of course, there are scores of Black youngsters and young adults who have no personal experience of racial discrimination, nor memory or knowledge of the Civil Rights struggles of their forebears. They are likely to give no thought to the possibility of experiencing racial prejudice. This is not a recent pattern. A decade ago Bennett (1978) addressed this matter in terms of a generation gap. He noted the decreased sharpness of racial antennae in young Blacks, many of whom did not expect to be rebuffed by the dominant society.

STRESSES GENERATED BY
OVERT RACIST PRACTICES

The current resurgence of overt racist practices on the campuses of sparsely integrated colleges has made for new experiences of stress for parents and their college-age children. Eighteen-year-old David, a freshman at a prestigious midwestern university, notified his parents that he wanted to transfer to his father's alma mater (a prestigious Black college). The call was precipitated by a series of incidents: the appearance and apparent campus-wide distribution of a flier on which Black students, described in derogatory terms, were urged to go home; groups of White students shouting racial epithets at Black students when they met outside the classrooms. David was troubled by the surging feelings of rage that he experienced; most alarming was the sense of potential violence. The efforts needed to suppress his rage left little energy for concentrated study. His parents' concern was justifiable; perhaps, the intensity of his mother's response was overdetermined in that she likened David's experience to that of an uncle who had been beaten badly during a student sit-in desegregation effort in the mid-1960s. David's situation triggered the resurfacing of a longstanding "battle" between the parents, a battle which pertained to David's education: public versus private elementary school, local private school versus an out-of-town preparatory school, traditional Black college versus one of the "big ten." When David was a second-grader, his father, observing that he was not working up to his ability, was persuaded to enroll him in a private school. He was strongly opposed to sending David to a boarding school and, when David approached college age, had campaigned strongly for David's enrollment at his alma mater, but David was persuaded by his mother's arguments that one of the "big ten" would provide broader opportunities.

Prior to the recent upsurge of blatant racism on the campuses of some of the "big ten" schools, Black students, especially women, expressed concern about isolation and experiences of being "put down." Not infrequently, a Black student would be questioned about her or his academic status or labeled as an "affirmative action student." Transfers to traditionally Black colleges were common after the freshman year. Parental reactions to the racist experiences of their college-age children are as varied as those of parents of younger children who have similar experiences. Anger, which is often the initial reaction, is followed by concerted efforts to provide emotional support. Parents do not tend to arrange for their child to leave school immediately; rather, like David's parents, they direct efforts toward learning more about the climate of the campus and the availability of counseling services. Some parents believe that these untoward college experiences can be useful in preparing students for their future world of work.

BLACK IDENTITY IN FLUX?

A growing number of Black parents have expressed some concern about their children's confusion or absence of Black identity. Journalist Patrice Gaines-Carter (1985) addressed this concern in an open letter to her daughter. Gaines-Carter labels her concern the "Post-Integration Blues." The daughter displayed disinterest in attending a program in memory of Martin Luther King, Jr. Her statement that that was the only morning she could sleep late added insult to the injury that the mother felt.

In addressing this matter of the dilution of the importance of Black history for many young Black people, Shervington (1986) made reference to those individuals who clearly proclaim their Black identity but have almost no knowledge of their roots. They may have heard of Spelman, Morehouse, or Talladega Colleges, but even then their knowledge is devoid of any information pertaining to the institutions as a rich part of their heritage. Their children's disregard of Black history is troublesome for some parents but of little concern to others.

Some parents contend that knowledge of Black history is of little value, if any, in getting accepted to an Ivy League college. It is likely that some behavioral scientists would sharply differ with those parents who feel it to be unimportant for their children to know about their Black heritage. The president of Howard University has mandated Black history as a required undergraduate course because of his growing sense of alarm about the lack of knowledge incoming Black students had about themselves as a people.

Shervington (1986) observed a particular pattern followed by some Black adolescent males who live in predominantly non-Black communities and who have failed to achieve academically. It is as if they have accepted the notion, prevalent among the youth in pockets of Black communities, that any effort directed toward academic achievement is equivalent to a drive to identify with the dominant group. For them, social development in a specific Black community has become a primary concern, and to their parents' distress, they make vigorous efforts to reject previously set goals that are now viewed as non-Black. This pattern is not limited to middle-class adolescent males. Findings from a recent study conducted by investigators at the University of the District of Columbia reveal this kind of behavior pattern to be commonplace in both males and females who live in the inner city (Fisher, 1987). Many of the subjects interviewed reported playing down their intellectual abilities lest their peers label them as "brainiacs" or "acting white." Based on our personal and professional experiences, we view the findings as familiar rather than new. The "brainiacs" in our youth were sometimes identified as "uppity." However, the differences within each group were noted in the past, as they should be noted in the present. It is likely that such differences will be in evidence in future generations.

SUBSTANCE USE AND ABUSE

Black middle-class parents are not immune to substance use or abuse. Emily and Samuel Brown are both highly competent in their respective professions and the proud parents of 10-year-old Samuel, Jr. The Browns have been separated for five years. They profess to love each other and have considered reconciliation several times. Mr. Brown is ambivalent about a reconciliation; Mrs. Brown is adamant that it wouldn't work because of her husband's drinking patterns. In fact, it was the drinking, associated with his unavailability, that prompted her to initiate the separation. The onset of the "excessive drinking" (Mrs. Brown's terminology) followed Mr. Brown's promotion to a "high-powered" position. He admitted to experiencing considerable stress because he was the first minority person to hold the position; "I felt that I had to do well — not to do well would have reflected on my race." He thought his wife was exaggerating about his drinking. However, he did admit to a change in his drinking pattern after the promotion. He recalled a "desire" which soon turned into a "need" to have several drinks before dinner, and maybe a "nightcap"; also, that he often felt "too wiped out" in the evening to give much time to his son or his wife. Both parents noted that he spent more time with their son since the separation. It was surprising to the therapist, to whom the son had been referred because of learning and behavioral problems, that neither parent was tuned in to the quality of the time that the father spent with the child; the distancing had continued. It was true that Samuel, Jr., was with his father on alternate weekends and an occasional overnight during the week. But, according to Mr. Brown, when they were together, much of the time was spent watching movies. Mr. Brown expressed no need for help for himself but was willing to see his son's therapist if it would be helpful to the child. However, his references to his personal history (reared by a dependent mother — reversal of roles; married a woman who, he felt, would provide some "mothering" — now felt his wife had abandoned him) suggested a reversal of his decision about treatment for himself.

PROBLEMS RELATED TO OVERINDULGENCE

Most parents want a better life for their children than they have had, especially if the childhood of the parents has been studded with experiences of deprivation. Middle-class Black parents who are from poor families frequently indulge or overindulge their children. Often, the overindulgence stems from intrapsychic conflicts of the parents and serves to meet their unmet needs. The pattern of overindulgence established by 17-year-old Nelson's grandparents is illustrative.

Nelson's mother, a highly valued only child, had died in his infancy. Her parents assumed guardianship of the child and throughout his life sought to realize the dreams and aspirations they had been seeking to make an actuality through their gifted daughter. Both grandparents had a limited formal education and had worked at low-level and low-paying jobs in the course of their struggles to achieve some of the comforts of middle-class status. It was clear that their overindulgence of their grandson served to fulfill some of the unmet needs and desires of their childhood and adolescence.

The patterns of giving by Nelson's grandparents served to thwart their conscious efforts to help him endure frustrations and to defer gratification, necessary elements in the development of a healthy ego and a mature capacity to consider alternatives. Shervington (1986) called attention to the growing numbers of Black adolescents in whom profound narcissism is prominent. Their growth has taken place in an environment which has fostered the development of a pattern of manipulation of others for the purpose of receiving immediate gratification.

SUMMARY

Case composites from the authors' clinical practices were used as the format for a review of selected examples of problems that middle-class Black parents experience in child rearing. Middle-class status, in itself, does not protect against stress in general and race-related stress in particular. However, economic stability allows for more alternative ways of seeking relief from stress-induced disorders. Utilization of self-selected mental health services is one such alternative. Job security also allows parents time and energy to address problems very soon after they become aware of difficulties that their children are experiencing. The authors provided glimpses of parents "taking charge" and ameliorating stresses on their own.

Reference was made to the complexities of the issues addressed, the ripple effects of upward mobility, and changes in the broader society. Undoubtedly, these changes will trigger other concerns in answering the question "What is best for our children?"

REFERENCES

Bennett, L. (1978). The lost/found generation. *Ebony, 33*(10), 35–42.

Comer, J. P., & Poussaint, A. F. (1975). *Black child care.* New York: Simon & Schuster.

Davis, G., & Watson, C. (1982). *Black life in corporate America.* Garden City, NY: Anchor Press/Doubleday.

Fisher, M. (1987, March 14). Peers inhibit Black achievers, study of D.C. schools find. *Washington Post*, p. 1.

Ford, D. L. (1978). The Black adult and the world of work. In L. E. Gary (Ed)., *Mental health: A challenge to the Black community.* Philadelphia: Dorrace.

Gaines-Carter, P. (1985). Is my "post-integration" daughter Black enough? *Ebony, 42*(2), 54–56.

Morgan, T. (1985, October 27). The world ahead: Black parents prepare their children for pride and prejudice. *The New York Times Magazine*, p. 32.

Shervington, W. W. (1986). The Black family: Clinical overview. *American Journal of Social Psychology, 6*(1), 6–10.

8

Adolescent Sexuality

Renee R. Jenkins

One of the most difficult yet common issues for all parents to manage during the adolescent years is sexuality. Statistics reported in the news media portray adolescents as sexually oriented and active. Parents feel threatened and powerless, and experience immense anxiety in approaching their own adolescents. Black parents are especially affected because of the disproportionate numbers of Black adolescents involved in early sexual intercourse and teenage pregnancy. Female-headed households are increasing for Black families, with teen mothers forming the poorest and most disadvantaged group (Edelman and Pittman, 1986). Consequently, the phenomenon of teen sexuality and its sequelae concerns Black parents, educators, administrators, sociologists, and all Black persons looking at the future of Black families in our culture.

Professional and popular publications have been flooded with articles on all aspects of teen sexual behavior. In the midst of this flood, there is still a drought in the area of the characteristics of Black middle-class adolescents and their parents. There is some additional consideration of socioeconomic status as an important variable in the current literature, compared with the majority of reports on Black lower-income adolescents in the 1970s. Nonetheless, there is still little detailed study of the effects of an upward shift in the socioeconomic status of Black families in the last decade and its impact on teen sexuality. In this chapter, I will review the current statistical trends in adolescent sexual behavior, including contraceptive use and pregnancy and its outcomes. I will focus on issues about and important to Black families and professionals who work with Black families. The chapter will conclude with recommendations to parents and professionals primarily directed toward reducing teen pregnancy and its negative impact on the future of Black adolescents.

TRENDS IN ADOLESCENT SEXUAL BEHAVIOR

General Trends

The most recent analysis of patterns of premarital sexual behavior in 13- to 19-year-old females shows a slowing in the rate of increase in sexual intercourse. However, teenagers continue to experience intercourse at younger and younger ages. For White teens there was a significant increase in activity for those entering adolescence during the late 1960s and early 1970s. Black teens showed a less significant increase, because of the already high levels of the previous decade. By 1982, the rates of increase appeared to be leveling off, and for Blacks there was a small (statistically nonsignificant) decline between 1979 and 1982 (Hofferth, Kahn, and Baldwin, 1987). When considering these trends we must remember that these statistics are for girls reporting intercourse at least once, and less than half of all unmarried United States female teens report any activity at all. The pattern of intercourse for younger teens is generally more sporadic and less frequent than for older teens and adults. Less detailed information is available on male teens; by most reports, however, boys initiate activity earlier than girls, but by the end of the teen years the percentage differences are much smaller (Hayes, 1987).

There has been an increase in the number of sexually active teenagers who have ever used a contraceptive method. In 1982, about 85% of female teens reported use, compared to 73% in 1979 and 66% in 1976. Although Black adolescents are less likely to use contraception than Whites, they are twice as likely to use a medical method (Hayes, 1987). The average delay between first intercourse and use of a prescription method is about one year (Zabin and Clark, 1981). Birth rates for teens are actually declining and are at their lowest levels since the 1940s. Racial comparisons show the greatest decline for Blacks aged 18 and under; the greatest decline for Whites was for teens aged 18 to 19 years. The reduction in births is attributed to a decrease in the size of the adolescent population since 1977, increased use of contraception, and increased number of abortions since the late 1970s.

About 30% of all abortions reported in the United States are performed on teens. For girls under age 15, there are 1.4 abortions for every live birth! Black teens are less likely to elect abortion as an outcome for a pregnancy. However, their pregnancy rates are higher than Whites; hence, their reported abortion rates are higher. For example, 40.3% of pregnant White teens aged 15 to 19 elected abortions in 1981, with a rate of 38.8 per thousand women; only 35% of pregnant Black teens elected abortion, but this resulted in a rate of 66.3 per thousand. Adoption as an option for unintended pregnancy has declined. Although comprehensive national data on adoption rates are not available, agency reports show a rise from 86% of teen mothers keeping their babies in 1971, to 93% of mothers in 1982. Blacks are less likely to adopt out their babies through agencies but often elect to have grandmothers or other relatives to rear their children (Hayes, 1987).

Trends within the Black Population

The literature provides few opportunities to look at differences within the Black population that would account for any differentials in the prevalence of sexual activity among Black adolescents. In their analysis of child and parent interviews from the 1976 and 1981 National Surveys of Children, Peterson, Moore, and Furstenberg (1985) found significant race and sex group differences in family determinants of early sexual activity, and recommended analysis of race sex groupings separately when studying these issues.

For Black teens the educational level of the mother is the variable for which there is the most significant body of data available on a national level. As one might guess, higher levels of maternal education are associated with lower rates of premarital intercourse, more frequent use of contraceptives, and fewer live births (Hogan and Kitagawa, 1985; Zelnik, Kantner, and Ford, 1981). The reverse is true for the relationship between abortion rate and maternal educational level (Zelnik, Kantner, and Ford, 1981). The difference in rates of teenage pregnancy by level of mother's education as a measure of socioeconomic status is probably the most disturbing because of its long-term effect on Black family formation. Teenagers with the fewest resources, both economic and educational, are the most likely to bear children. Early childbearing anchors most of these young men and women to the poverty cycle. With the concurrent trend of greater economic opportunity and progress among young Blacks during the 1970s, many observers are concerned about a potentially widening gap in socioeconomic status in young Blacks.

INDIVIDUAL AND FAMILY FACTORS AS
DETERMINANTS OF SEXUAL BEHAVIOR

Certain individual and family factors show consistent relationships with the timing of sexual activity, contraceptive use, pregnancy, and the decisions a girl and her family make about resolving a pregnancy. Looking at these relationships helps to formulate hypotheses as to the way that socioeconomic status operates to influence sexual behavior. A program or an individual is less able to change a young person's socioeconomic status than to change some of the factors that operate through social class status. For example, young girls who are motivated toward high educational expectations are more likely to use contraception than girls who are not. A program that is designed to increase contraceptive use among teens should look at how this factor affects its clients and consider modification of this factor in setting its program goals.

Sexuality is one of the major psychosocial issues in normative adolescent development. Sex roles are learned prior to adolescence, with the solidification of gender identity and social roles, as related to sexual behavior, becoming a primary focus during adolescence. The most common outcome anticipated by late adolescence is the establishment of a relationship with a chosen mate, which may or may not involve sexual intercourse.

Research into the individual factors associated with the initiation of sexual intercourse shows some obvious and some not-so-obvious relationships. The older the adolescent, the more likely he or she is to engage in intercourse. Teenagers who report themselves as being less religious, placing less emphasis on educational goals, and dating early and frequently are at risk for early intercourse. Some of the same factors also tend to influence the use of contraceptives. In addition, a girl's perception of needing contraception, as manifested in her having a stable romantic relationship with frequent sexual encounters, enhances the likelihood of her using birth control. She has accepted sexuality as part of her life and has less guilt about it (McAnarney and Schreider, 1984). Once a teenager becomes pregnant her decision to continue or terminate the pregnancy is also influenced by her future educational plans. Girls with good academic performance and plans to complete more schooling are more likely to abort than girls with lower educational expectations. The parents' high level of education also operates to increase the likelihood of opting for abortion (Hayes, 1987).

The association between family structure and sexual behavior is often examined, with children of the single-parent family expected to be at higher risk. Peterson, Moore, and Furstenberg (1985) constructed a model using a national data base which considered additional information about dating behavior of parents. Differences were observed in separate race and sex groups. White daughters of infrequently dating single mothers reported an incidence of sexual activity similar to that of daughters living with both parents. Daughters of remarried and dating mothers were more likely to be sexually experienced. Black daughters were more likely to be sexually active when living apart from the father. For White females, neighborhood factors, educational aspirations, and attitudes did not affect the association between family structure and sexual activity. However, for Black females, parental education, family income, neighborhood quality, and educational aspirations reduced the effect of family structure on sexual activity; the degree of affection between mother and daughter nearly eliminated this association. The findings for Black males were influenced by family structure, and this influence was not changed by other factors. The relationship for White males was completely different: sons who resided with the biological or adoptive father were more likely to be sexually active. Again, these observations, though exploratory, point to the necessity of studying race/sex groups separately.

Contrary to the belief that parents do not have control over their teenager's sexual behavior, consistent relationships demonstrating the impact of parental influence have been reported. Teenagers who perceive more parental approval of sexual behavior and experience fewer parental controls report intercourse more frequently than those with opposite perceptions (McAnarney and Schreider, 1984). Although the influence of parental communication on behavior is of critical import in advising parents, the information on it is not consistent. Close family relationships appear to delay the initiation of intercourse, but whether direct communication is the method of influence is not clear. Part of the uncertainty concerns what is communicated and when. Is there more communication after a parent suspects interest in sexual intercourse? Are the conversations about moral guidelines or specific information on use of contraception? The impact of communication with mothers is different from that of communication with fathers, especially for boys, with father-son communication more likely to be associated with being sexually experienced (Hayes, 1987). Most programs and professionals support the approach of encouraging parent-teen communication, with strong suggestions toward more specific supportive information sharing rather than admonitions and threats.

Greer Fox's (1986) most recent work in intrafamilial sexual communication begins to provide a framework for characterization and further study of communication patterns. Her sample included primarily middle-income Black and White families, in which the teenagers were of both sexes. Through in-depth interviews she was able to identify communication patterns in dual-parent families. Patterns are described as:

1. *Complementary:* separation of husband and wife responsibilities for certain types of communication, often following same-sex lines
2. *Duplicative:* one parent's actions or words are reinforced by the other
3. *Compensatory:* one parent compensates for the incompetent communication attempts by the other
4. *Crossover:* interchangeability of the parents' roles

Parents also have distinguishing patterns of communicating with each other. The patterns described are self-explanatory and include active discussion, occasional reporting, passive assumption, and mutual ignorance. Fox has yet to correlate these patterns with sexual behavior in the teenager. However, they do provide a heretofore unavailable structure within which to consider the quality and style of communication. These aspects of communication are expected to have some impact on the effectiveness of the message transmitted. Fox explicitly cautions against placing too much emphasis at this point on the quantitative rather than the qualitative analysis of the complex interaction of parental role and teen sexual behavior (Fox, 1986).

SUMMARY

Common demographic variables that explain differences in behavior in many populations continue to explain differences in sexual behavior patterns of teens. Race, gender, and socioeconomic status are most commonly described, with predictable variations. What we are still missing is the in-depth intragroup comparisons which help us understand why teens with the same demographic background do or do not put themselves at risk for adverse sexual experiences. Handling one's sexuality is part of the normal developmental task of humans.

Developmental competence in this area appears to be influenced by developmental competence in other areas, such as achievement orientation. In addition, factors that support developmental competence in other areas, such as positive parental supports, carry over to sexuality. As we gain further insight into adolescent sexuality, the commonalities among factors that further the development of competent, responsible, and successful adults will provide clearer directions for parents and professionals in their efforts to assist in this developmental process.

RECOMMENDATIONS

To Parents

Different parenting capabilities are necessary at different stages in a child's life. The key to adaptation is anticipation of the issues to be dealt with at each stage and appropriate interaction with the child. The character of the interaction must change as the child matures, and parental flexibility is necessary in order to make these changes. The most consistent patterns of interaction that appear to influence the mature handling of a teen's sexual development are early open (two-way) communication; sensitivity to the adolescent's perspective; consistency in management style, rules, and role-modeling behavior; support and guidance in decision making; and persistence in the face of apparent rejection (Fox, 1986; Jenkins, 1982). This is by no means an exhaustive list, but these are the qualities of the parent-adolescent interaction that are most commonly cited.

The quality of the interaction may have a greater influence than the details of what is communicated, but most parents are more confident in their communication when they feel they have accurate information. There is an abundance of publications on sexuality, pubertal development, conception, contraception, and so forth, available through public agencies and commercially, that are age-appropriate for a child and sufficient for a lay parent. Health professionals can be of assistance in suggesting methods to obtain this information.

To Professionals

On an individual family level, assessment of a request being made by the family or the family problem being addressed is best looked at in the context of the total family functioning. Rarely is a request or a problem related to teen sexuality an isolated phenomenon. Sometimes the request is rather superficial, for information (e.g., literature or referrals for routine health-related care). Often, however, a request in this area is of a crisis nature. Although resolution of the crisis is primary, the crisis provides a window of opportunity to address other issues about the family's functioning, such as communication, and distribution of responsibility and roles in childrearing. An opportunity to address these more global issues for a family may serve to prevent further crises and have a longer-lasting impact when the crisis is over.

On a programmatic level, educators and service providers have to increase their efforts to reach parents and assist them in the task of managing their children's sexuality. Such efforts may include parental sex education, parental child and adolescent development education, and assistance with communication skills for teens and families. In addition, efforts in other nonhealth settings such as schools and recreational programs should seek parental endorsement of these types of activities. Early parent involvement tends to decrease the negative reactions to these educational activities generated by a few parent resistors.

The most productive means of assisting Black middle-class families in coping with their adolescents' sexuality is confrontation and, then, support in the parental assumption of an early, more active role in their children's sexual education.

REFERENCES

Edelman, M. W., & Pittman, K. J. (1986). Adolescent pregnancy: Black and White. *Journal of Community Health, 11,* 63–69.

Fox, G. L. (1986). *Intrafamilial sexual socialization patterns and outcomes* (Final Report. Grant No. APR000925-01). Washington, DC: Office of Adolescent Pregnancy Project, Department of Health and Human Services.

Hayes, C. D. (Ed.). (1987). *Risking the future: Adolescent sexuality, pregnancy, and childbearing, Vol. 1.* Washington, DC: National Academy Press.

Hofferth, S. L., Kahn, J. R., & Baldwin, W. (1987). Premarital sexual activity among U.S. teenage women over the past three decades. *Family Planning Perspectives, 19*(2), 6–53.

Hogan, P., & Kitagawa, E. (1985). The impact of social status, family structure, and neighborhood on the fertility of Black adolescents. *American Journal of Sociology, 90,* 825–855.

Jenkins, R. R. (1982). Adolescent sexuality and the family. *Pediatric Annals, 11,* 740–742, 746.

McAnarney, E. R., & Schreider, C. (1984). *Identifying social and psychological antecedents of adolescent pregnancy: The contributions of research to concepts of prevention.* New York: William T. Grant Foundation.

Peterson, J. L., Moore, K. A., & Furstenberg, F. F. (1985). *Starting early: The antecedents of early premarital intercourse* (Final Summary Report Contract No. APR000916-01-1). Washington, DC: Office of Adolescent Pregnancy Programs, Department of Health and Human Services.

Zabin, L. S., & Clark, S. D., Jr. (1981). Why they delay: A study of teenage family planning clinic patients. *Family Planning Perspectives, 13,* 205–217.

Zelnik, M., Kantner, J., & Ford, K. (1981). *Sex and pregnancy in adolescence.* Beverly Hills, CA: Sage Publications.

9

Parenting of the Elderly

Audreye E. Johnson

Family responsibility for the elderly has often been taken for granted. Hanson, Sauer, and Seelbach (1983) studied filial responsibility among Blacks and Whites. Neither group was found to "support filial norms very strongly [which] suggests that the elderly of both races need alternative sources of support which must come from other groups and organizations in the community." Clark and Rakowski (1983) pointed out that there may be the need for methods to enhance the helping skills of family caregivers as the needs of the elderly increase. Treas (1977) noted the need to consider subsidies to families who care for the elderly.

Assumption of the role of caregiver for elderly parents by children represents a discontinuity in a lifetime of different expectations. Filial responsibility for Blacks has usually been viewed through a White Anglo-Saxon lens. The adult African-American middle class and their elderly parents has been given scant attention. I report here a study of mine that begins to explore Black thinking on aging of self and parent.

AN OVERVIEW OF AGING

The graying of America in the 1970s and 1980s has been rapid, and has been occurring within all racial, cultural, and ethnic groups in the United States. The fastest-growing segment of the population is those 65 years of age and older. It has been estimated that by the year 2030 those 65 years and over will be 21.1 percent of the population, and by 2050, 21.7 percent. This growth has fostered concern for the mental health of the aged (Birren and Sloane, 1980).

99

The difference in the quality of life of the aged as related to minority and ethnic groups has also been given some attention (Brubaker, 1985; Butler, 1975; J. Jackson, 1980; Kobata, Lockery, and Moriwaki, 1980; and Lowy, 1985).

The age at which one is labeled as elderly has been arbitrarily determined. The Social Security Act, which became law in August 1935, defined 65 years as the age for entitlement for Old Age Assistance. Since 1978 it has been possible to extend the retirement age to 70 years. The aging process cannot be tied only to chronological years; cultural, genetic, socioeconomic, and neurobiological factors are also important.

Advanced medical technology has increased the longevity of Americans. Other influences have been safer and improved working conditions, more leisure time, better nutrition, and other lifestyle improvements. Additionally, such changes as geographical mobility, smaller families, and the change in caregiving roles have placed in sharp focus the manner in which the elderly will be cared for, and by whom, should they falter and need help. The loss of control over one's life may happen before age 65 or years later. It may never happen, regardless of the longevity of a person. Those unable to assume responsibility for themselves are likely to need in-home or institutional care. Regardless, the question arises as to who will be the caregiver, the person in charge, the one who will make the needed decisions, the one to pay the bills when funds are limited. What are the consequences of children parenting parents?

The aging of America has caused adult children to become the guardians, caregivers, and final decision makers for their parents. Moving from the role of a child to that of a parent of one's own parent calls for an adjustment in thinking and behavior. Some of the variables that influence this role change in the African-American community are race, socioeconomic status and position, and gender. The issue of race appears to be of particular significance. The common denominator of race based on color has been the central cord which has bound African-Americans together. The racism of oppression and denial of opportunity might be defined as

> . . . the systematic exclusion of a people from societal participation, psycho-social and economic, based on color; using oppression and discrimination to ensure prejudice of people and institutions against those of color, formally and informally, by any means possible. Such behavior resulting from this is both individual and institutional racism. (A. E. Johnson, 1978, p. 212)

ELDERLY AFRICAN-AMERICANS

The life expectancy for African-American males in 1900 was roughly 33 years, and for women 35 years. In 1982 the life expectancy for Black men had reached 65 years, and 74 years for Black women, who constitute 52.7 percent of the Black population (Dion, 1984). Blacks continue to have a shorter life expectancy than their White counterparts, by roughly 6 years (D. L. Johnson, 1986). In 1980 the Blacks 65 years and over constituted almost 8% of the Black population, or about 2.1 million. Moreover, 7.5%, or 157,500, were 85 years and older. Blacks reaching about 75 years of age tend to disproportionately outnumber others 75 years and older (Cornely, 1970). Unfortunately, though he suggested further researching the area, there remains a paucity of study of this phenomena, despite gradual recognition of Cornely's finding. The fact that elderly African-Americans were the fastest-growing part of their population group in the decade of the seventies, increasing 34%, also warrants exploration, especially because the increase for the total Black population was only 16%. Unfortunately, those few scholars engaged in this type of research have been hampered by lack of resources, both monetary and personnel.

The socioeconomic status and position of Blacks within the United States must be addressed in considering issues affecting the care of elderly African-Americans (Bennett, 1982; Franklin, 1974; Higginbotham, 1980). The overt and covert aspects of the various forms of racism have been instrumental in determining both the status and position of the Black elderly. The engineered human degradation and oppression of racism have taken their toll on the current population of Black elderly, and will influence the well-being and quality of life of all Black Americans for the foreseeable future.

The economic disparity in the African-American community can be seen at all class levels and in all types of families. "Black family median income was 56 percent of White family income in 1984," (D. L. Johnson, 1986, p. 6). This difference in income was also found among the elderly who have generally earned less throughout their life span. "The rate of poverty among older Blacks is twice that of older Whites. In 1984 the median income for Black males over the age of 65 was $6,163 compared to $10,890 for White males. For Black females the 1984 median income was $4,345. For White females the figure was $6,309" (NIA Sponsors Workshop, 1986).

The majority of African-Americans, 60%, live in the central city urban areas, and about half reside in the South. Most of the Black elderly, 96%, live with a daughter. Only a small percentage, 3 to 4, are institutionalized. This figure, reported by Brody (1974), has remained rather constant over the years. Even at the upper age level, 85 years and over, only 12% of African-Americans live in institutions. And, about 13% of Blacks continue to work after age 65. Elderly African-Americans have been undereducated; about 17% have finished high school.

"Of 26.3 million Americans over the age of 65 who are not in hospitals or nursing homes, almost a third (8 million) live alone" ("Senior Citizens," 1986). For those living alone there is usually contact with relatives or close friends. Some elderly live in their own homes or with relatives. Over half of African-American families, 53%, are composed of married couples. The marital status of the Black elderly in 1980 was as follows: 56.9% of the men were married, 22.1% were widowed, 14.7% were divorced or separated, and 6.5% were single, never married; for the women 25.0% were married, 57.7% were widowed, 11.6% were divorced or separated, and 5.6% were single, never married. Since women outlive men they also tend to be without a mate.

THE STUDY

Education and gainful employment were the focus of an exploratory descriptive study. The premise was that these two characteristics made for middle-class status of Blacks. Two major issues were addressed: Black professionals' perception of health care, and aging for themselves and significant others. It was hypothesized that there would be no difference between the perceptions of middle-class Blacks and Blacks who are less well off.

Questionnaires related to the above issues were circulated to individuals in two groups: (1) Group A, 104 faculty and staff at a predominantly White Southern university, and (2) Group B, a random sample of 120 persons, from a pool of 360 known to have been human service practitioners. The return rate for the mailed questionnaire was good for each group: 67 or 64.4%, and 79 or 65.8%, respectively.

Assumptions and Limitations

The study was directed toward Blacks by a Black for comparison with other Blacks. The use of mail questionnaires depended upon the cooperation of the respondents, with recognition of the diversity of the Black experience. However, the topic was thought to be significant enough to secure a response.

The small sample was a limitation of the study. Other limitations relate to the interpretation of the instrument by the respondents, and the accuracy of the responses.

Demographics

The age of the respondents ranged from under 25 years to 65 years and over. Group A (faculty and staff) was younger than Group B (a random sample); however, when the groups were combined, 92 individuals, or 63%, were 25 through 44 years of age. There was a total of 72 men and 74 women, 49 and 51%, respectively. Nearly two-thirds, 66%, were married. The fathers of both sets of respondents had been mostly blue-collar workers, laborers and service workers. The mothers were mostly employed, primarily in blue color jobs. More than half, 56% of all respondents, had incomes in excess of $30,000 per year. Those in Group A earned less than those in Group B.

The total group was well educated; 98% of the 146 respondents had college or graduate degrees. Overall, 95% of Group B had completed postgraduate education, compared with 79% in Group A.

Findings

Kinship Bonds. The respondents were in touch with their relatives. Some contributed financially and made decisions for their relatives. Sixty-six percent in each group anticipated having to make a financial contribution to a significant adult. Each group further anticipated they might have to take on decision-making responsibilities (69% of Group A and 75% of Group B).

Health Care. Less than one-third of Group A thought that hospitals provided good medical care to Blacks. Just over one-third, 39%, of Group B thought that medical care in hospitals for African-Americans was good. Both groups of respondents were decisive in responses regarding experimentation on African-Americans in hospitals. Just over one-half, 51%, in Group B thought that experimentation took place on Blacks. In Group A 43% thought that experimentation occurred. Both groups would be comfortable in questioning a physician's advice.

Almost one-half, 48%, of Group A had faced a health crisis in relation to a significant adult. Group B had a much larger percentage, 60, who had faced such a crisis. Less than one-half of each group had faced the need to make a decision regarding a health crisis. Almost one-half, 49%, in each group reported that it would be a family decision should it be necessary to consider placement of a significant adult because of a medical problem. Few would have sole decision-making responsibility (6% of Group A and 18% of Group B).

The Elderly. Nursing homes were not viewed positively by the respondents. Only 12% of Group A thought that nursing homes provided good care to African-Americans, and 18% of Group B thought this to be so.

Few in Group A had faced a crisis due to the age of a significant adult (6 persons, or 9%). Just over one-fourth, 21 individuals, or 27%, of Group B had faced a crisis with an elderly adult. The need for decision making regarding an elderly adult had not occurred often (7% of Group A and 20% of Group B). Over one-half of both groups (58% of Group A and 53% of Group B) reported that the family would be involved in any decision-making deliberations. Few would be left with the sole decision-making responsibility in either group.

Discussion of Findings

Regardless of age, there was congruency of the responses regarding health care and the elderly in institutional care settings. African-American self-help in health care, as well as social issues, was early influenced by the society in which they lived. Folk medicine was a must for Blacks in the struggle for survival (Morais, 1976). The pharmacopoeia developed was more often orally transmitted through the community healers, as well as within family constellations. The currency of the practice has been discussed, too, by Dennis (1985). Self-treatment has been a main means of cure in the Black community (Watson, 1984). Mechanic (1972) noted, "The idea implicit . . . is that primitive conceptions of illness are part of a learned cultural complex and are functionally associated with other aspects of cultural responses to environmental threats" (p. 129). The same conceptual framework and ideation could be applied to the care of and concern for the elderly, who have in the past been held in high esteem in the African-American community.

The health and nurturing belief systems of African-Americans appear to cut across class lines. It would seem to be important to consider these systems of belief individually and collectively when attempting to treat with modern medicines or to recommend placement in nursing home facilities for the elderly.

Population size, age and sex structure, socio-economic composition, and other characteristics differentiate minority groups from the White population. Because these characteristics influence health, they must be considered when assessing the health status of minority groups. (Office of Health Research, Statistics, and Technology, 1980)

Although there has been a slight decline in the poverty of the Black elderly, from 39.1% in 1983 to 33% in 1986, this represents a figure of well over 700,000 persons aged 65 and over (The Economic Plight of Older Blacks, 1983). The fact that the Black elderly population is growing indicates the middle-class will have an uphill struggle to actualize their kinship bonds in caring for their parents and significant others. The lower income levels in the African-American middle-class (as compared to the majority group), the continued escalation of the cost of living, mobility of family members and significant others, fixed income dependence, and other economic factors will make it increasingly difficult for middle-class African-Americans to take care of their own.

The recent publication on *Black Initiative and Governmental Responsibility* (1987) clearly notes the self-help tradition of the Black community, but also calls attention to the widening disparities of income of African-Americans as compared to the majority group. Thus, self-help programs are likely to need some bolstering from the wider society.

This study would seem to have relevance for social workers and other human service practitioners and health care providers, as well as policy makers and planners. If highly educated, middle-class African-Americans have limited trust of outside care of the elderly and of health care given to Blacks, then the barriers to those less educated and knowledgeable are indeed difficult. These barriers, which influence the use of needed services by African-Americans, require constant attention.

CONCLUSION

There are a number of reasons why it might be necessary for the adult child to take on parenting responsibilities for her/his parent.

All of them add up to the fact that the parent is no longer able to function independently. Although it is true that partial care or closer attention is not nearly as time consuming as total care, there is still disruption to the life of the caregiver. It becomes an addition to the life pattern which has already been established (Solldo and Myllyluoma, 1983; Cicirelli, 1983; Lopata, 1978). Incidents of total disruption occur when the parent must move into the home of the adult child, when the parent must be placed in an institution, and when the parent needs daily help in the parent's own home.

Having anticipated the change in role can make a difference in adjusting to this new relationship between parent and child. Given the geographical mobility of the African-American middle-class, living a distance away from one's family of origin is not unusual. The African-American middle-class is a part of the American mainstream and is caught up with getting ahead, keeping up with the Joneses, getting that promotion, rearing one's children and seeing that they are protected from many of life's hardships — in other words, pursuing the American dream. Therefore, denial may come into play, and become the means of avoiding recognition of the breakdown of an elderly parent. Living away from the parent may bolster this defense mechanism even though frequent phone contact may be present and yearly, or more frequent, visits may be the pattern.

Usually, initial efforts in the planning of care focus on keeping the parent within the parent's own home. The next step is to move the parent into the home of the adult child. Even at great physical, financial, and emotional sacrifice, efforts are usually directed toward keeping the parent in the child's home. The decision to place a parent in an institution is done after all other efforts to adequately address the parent's needs have failed (Smallegan, 1985).

More often than not, the adult child needs assistance from family, friends, and sometimes social agencies in meeting all the needs of an ill parent in the home. Public assistance to lighten the burden has been suggested (Arling and McAuley, 1983). The need for social agencies to be sensitive to serving the elderly Black is crucial (A. E. Johnson, 1982, 1983a, 1983b, 1985), especially because of the low usage of nursing homes by Blacks.

Respite care, which would allow time out for the caregiver family member, is not uniformly or easily available. Of course, such respite care becomes an added financial expense. Paying for additional help in the home, a parent sitter for a night out, in addition to the paid help that may be needed on a daily basis, can readily drain the financial resources of all involved. This can reduce the middle-class status of the family. Temporary placement of the parent in a nursing home would allow the caregiver a brief respite, but it is a financial burden that many African-American caregivers are not able to afford.

The social, physical, and mental problems of the African-American elderly need attention within the Black community and in the wider society. The absorption of the Black elderly into the family by the middle-class has, in part, masked the severity of the problems of their care needs. Consideration has not been given to the poverty that hovers over the middle-class as it strives to maintain the kinship bonds of love, concern, caring, and commitment, which are a part of its heritage, and at the same time to maintain middle-class status.

Alzheimer's disease, for which there is no known cure, affects 2.5 million of the elderly. The ravaging of the basic functioning abilities of the afflicted elderly places the adult child caregiver in the living hell of watching the deterioration of a loved one.

"The social networking operative within the Black community might be described as a nurturing and mutually beneficial relationship between individual and/or groups related to their coping with life issues" (A. E. Johnson, 1983a). Networking and kinship bonds have been studied repetitively by African-Americans and others to the extent that a new vocabulary has resulted: *kinship ties, fictive kin, extended family*. These terms have forged relationships of meaning in the African-American community and have been intricately involved with its survival. This support system has been noted by many investigators (Jackson, Rhone, and Sanders, 1973; Billingsley, 1968; Ladner, 1972; Hill, 1972, 1977; Staples, 1971, 1973; Liebow, 1967; Stack, 1974; Gutman, 1976; Johnson and Billingsley, 1983).

There is a need for the informal and the formal systems of caregiving to come together if the quality of life of the elderly Black is to be improved. Formal systems such as Social Security, senior citizens groups, Medicare, Medicaid, nursing homes, and hospitals will need to be augmented by the informal networks of kinship, friends, church, neighbors, club groups, and the like. But the informal system should not be expected to carry the full responsibility for care of the Black elderly. There is the need for a formal system of support and help in a professional manner (Solomon, 1976, 1983) to empower the African-American community toward an improved quality of life for all of its citizens.

The summary, conclusions, and recommendations put forth here have implications for public policy initiatives regarding the family, the elderly, and health care. Questions are also implied regarding what will happen with the African-American middle-class if the burden of caring for the elderly is placed solely upon their shoulders. The wealth disparity between Blacks and other groups will continue, especially in those households headed by women, who are the primary caregivers of the elderly in the African-American communities.

True peace is not merely the absence of tension; it is the presence of justice. (King, 1987)

REFERENCES

Ackoff, R. (1967). *The design of social research.* Chicago: The University of Chicago Press.
Arling, G., & McAuley, W. J. (1983). The feasibility of public payments for family caregiving. *The Gerontologist, 23,* 300–306.
Beaver, M. (1979). The decision-making process and its relationship to relocation adjustment in old people. *The Gerontologist, 19,* 567–574.
Bennett, L., Jr. (1982). *Before the Mayflower: A history of Black America* (5th ed.). Chicago: Johnson Publishing Company.
Billingsley, A. (1968). *Black families in White America.* Englewood Cliffs, NJ: Prentice-Hall.
Birren, J. E., & Sloane, R. B. (Eds.). (1980). *Handbook of mental health and aging.* Englewood Cliffs, NJ: Prentice-Hall.
Black initiative and governmental responsibility. (1987). Washington, DC: Joint Center for Political Studies.
Brody, E. (1974). *A social work guide for long-term care facilities.* Rockville, MD: NIMH.
Brubaker, T. H. (1985). *Later life families.* Beverly Hills, CA: Sage Publications.
Butler, R. (1975). *Why survive! Being old in America.* New York: Harper & Row.
Chou, Y.-L. (1963). *Applied business and economic statistics* (p. 348). New York: Holt, Rinehart and Winston.
Cicirelli, V. G. (1983). A comparison of helping behavior to elderly parents of adult children with intact and disrupted marriages. *The Gerontologist, 23,* 619–625.
Clark, N. M., & Rakowski, W. (1983). Family care-givers of older adults: Improving helping skills. *The Gerontologist, 23,* 637–642.
Cornely, P. B. (1970, April). Community participation and control: A possible answer to racism in health. *The Milbank Memorial Fund Quarterly, 48,* 347–363.
Dennis, R. E. (1985). Health beliefs and practices of ethnic and religious groups. In E. L. Watkins & A. E. Johnson (Eds.), *Re-*

moving cultural and ethnic barriers to health care (pp. 12–28). Chapel Hill, NC: Schools of Public Health and Social Work.

Dion, M. J. (1984). *We, the American women.* Bureau of the Census. Washington, DC: US Government Printing Office.

The economic plight of older Blacks. (1983, February). Washington, DC: National Caucus and Center on Black Aged.

Fogel, R. W., Hatfield, E., Kiesler, S. B., & Shannas, E. (Eds.). (1981). *Aging: Stability and change in the family.* New York: Academic Press.

Franklin, J. H. (1974). *From slavery to freedom: A history of Negro Americans* (4th ed.). New York: Alfred A. Knopf.

Gary, L. E. (1983). Utilization of network systems in the Black community. In A. E. Johnson (Ed.), *The Black experience: Considerations for health and human services.* Davis, CA: International Dialogue Press.

Gelman, D., Hager, M., Gonzalez, D. L., Morris, H., McCormick, J., Jackson, T., & Karagians, E. (1985, May 6). Who's taking care of our parents? *Newsweek,* pp. 61–68.

Glasgow, D. (1980). *The Black underclass.* San Francisco: Jossey-Bass.

Gutman, H. G. (1976). *The Black family in slavery and freedom, 1750–1925.* New York: Pantheon Books.

Hanson, S. L., Sauer, W. J., & Seelbach, W. C. (1983). Racial and cohort variations in filial responsibility norms. *The Gerontologist, 23,* 626–631.

Health Resources Administration. (1980). *Health of the disadvantaged: Chartbook II.* Washington, DC: US Government Printing Office, Department of Health, Education and Welfare.

Higginbotham, A. L., Jr. (1980). *In the matter of color: Race and the American legal process, the colonial period.* New York: Oxford University Press.

Hill, R. B. (1972). *The strengths of Black families.* New York: Emerson Hall.

Hill, R. B. (1977). *Informal adoption among Black families.* Washington, DC: National Urban League Research Department.

Jackson, J. J. (1980). *Minorities and aging.* Belmont, CA: Wadsworth Publishing Company.

Jackson, W. S., Rhone, J. V., & Sanders, C. L. (1973). *Social service delivery system in the Black community during the ante-bellum period (1619–1860).* Atlanta: Atlanta University School of Social Work.

Jahoda, M., Deutsch, M., & Cook, S. W. (1951). *Research methods in social relations: With special reference to prejudice: Vol. 1. Basic Processes.* New York: Dryden Press.

Johnson, A. E. (1978). The organization of mental health services delivery. In L. E. Gary (Ed.), *Mental health: A challenge to the Black community.* Philadelphia: Dorrance & Company.

Johnson, A. E. (1982). *Social work intervention with the Black elderly.* Paper presented at the 110th Annual Meeting of the American Public/Health Association, Montreal, Canada.

Johnson, A. E. (1983a, Spring). The Black elderly and social work services. *Black Caucus: Journal of the National Association of Black Social Workers.*

Johnson, A. E. (1983b). *The elderly Black female: a forgotten treasure.* Paper presented at the Annual Conference of the National Association of Black Social Workers, Miami Beach, FL.

Johnson, A. E. (1984). *Selected Black professionals' view of health care and the elderly.* Paper presented at the National Health Conference of the National Association of Social Workers, Washington, DC.

Johnson, A. E. (1985). *Preparing to be Black and elderly.* Paper presented at the Annual Meeting of the Council on Social Work Education, Washington, DC.

Johnson, A. E., & Billingsley, A. (1983). The Black family curriculum need. *Proceedings of the 14th Annual Conference of the National Association of Black Social Workers* (pp. 267–276). New York: NABSW.

Johnson, D. L. (1986). *We, the Black Americans.* Bureau of the Census. Washington, DC: US Government Printing Office, p. 6.

Kobata, F. S., Lockery, S. A., & Moriwaki, S. Y. (1980). Minority issues in mental health and aging. In J. E. Birren & R. B. Sloane (Eds.), *Handbook of mental health and aging.* Englewoods Cliffs, NJ: Prentice-Hall.

King, C. S. (Ed.). (1987). *The Words of Martin Luther King, Jr.* New York: Newmarket Press.

Ladner, J. A. (1972). *Tomorrow's tomorrow: The Black woman.* Garden City, NY: Anchor Books.

Lastrucci, C. L. (1967). *The scientific approach: Basic principles of the scientific method.* Cambridge, MA: Schenkman.

Liebow, E. (1967). *Tally's Corner.* Boston: Little, Brown.

Lopata, H. Z. (1978, May). Contributions of extended families of the support systems of metropolitan area widows: Limitations of the modified kin network. *Journal of Marriage and the Family, 40,* 355–364.

Lowy, L. (1985). *Social work with the aging: The challenge and promise of the later years* (2nd ed.). New York: Longman.

Manuel, R. C. (1986, September 3). A socio-demographic profile of the Black aged. Submitted to the House Select Committee on Aging, Washington, DC.

Martin, J. M., & Martin, E. P. (1985). *The helping tradition in the*

Black community. Silver Spring, MD: National Association of Social Workers.

Matney, W. C., & Johnson, D. L. (1984). *American's Black population: A statistical view, 1970–1982* (Special Publication PIO/POP-83-1). Bureau of the Census. Washington, DC: US Government Printing Office.

Mechanic, D. (1972). Response factors in illness behavior. In E. Gartly Jaco (Ed.), *Patients, physicians, and illness* (2nd ed.) (p. 129). New York: Free Press.

Morais, H. M. (1976). *The history of the Afro-American in medicine.* The Association for the Study of Afro-American Life and History. Cornwells Heights, PA: Publishers Agency.

NIA Sponsors Workshop on Black Aging Process. (1986, September 25–26). Unpublished notes from the Workshop Research on Aging Black Populations sponsored by National Institute on Aging, Office of Minority Affairs Initiatives, American Association of Retired Persons, Office of Minority Health, U.S. Department of Health and Human Services, Washington, DC.

Office of Health Research, Statistics, and Technology. (1980). *Health United States 1979* [DHEW Publication No. (PHS) 80-1232]. Washington, DC: US Government Printing Office.

Seelbach, W. C., & Aauer, W. J. (1977). Filial responsibility expectations and morale among aged parents. *The Gerontologist, 17,* 492–499.

Senior citizens: On their own. (1986, October 27). *Newsweek,* p. 5.

Shanas, E. (1979). The family as a social support system in old age. *The Gerontologist, 19,* 169–174.

Smallegan, M. (1985). There was nothing else to do: Needs for care before nursing home admission. *The Gerontologist, 25,* 364–369.

Solldo, B. J., & Myllyluoma, J. (1983). Caregivers who live with dependent elderly. *The Gerontologist, 23,* 605–611.

Solomon, B. B. (1976). *Black empowerment: Social work in oppressed communities.* New York: Columbia University Press.

Solomon, B. B. (1983). Innovations in service delivery to Black clients. In A. E. Johnson (Ed.), *The Black experience: Considerations for health and human services.* Davis, CA: International Dialogue Press, pp. 75–93.

Stack, C. B. (1974). *All our kin: Strategies for survival in a Black community.* New York: Harper Colophon Books.

Staples, R. (1971). In S. Fullerton (Ed.), *The Black family: Essays and studies.* Belmont, CA: Wadsworth.

Staples, R. (1973). *The Black woman in America: Sex, marriage, and the family.* Chicago: Nelson-Hall.

The state of Black America. (1987). New York: The National Urban League.

Treas, J. (1977). Family support systems for the aged: Some social and demographic considerations. *The Gerontologist, 17,* 486–491.

US Department of Commerce. (1979). *The social and economic status of the Black population in the United States: An historical view, 1790–1978.* Bureau of the Census. Washington, DC: US Government Printing Office.

US Department of Commerce. (1983). *America in transition: An aging society.* Bureau of the Census. Washington, DC: US Government Printing Office.

Watson, W. H. (Ed.). (1984). *Black folk medicine: The therapeutic significance of faith and trust.* New Brunswick, NJ: Transaction.

White, J. L. (1984). *The psychology of Blacks: An Afro-American perspective.* Englewood Cliffs, NJ: Prentice-Hall.

Introduction to Part IV

EDUCATIONAL ISSUES

Alice F. Coner-Edwards

The analyses of the various educational issues with which Black middle-class families are confronted begins with conceptualizations by Adelbert Jenkins. This chapter sets the stage for examination of the broader educational issues by focusing on a special nurturing capacity that is found within Black middle-class families. Jenkins outlines the specific activities in which Black middle-class parents engage to further the education of their school-age children. He proposes that Black children have survived psychologically in the context of a racist society by separating their personal sense of worth from the negative role ascriptions attributed to them by the dominant society. The Black family, as contributor to this process, has nurtured the child's sense of self and has expanded the child's range of possible selves. Of particular significance is Jenkins's message that oppression does not necessarily equate with being at the mercy of events.

Jean Wheeler Smith's work on select issues confronting middle-class Blacks in the process of educating their offspring gives a process-centered analysis of major stressors presented by the educational system. Smith examines the school system as a complex bureaucracy requiring discrete navigation skills to successfully negotiate the educational process, as well as parental ambivalence that serves as a barrier to a child's successful educational experience. Like Jenkins, Smith emphasizes select aspects of the home environment and the extended family as nurturing, supportive, and critical to the child's success in school. This most contributive analysis is reality based in case illustrations and vignettes of real-life experiences of Black middle-class parents in their efforts to educate their school-age children.

113

Marilyn Benoit continues the theme of critical educational issues facing the Black middle-class with a focus on the role of the child advocate in educational systems. Benoit provides a brief historical review and definition of the problem which substantiates the need for child advocacy. Like Smith, Benoit points out that the school system may lack the resources needed to provide the time to handle the myriad of special problems presented by many children. Benoit emphasizes the importance of the objective perceptions of the child advocate, an outsider who is less in conflict with divergent school rules and child needs. This analysis addresses the critical question of "Why should the mental health professional act as advocate?" The analysis also helps to reclarify the role of the mental health advocate among other school personnel, many of whom view themselves as advocates.

10

Black Families:
The Nurturing of Agency

Adelbert H. Jenkins

Recent scholarship has come to recognize strengths in the Black family, particularly in middle-class and stable working-class contexts. This approach to the Black family is at variance with the tradition in the social sciences, which has tended to focus on the weaknesses in the psychosocial adaptation of Black Americans. The trend toward a more balanced view of Blacks can be examined in the context of emerging "teleologic" themes in psychology. Such perspectives emphasize the idea that active human agency is an essential contributor of human behavior.

More specifically, it is proposed in this chapter that Blacks have survived psychologically in the context of a racist society by finding ways of separating their personal sense of worth from the negative role ascriptions attributed to them by Whites. The Black family has contributed to this process by nurturing Black children's sense of agency, a sense of themselves as participants in the events around them. Through the enhancement of children's "self-awareness" and the expansion of their range of "possible selves," children come to learn about their capabilities and to know that they can carry out their own intentions or influence the events around them.

One of the major functions of the family is providing for the healthy emotional and psychological development of its children. There has been a tradition in social science writing to raise questions about the capacity of the typical Black family to perform this function (Slaughter and McWorter, 1985). However, recent scholarship indicates that both during and after slavery Blacks often found ways of organizing stable and supportive contexts for themselves and their children (Billingsley, 1968; Gutman, 1976; Slaughter and McWorter, 1985).

The task of encouraging healthy psychological development has included the need to provide a buffer against the psychological assaults posed by racism. Many Black families, particularly middle-class families, have understood this and have been able to perform this function quite well against the pressures exerted by the dominant society (Billingsley, 1968). As Spencer (1987) notes in her discussion of resilience in minorities, "in the face of many obstacles, African American children seem to have an amazing capacity to cope and to rise above circumstances" (p. 114). However, she goes on to note, "data remain unavailable that might more clearly delineate how minority group parents at the microsystem level prepare children for external threats perceived to be at the macrosystem level. Specifically more information is needed on what minority parents teach their children [about how to cope]" (p. 114). In this chapter I will address the question of what Black parents do that might be effective in preparing their youngsters for dealing with the American society. I will not present new data here but, rather, will refocus previous literature on this topic from a particular theoretical point of view.

In previous writing I have suggested that Blacks have survived as a group historically by developing and exercising what amounts to basic human capacities for psychological "agency" (Jenkins, 1982). Here I will propose more specifically that one of the ways Black families have contributed to their children's capacity to cope is through nurturing in them this sense of agency. I will first briefly define the concept of agency in terms of a current "teleologic" approach to psychology. I will then discuss the Black family's role in sustaining self-esteem in the child and contributing to a sense of self as agent. Finally, I will suggest that the family does this partly by helping the child develop "self-awareness" and a conception of "possible selves."

TELEOLOGY IN PSYCHOLOGY

The particular teleologic or "telic" psychological position that will be used here is consistent with "humanistic" approaches to psychology, broadly defined (Rychlak, 1977, 1979). It proposes that human beings are active contributors to the outcomes of situations that affect them; they are not just passive responders to environmental and internal (physiological) forces acting on them, as the more traditional views in social science would have it. Although telic-human-istic theorists have somewhat differing vantage points on this issue, the tie binding them is the "assumption that the individual makes a difference or contributes to the flow of events" (Rychlak, 1976, p. 128). In the perspective being adopted here, there are several basic issues that characterize a telic point of view. These have to do with causation, meaning and a "construing" mentality.

Determinants of Behavior

First of all, a telic position recognizes that people have an active causal influence on their lives by the intentions and purposes they bring to the circumstances in which they find themselves. People do not act only in response to the stimuli impinging on them. The term *teleologic* derives from the Greek word *telos*, or "end." This term draws attention to the fact that ends or goals that people conceive as the "reasons" for their behavior become powerful motivators of their actions.

Of course, external factors do exert considerable force on a person. However, subjectively held intentions also have considerable power to affect behavior. We might imagine, for example, a poor Black youth who has the heartfelt wish to become a doctor. Even if no one in her family has gone to college and even if it is the girl's aspirations in the family which are favored, her intentions may fuel her hard work and enable her to achieve her goals in spite of hampering circumstances around her. The capacity to set intentions that can have motivating effect on behavior is one important aspect of human agency. Traditional social science has often failed to understand this dimension in human action. This is because it has emphasized almost exclusively those factors which act *on* the person, such as internal drives and environmental stimuli.

The importance of intentionality is implicit also in Robert White's discussion of "competence motivation," which he suggests begins to develop in early infancy and gradually takes shape in later life (White, 1963). He suggests that some of the young infant's important early interactions with the world are not primarily drive dominated. Rather, they reflect the baby's effort to reach out and have a satisfying effect on the world. Such action represents, in essence, an urge to be *effective.* This feature of behavior develops into a life-long motivation to become ever more *competent* in one's broader transactions with the physical and social world. This is an example, then, of a powerfully motivating intention that governs all people's lives, including, of course, the lives of Black persons.

Meaning in Events

A second feature of the telic framework is an expanded view of meaning. This issue is particularly important to our discussion here. From one standpoint the effort to specify the meaning of an item in experience is based on describing that event precisely. By characterizing its uniqueness, we differentiate it clearly from other events encountered. This has been called a "demonstrative" approach to meaning, and it is the one most familiar in traditional science.

In contrast, people have the capacity to take a "dialectical" approach to meaning as well. From this point of view many concepts of interest to people cannot be pinned down with precision. Rather, the meaning of an item is "framed" by the opposite or alternate implications of the concept. Thus, the "beauty" of an object is determined with respect to some conception in the viewer's mind of what "ugliness" is. Similarly, a "just" act is defined partly in terms of a conception of an "unjust" act. A notion of "left" depends on the conception of "right," "up" implies "down," and so on. Without trying to spell out all the implications of this notion here (see Rychlak, 1979, for a more extended discussion of dialectical thinking), we can say that people have the ability, in the presence of a given situation, to conceive of its opposite — something not present in that situation. They then can act to bring that conception into being if they choose. For example, seeing an empty lot I can imagine a space filled with a shopping center or an industrial park; then I can embark on the necessary activities to bring this image into being.

Clearly, this is another important aspect of the nature of agency that we are seeking to outline here. Human beings, by drawing on their capacity to view situations differently from how they are presented, can determine which conception they will emphasize. This choice is governed by their intentions in that situation. There is always more than one way of conceiving a given situation in reality. Throughout history, Blacks have used their adaptive abilities not only to respond to situations objectively and accurately — with demonstrative thinking — but also to go beyond the givens. They have used their dialectical thinking abilities to envision alternative conceptions of themselves, different from those imposed on them by a racist society. When labeled incompetent and unworthy, Blacks have often conceived the opposite about themselves, and then they have acted in competent and worthy ways.

Active Mentality

A third issue that helps us characterize the telic approach to agency is one that distinguishes between two views of the development and functioning of mentality. One approach to theorizing characterizes the mind metaphorically as a kind of blank slate. Experiences with the physical and social environment are seen as leaving "traces" on a relatively passive organism; such events are typically seen by social scientists as *the* way in which the organism's development is shaped. Such a view is useful to a degree, but a psychological perspective that is attempting to support an active image of agency requires an additional conception. This is one that sees the human being as cognitively active from birth in structuring experience, although this activity is carried on in rudimentary ways at first. Mind develops from the activity the child brings to the world that he or she finds. These transactions lead to the development of a conceptual framework through which the individual approaches the world. Blacks have used their native human capacities to actively fashion a sense of "reality" that is more in keeping with *their* understanding of *their* intentions for themselves and their children.

HUMANISM AND BLACK PSYCHOLOGY

Psychology has traditionally portrayed Blacks as being reactive responders to the things that happen to them, and thus as having little control over their destinies (Jenkins, 1982, chap. 1). In addition, Blacks have been portrayed as deficient in what they need to be fully effective in society (Crain and Weisman, 1972, p. 26; Kardiner and Ovesey, 1962, p. 297). Although Blacks have certainly shown problematic styles of adapting, this perspective overlooks the many positive qualities, as Ralph Ellison says, ". . . which the American Negro has developed despite and in rejection of the obstacles and meannesses imposed upon us" (1964, p. 21). The more explicit conception of agency being presented here adds the needed supplement to our conception of how Blacks have sustained their humanity. In many instances Afro-Americans have actively and intentionally brought to their lives conceptions of their competence that have been at variance with the judgments made of them by the majority society. Blacks have survived by exercising their human capacity for agency in many of the circumstances in which they have found themselves historically.

THE BLACK FAMILY AND THE SENSE OF SELF

The main contention of this chapter is that in preparing the child for the "external threats . . . at the macrosystem level" (Spencer, 1987, p. 114), an important function of the Black family has been to awaken the recognition in the Black child that he or she can have an active impact on life by setting intentions, intentions that can be at (dialectical) variance to those circumstances that society has set before the child. From a psychological point of view, one way in which the family nurtures this attitude is through the support it gives to the child's sense of self.

Self-Concept

The notion of self, particularly as embodied in the idea of "self-concept," has been an important one in psychology. The self-concept is, as Keen (1970) puts it, the sense of "what I am." The self-concept can be described as a multifaceted construction or *theory* one has about oneself (Epstein, 1973). We recognize various role performances we engage in and skills that we have as being relatively independent yet connected aspects of ourselves. For example, important components of a person's self-concept might include the recognition of being a parent, an engineer, an Afro-American, an avid although not especially skilled skier, a devout Christian, and so on. Associated with one's self-concept is a certain level of *self-esteem*, the personal evaluation of one's worth, which is an important index of a person's coping effectiveness. People who express a positive self-concept and have high self-esteem are usually thought to be showing important elements of a healthy psychological adaptation.

Over the years there have been conflicting interpretations of the research literature concerning the level of self-esteem in Black children (Cross, 1985). Some data had seemed to indicate that Black children feel less positively about themselves than do White children, whereas other data have appeared to reflect a quite high level of self-regard among Black children. More recent scholarship has tended to recognize the multifaceted (dialectical) nature of the self-concept and the fact that Black children, like everyone, have different reference points from which to evaluate their sense of self. It appears that prior studies done in this area were tapping different aspects of the multifaceted sense of self. Thus, the data seem to indicate that Black children always have felt as positively as White children about many aspects of themselves as *persons,* a sense of self that is without particular reference to racial identity. However, prior to the Black pride movement of the sixties, Black children may have harbored varying degrees of ambivalence about that aspect of themselves that pertained to their ethnic classification, their "racial reference group orientation" (Cross, 1985, 1987). (In recent years it is likely that reference group orientation for Black children has grown to be more consistently positive, also.)

Maintaining such a separation between personal identity and negative aspects of reference group orientation has helped the adaptation of Black children historically. But the independence of these two facets of the sense of self has not been simply an accident of history. Intact Black families have worked hard to support the various components of personal self-concept and self-esteem in order to keep them separate in the child's mind from the negative racial ascriptions toward the self that White society has tried to impose.

Maintenance of Positive Self-Esteem in Crises

This issue can be illustrated by Robert Coles's moving portrait of a 6-year-old Black girl named Ruby, presented in the first volume of his series *Children of Crisis* (1967). In this book Coles's aim was to try to understand the effect of the turbulence of the early desegregation struggles in the South on Black and White children and their families. His method with the children was to engage them in play sessions and hold informal conversations with them. A particular focus of interest was the children's crayon drawings and what these productions seemed to reveal about their evaluation of themselves and each other. Interpreted carefully, according to established clinical principles, drawings of human figures can be useful in getting an idea of a child's sense of self.

When Coles first met Ruby she was one of the few Black children going to a newly desegregated public school in New Orleans. This meant daily trips through a gauntlet of boisterous and angry White adults who were picketing the school. Regarding Ruby's drawings Coles noted that:

She drew white people larger and more lifelike. Negroes were smaller, their bodies less intact. A white girl we both knew to be her own size appeared several times taller. While Ruby's own face . . . lacked an eye in one drawing, an ear in another, the white girl never lacked any features. (1967, p. 47)

Thus, it seemed that one aspect of Ruby's sense of self, her self-image referrable to racial group orientation, had been somewhat negatively affected by her experiences in her first 6 years. These portrayals of self were seemingly not just responses to the traumatic incidents she was facing daily. When Coles examined similar drawings of hers before he or the desegregation crisis entered her life, he found a similar diminution of Blacks as compared to Whites.

However, consistent with the multifaceted view of the sense of self being presented in this chapter, Coles had other things to say about Ruby as well. She was the oldest of five children in an intact family that loved and supported her in every way they could, although they all were feeling the effects of the crisis. Her mother would remind her of Ruby's maternal grandfather, who lived on his farm not too far away: "Momma . . . says her daddy is the strongest man you can find. She says . . . he can lick anyone and his brother together. She says not to worry, we have a hiding place and I should remember it every day" (Coles, 1967, p. 49). In spite of the crises she faced daily she slept well, did well in school, and engaged avidly in her regular playtimes when school was out. These are important behavioral indices of a child's adjustment. Thus, except for a temporary eating problem directly related to the turbulence she was going through, in general she gave evidence of being able to enjoy many aspects of a normal childhood. It seemed that personal identity, composed of attributes not referrable to race, was quite healthy on the whole.

Clearly, Ruby's parents tried to create an atmosphere in their home that would be a healing contrast to the negative things she experienced every day in the world outside. W. E. B. DuBois, writing to Black parents in *Crisis* magazine in 1926, suggested that this is a continuing task for Black parents even when times are less manifestly turbulent:

At least in your home you have a chance to make your child's surroundings of the best; books and pictures and music; cleanliness, order, sympathy and understanding; information, friendship and love — there is not much of evil in the world that can stand against such home surroundings. (In Diggs, 1976, p. 390)

Thus, historically an important way that Black families have bolstered their children's sense of self and helped build a sense of competence has been by providing positive alternatives in that part of the environment that they could control.

Self as Agent

In addition to the quality of the surroundings for their children, Black families have affected the sense of self in their children by direct influence on the child's sense of "agency." For the telic-humanistic view being proposed here, the sense of agency is a particularly important aspect of the individual's sense of self. Rather than the content of the self — the sense of "*what* I am" — agency has more to do with the sense "*that* I am" (Keen, 1970). This experience presumably begins to emerge as children start to develop a sense of themselves as a cause of events around them by means of the growing ability to carry out the intentions they set.

As noted earlier, from a psychological point of view many situations in our lives from our earliest days are full of possibilities for action.

> This quality of open alternatives in experience demands that the human being *affirm* [emphasis added] some . . . meaning at the outset for the sake of which behavior might then take place. [Affirmation is] one of those active roles assigned to mind by humanists because which item . . . of . . . experience is singled out for identification is up to the individual and *not* to the environment. (Rychlak, 1977, p. 295)

Gradually, as we act in life circumstances, we come to recognize ourselves as beings who take initiative and make decisions, and as we carry out this agency we shape the course of our lives.

One important implication of this point is that we are self-creating beings and thus bear some responsibility, in one sense of the word, for what we become. This is true even of young children, whose predilections are often based on what seems to them to advance their sense of efficacy and their developing sense of competence, even sometimes in spite of what their parents may wish for them (Jenkins, 1982, pp. 31–35). Because we make critical contributions to the course of our lives as agents, it is important that we come to realize it. An important function that stable families provide for their children's psychological development is helping them to become *aware* of their agency in their own lives. This is what Black families have done for their children in many instances.

THE BLACK FAMILY AND SELF-AWARENESS

The term *awareness* has a special meaning in the particular telic-humanistic perspective being used here. Although all people are more or less "conscious" of many of the things that they do, many people do not have a sense of "awareness" regarding their actions. Awareness refers to an "appreciation of the arbitrariness in experience," in other words, "knowing that something else might be taking place in a life circumstance" (Rychlak, 1977, p. 354). A *self-aware* person recognizes that although I am *this* way in this situation, I *could* be or do something else. Thus, as we have seen, the individual plays an important role in the development of his or her own self-concept.

When a person realizes that who (s)he is becoming is composed to an important degree of choices that (s)he is making, then one is [self-aware], as that term is being used here. . . . While self-awareness concerning all of one's behavior is not always desirable, for most people and for the developing child, broadening awareness of the degree to which (s)he is an active contributor to his or her own life is a worthwhile goal. (Jenkins, 1982, p. 41)

Thus, it is likely that parents in stable Black families provide circumstances and act toward their children in ways that enhance their self-awareness. In spite of being immersed in a larger society that reflects back to the child negative images about Blacks, the family nurtures a process within its children that encourages them to take a dialectic perspective on their lives and realize that they can have some impact on their lives. One does this partly by giving children choices over their affairs when possible, and respecting these choices (Comer and Poussaint, 1975). The significance of such choices will change as children grow, of course. Exposing them to an enriched environment, as DuBois suggests, undoubtedly enhances the notion that choices are available, especially when information about how other Blacks have succeeded is included.

"Possible Selves"

The telic notion of self-awareness bears on another area of research in psychology. This is the domain of "possible selves" recently articulated by Markus and Nurius (1986). This concept refers to the way that people think about themselves in terms of both positive and negative possibilities. It seems to be built around the notion of alternative options for development. The idea of possible selves seems quite consistent with the concept of the dialectic as I have used it here, although Markus and Nurius do not use that term explicitly:

> Possible selves are the ideal selves that we would very much like to become. They are also the selves we could become, and the selves we are afraid of becoming. . . . An individual's repertoire of possible selves can be viewed as the cognitive manifestation of enduring goals, aspirations, motives, fears, and threats. (Markus and Nurius, 1986, p. 954)

This idea includes in it the notion that by their choices people are active in their own creation: "Through the selection and construction of possible selves individuals can be viewed as active producers of their own development" (p. 955). Although the construction of possible selves is an individually inventive process, people draw on the social milieu of which they are a part:

> The 1984 Olympic games probably created powerful possible selves for some young runners. Many no doubt absorbed the performance of Carl Lewis within the realm of their own possible selves, just as Carl Lewis claimed to have used the early track victories of Jesse Owens to create a possible self and to give a specific cognitive form to his desire to become the world's fastest runner. (Markus and Nurius, 1986, p. 955)

In addition to the media and the images of influential people they transmit, I also maintain that parents, through their interaction with children in the family, are singularly important contributors to the evolution of self-awareness in the young child and to the openness toward the possibility of alternatives for self-development.

Growth of Self-Awareness Under Oppression

The notions of "possible selves" and "self-awareness" that have been discussed here can be illustrated to some extent by a vignette from *The Autobiography of Malcolm X* (1965). His life as portrayed there depicts his continual stance of dialectical opposition to the oppression he experienced in the American society. However, looking more closely, one can also see the positive strivings for self-creation and competent self-development (Jenkins, 1982, pp. 132–135). Although most of his years of growing up did not take place in the context of an intact middle-class family, some aspects of his early family life combined with his native intelligence seem to have given him the background to develop self-awareness and the capacity to contemplate alternatives for himself.

According to him one crucial turning point in the development of his self-awareness came in his eighth-grade year. He had become an accommodating and well-liked youngster in the predominantly White Michigan community in which he was growing up and by the eighth grade he was one of the best students in his school. One day, in discussing his career aspirations with one of his teachers, Malcolm shared his thoughts about eventually becoming a lawyer. The teacher, who had previously been quite supportive of him, chided Malcolm about not being "realistic" in his thinking. He startled Malcolm with his comment that wanting to become a lawyer was "no realistic goal for a nigger." He urged Malcolm to capitalize on his manual skills, which he said boded well for his becoming a first-class carpenter. Reminiscing about that event later, Malcolm noted,

> It was a surprising thing that I had never thought of it that way before, but I realized that whatever I wasn't, I *was* smarter than nearly all of those white kids. But apparently I was still not intelligent enough, in their eyes, to become whatever *I* wanted to be. It was then that I began to change — inside. (Malcolm X, 1965, p. 37)

This is a clear example of a dialectic self-awareness accompanied by a conception of possible selves that was beginning to emerge in Malcolm. That is, his understanding of what he could be differed from what his teacher thought he should be. Although his teacher saw him (probably correctly) as being good with his hands, Malcolm understood himself to also have verbal and thinking abilities that could lead him in other productive directions. The budding aspects of himself as a potential lawyer which he affirmed were determined by *his* mental constructions about himself and the future possibilities. Of course a person's ability to actually carry out the ideas he or she envisions depends greatly on social barriers and supports, but in principle the individual can still sustain the idea of how things *could* be. It is likely that Malcolm was such an effective leader, especially in his post-prison years, because of his capacity to sustain and carry out a (dialectic) conception of himself that was not deterred by what Whites, and sometimes other Blacks, thought of him.

CONCLUSIONS

It has been proposed here that a telic-humanistic perspective on behavior makes a contribution to understanding the psychological coping skills of Black Americans. This point of view, which emphasizes the person's contribution as a causal factor in his or her life, is meant to enrich our view of the human being by supplementing the typical psychological depictions that characterize the individual as being only a respondent to stimuli. Thus, people act on the basis of subjectively derived intentions selected from among the alternative possibilities presented in life.

Consistent with the overall thrust of Black adaptation to life in the United States, stable and middle-class Black families, free of the stresses of economic instability, have been in a better position to help their children develop a sense of themselves as effective agents in their lives. They have helped children develop the *awareness* that they can actively select what they will focus on conceptually from inevitable options in their experience. Even as members of an oppressed group they are not simply at the mercy of events. Black families have functioned to enhance the child's cognitive awareness of the alternate possibilities for self-development notwithstanding the racist society in which they live.

REFERENCES

Billingsley, A. (1968). *Black families in White America.* Englewood Cliffs, NJ: Prentice-Hall.

Coles, R. (1967). *Children of crisis: A study of child care.* New York: Simon & Schuster.

Comer, J. P., & Poussaint, A. F. (1975). *Black child care.* New York: Simon & Schuster.

Crain, R. L., & Weisman, C. S. (1972). *Discrimination, personality and achievement: A survey of northern Blacks.* New York: Academic Press.

Cross, W. E., Jr. (1985). Black identity: Rediscovering the distinction between personal identity and reference group orientation. In M. B. Spencer, G. K. Brookins, & W. R. Allen (Eds.), *Beginnings: The social and affective development of Black children* (pp. 155–171). Hillside, NJ: Lawrence Erlbaum.

Cross, W. E., Jr. (1987). A two-factor theory of Black identity: Implications for the study of identity development in minority children. In J. S. Phinney & M. J. Rotheram (Eds.), *Children's*

ethnic socialization (pp. 117–133). Newbury Park, CA: Sage Publications.
Diggs, I. (1976). Dubois and children. *Phylon, 37,* 370–399.
Ellison, R. (1964). That same pain, that same pleasure: an interview. In R. Ellison, *Shadow and act* (pp. 3–23). New York: Random House.
Epstein, S. (1973). The self-concept revisited: Or a theory of a theory. *American Psychologist, 28,* 404–416.
Gutman, H. G. (1976). *The Black family in slavery and freedom: 1750–1925.* New York: Vintage.
Jenkins, A. H. (1982). *The psychology of the Afro-American: A humanistic approach.* Elmsford, NY: Pergamon.
Kardiner, A., & Ovesey, L. (1962). *The mark of oppression.* Cleveland: Meridian Books. (Original edition, New York: W. W. Norton, 1951)
Keen, E. (1970). *The three faces of being: Toward an existential clinical psychology.* New York: Appleton-Century-Crofts.
Malcolm X. (1965). *The autobiography of Malcolm X.* New York: Grove.
Markus, H., & Nurius, P. (1986). Possible selves. *American Psychologist, 41,* 954–969.
Rychlak, J. F. (1976). Is a concept of "self" necessary in psychological theory, and if so why? A humanistic perspective. In A. Wandersman, P. J. Poppen, & D. F. Ricks (Eds.), *Humanism and behaviorism: Dialogue and growth* (pp. 121–143). Elmsford, NY: Pergamon Press.
Rychlak, J. F. (1977). *The psychology of rigorous humanism.* New York: Wiley.
Rychlak, J. F. (1979). *Discovering free will and personal responsibility.* New York: Oxford University Press.
Slaughter, D. T., & McWorter, G. A. (1985). Social origins and early features of the scientific study of Black American families and children. In M. B. Spencer, G. K. Brookins, & W. R. Allen (Eds.), *Beginnings: The social and affective development of Black children* (pp. 5–18). Hillsdale, NJ: Lawrence Erlbaum.
Spencer, M. B. (1987). Black children's ethnic identity formation: Risk and resilience of castelike minorities. In J. S. Phinney & M. J. Rotheram (Eds.), *Children's ethnic socialization: Pluralism and development* (pp. 103–116). Newbury Park, CA: Sage Publications.
White, R. W. (1963). Ego and reality in psychoanalytic theory. *Psychological Issues, 3* (Serial No. 11).

11

Black Middle-Class
Education in the 1980s

Jean Wheeler Smith

There are many issues relative to the process of educating Black middle-class children that have received little attention by scholars of the educational process. The issues that have most often been the focus of attention include educating the disadvantaged, low-grade achievement, genetic endowment, and home environment (Bloom, Davis, and Hess, 1965; Coleman, 1966; Jensen, 1969; Guthrie, Kleindorfer, Levin, and Stout, 1971). In these studies emphasis was placed on the intellectual deficits of Black children, chaotic home environments, or inferior Black children, and their parents were often blamed for the negatives.

More recently, a cultural discontinuity perspective (Ogbu, 1981) has emerged, which emphasizes the failure of the school system to recognize and utilize Black children's competencies directly associated with the teaching and testing process, and the child's unique learning style (Gibson, 1976; Boykin, 1980). Although the cultural discontinuity perspective appropriately takes the blame away from Black children and parents, this perspective, like earlier ones, focuses on the failures. All have failed to look within Black family groups for comparative understanding of the groups or to offer some analysis of the successes of Black children who do quite well, even in school settings involving a high incidence of failure.

In attempting to provide additional insight into the educational issues of Black children, this chapter presents a more process-centered analysis of issues facing Black middle-class families as they attempt to educate their children. The discussion includes issues such as the school as a bureaucracy, the authority of school personnel, account-

129

ability in public and private education, the nurturing home environment, and extended family support. Several case illustrations are presented to highlight key issues of the educational process.

Black middle-class parents, clinicians, and scholars alike are concerned with the educational process of school-age children. From the perspective of a Black child psychiatrist in a large urban setting, wherein over half of the referrals involve a history of school difficulties, these problems appear grave and the answers not immediately obvious. The following vignette illustrates this point.

An elegant Black couple, an obviously high-functioning pair, came into my office escorting a sullen, unhappy child who was failing in school. The scene was a study in contrasts: The mother, who managed a government human services program, was dressed in vibrant pinks, with just the right number of gold chains. She kept a comfortable home, got consistent promotions at work, and found time to swim three times a week and still have a great hairdo. The father wore an Italian cut suit that fit smoothly over his athletic frame. He found time for sports (tennis on the weekends; weights during the week) while he moved up in his law firm. Both were smiling, intelligent people who gave good eye contact and have always done well in any educational or work setting.

Sitting incongruously between them was a very unhappy 10-year-old boy, dressed in designer jeans, who stared at the floor, answered in monosyllables, and tried to defend against his rage at having his school failure exposed. He did not have the slightest idea why he could not master the times tables, and he was overwhelmed with anxiety when he was required to write an essay.

The parents were baffled. He had been in public and private Black schools, and alternative schools, in the effort to find a place where he could work productively. He had been to Paris with his grandmother and he went skiing three times a year. In contrast, his father and mother never went 20 miles beyond their places of birth in Mississippi before age 18; they had not been to Paris yet, and they had never been on a pair of skis.

"What is going on with this child?" the parents asked. "With all these resources, why can't he pull himself together to learn the darn multiplication tables?" That was their direct question.

Their indirect question, and the subject of this chapter, is: "Why have Black middle-class parents been unable to pass on to our children the fruits of our labor? We worked hard in school. We struggled.

We sat in at lunch counters and registered voters. We ran Black awareness programs on our campuses and helped inner-city children. And we assumed that in our hands, freedom would translate into a happy life, with happy, highly functioning children. Yet that is not how things turned out. Why is this, and what can we do to make education work for our children?"

For any Black family the answer to this question may lie in the problem of individual variation. Any single child may be suffering from a depression that reduces self-esteem and ability to be interested in school; the child may have an attention deficit disorder, which reduces the ability to concentrate on schoolwork. The child may be psychotic and hear voices that say the teacher is a demon-witch, or the child may have a learning disability that sets her or him up for failure in school. These problems would be addressed in individual consultation with child mental health and educational professionals.

Aside from individual variation, however, the Black middle class of the 1980s is experiencing a problem as a group in trying to educate school-age children. The problem is related to a failure to assess the negative impact of urbanization, upward mobility, loss of extended family, and the breakdown of authority and family structure on our children. Some of these themes are echoed elsewhere in this volume. However, in the area of education the themes have certain manifestations: (1) some Black parents, who have a history of combating authority, tend to "derail" their children's education by undermining the authority of teachers and principals; (2) school systems have become big business, with a complex bureaucratic structure that even the most persistent person cannot navigate; (3) young people are growing up without the kind of "peace and quiet" and the kind of secure emotional background that preceding generations had; and (4) young people do not have the advantage of an extended family to turn to for help.

AUTHORITY

It is very difficult for a Black parent who has spent five, or ten, or even more years marching and organizing against a racist society, which uses authority and power as a tool of oppression, to then turn a child over to people who appear to be representing that structure of power and authority. Many teachers and principals represent that structure. The irony of the situation is that surrendering of parental authority to teachers, principals, librarians, and hall guards is essential for education to go forward. The child *must* see his or her teacher as an extension of parental authority, and education must go on in an atmosphere of trust. After all, why should a child believe that 10 to the power of 2 is 100, unless he or she is told by someone who can be trusted, someone who is believed by the parents to be right most of the time?

A 9-year-old Afro-American boy was recommended for psychiatric evaluation because of school failure in the face of an above-average IQ. He demonstrated sad, withdrawn behavior alternating with random attacks on schoolmates and frequent vomiting that appeared to be self-induced.

His mother, an attractive Afro-American woman in her early thirties, came to the psychiatrist's office in a flurry, with high heels clicking and a loosely belted cape. She began by saying that she was sure her son was a victim of a racist plot by his White teachers to label him as dumb and crazy. She demanded a document stating that he was completely normal, so that she could sue the teacher and all those related to her. On interview with this sad fellow, I learned that he was clinically depressed over several recent losses in his life. He had moved with his mother to a very sparsely integrated neighborhood, which had plenty of green grass but no children who knew or liked him. He had left behind a less prestigious Black neighborhood, where he had friends and where he had a continually present grandmother and grandfather, who gave him cookies and talked to him. Also, in the old neighborhood he had had many opportunities to run into his father (whom his mother hated with a vengeance and about whom no kind word had been spoken in six months). In the new house he was alone from 4 to 7 P.M., at which time his mother rushed in, prepared a quick meal, and went to sleep.

Mother could not be convinced (at least, not by me) that anything could possibly be worrying this boy. After all, he had the ability; "The tests proved it, didn't they? It must be the case that the teachers are discriminating against him." Since the psychiatrist could not provide mother with documentation for her lawsuit, she marched out angrily. In a follow-up call I learned that the boy continued his vomiting, fighting, and failing, while mother continued her lawsuit. It is apparent that this child could not be educated by teachers whom his mother could not trust.

Perhaps society has driven many Black parents to distrust educators. However, this attitude does not permit young people to get a good education. Three alternatives are suggested for parents who cannot trust their child's teachers and people in charge: (1) reexamine other effects of one's own actions on the resulting situation; (2) move the child to a new system, or, if a move is impossible, (3) try, in some collegial and cooperative way, to appropriately change the system that is educating the child.

The conclusion here is valid, but the cases presented do not really allow the conclusion to be deduced. The last case documents what we see as a failure of the mother to help us understand the impact of her actions. Moving the child to a new system or changing the system would not help this child.

THE EDUCATIONAL BUREAUCRACY

The second problem in Black middle-class education is one that is shared with our White middle-class counterparts. Education is too big (some public high and junior high schools in large cities look like automotive factories or a space shuttle center), and no one can be held accountable. One must search through these factories for someone to talk with about the child, and then pray that the same person will be there next month for a follow-up appointment. Private educational facilities tend not to be so big, but many of them are demonstrating a big business mentality in the 1980s. A result is that classes are too large and children are treated like budget items. In particular, private Catholic schools have become much less of a resource for Black middle-class families as a result of these changes.

The big business aspect of education is less of a problem if all one's children are top-of-the-line scholars. (If they are, congratulations!) Black children with IQs of 115 or over who are hard workers, attractive, well mannered, and competent in at least one sport, who have no disabilities, who make friends easily, and who have a stable, supportive home life, can do well in a classroom of thirty children in a school that operates like a factory or a space shuttle. Parents who have children who fit this description only have to show up for one parent conference and one fund raiser a year.

The problem comes when a child has a special problem — a learning disability in reading or math, depression or anxiety, a physical handicap, or just average intelligence. Then it becomes difficult to navigate the school bureaucracy. In large bureaucratic school settings it may take years for the child's problem to surface. Many parents who have come for an evaluation of their child's attention deficit disorder have noted, in retrospect, that their child has had problems in "attending to tasks" for years. They can pull out report cards of the previous four years, all of which make reference to the problem. But in a big educational bureaucracy the job is often considered to be "done" once the problem has been given a name and listed on a piece of paper. The teacher, and the system, appear to believe that they have done their job by noting the child's lack of concentration. After this, the teacher is not responsible. Perhaps the teacher is not responsible, but the question remains: who is the responsible party?

A major problem in a big bureaucracy is discovering who is responsible to help solve the problem. Parents are forced to spend long hours in attempting to solve this dilemma. Often, there is a centralized office for "special education," with an obscure route of entry. First, walk-ins are prohibited. Moreover, one must be referred by a local school person, who may be informally penalized for making the referral. Because the presenting problem creates a load on the system, an additional issue involves proving that the child is engaged in remedial activities when, in fact, the personnel hardly know the child's name. Usually, a big paperwork structure is developed that includes an "individualized education plan," but no one person who really cares whether or not the plan has been implemented.

On a more positive note, the bureaucrats on top do tend to be understanding and helpful if a parent can get to them. The answer is to persevere in the quest for appropriate public education for the child without becoming bitter and driven to undercut the people who take care of one's child. Should a parent reach the point of bitterness and cynicism, one is in a position of the mother who could seek no viable action other than to file a lawsuit.

Ideally, parents should be more visible. Their presence can be helpful even though they may not have educational expertise. Teachers cannot continually forget to mark a child's English papers if that child's parent is sitting in the office answering the phone, or involved in accompanying a group of children on a field trip. A parent who is politically inclined can become an officer of the PTA, or a member of the Board of Directors of the private school in which the child is enrolled. Such efforts can modify the perception of teachers and school administrators; that is, it can get them to see Black children and their parents as *human* and deserving to be educated carefully.

PUBLIC VERSUS PRIVATE EDUCATION

Many middle-class Black parents turn to the private sector for their children's education. There are many reasons for this choice; not the least among them is status and the presumed benefits of exposing the children to the dominant group. Another reason concerns accountability. The leadership of private schools is accountable to parents for the handling of a problem that they are being paid to handle. If this cannot be done, the parents are free to take the yearly four, or five, or seven thousand dollars elsewhere. In most private school settings one can make contact with the principal in the parking lot or at the Friday assembly, and she or he will problem solve with the parent on the spot. The principal wants to solve the problem if possible. Unfortunately, there is little direct, personal accountability in the public system.

Another reason for Black middle-class parents choosing private education is similar to the motivating factors of other groups: to enhance moral values. A potential problem here, of course, is that in other groups, particularly in large pockets of the dominant group, morals can be intertwined with racism. There are some strong moral values that Black middle-class parents want for their children, including respecting others, treating people the way one would like to be treated, and being honest. These are some of the values that one gets in good private schools, including alternative Afro-American schools.

When sincere, interested Black middle-class parents have gotten involved in public education, they stress the importance of accountability and a positive moral environment. We can speculate that a primary reason for the decline in the effectiveness of Catholic education for the Black middle class has been the abandonment of these two features by that system during the last ten to twenty years.

EMOTIONAL SUPPORTS

Black middle-class children of today are not growing up with the kind of peace and quiet and opportunity for reflection that was available for their parents in their youth. A vignette from my childhood illustrates this difference.

I was seventeen years old before I knew what my front door

key looked like. I didn't need it. My household was composed
of a mother, two sisters, a grandmother, and myself. (My father
had been killed in World War II.) My mother was our sole
support. She made it possible for my grandmother to be at home
and within the sound of my voice when I returned from school.

Today, children may not be so lucky. The younger ones may have
extended days in some institutional setting. The older ones have
owned many house keys (sometimes one a month). What difference
does this make educationally? It means that there is a period of
anxiety and resettling (when they arrive home from school) between
3:30 and 6:00 P.M. during which it's difficult for a child to be
productive. Although some children do beat the odds, this period is
a kind of aimless, nonproductive time for others; it triggers problems
that are hard to overcome. Because of pressures that they have
experienced in their workplace, parents are not always emotionally
available to meet the psychological needs of their children at the
end of a long day. Frequently, children do not know what to expect
from their working parents; that is, there may be a reaching out and
effusive praise, or an emotional withdrawal and a lack of interest (as
perceived by the children). When the latter atmosphere is created,
many children find it difficult to turn their attention to their homework. Unlike a generation ago, extended family members are usually
not available to pay attention to the children, or to act as buffers for
parental extremes. Some middle-class parents have housekeepers or
nannies, who can serve some of the functions of the extended family,
but it is difficult for employees to be as effective as a grandparent,
or Aunt Ethel, or Uncle Joe, or cousin Sue.
    Many roles can be played by available extended family members.
They can help our children with problem solving, give advice on
how to approach a teacher who has expressed disappointment in the
child's work, and advise how to handle aggressive or mean peers.
They can be available for minor, but urgent, calls. Teachers and
children get very uptight when the child has a fever and the parent
is in a board meeting and will not be available for an hour. Extended
family members can be there to "ooh and aah" over a good chemistry
test grade, or over a star which has been pasted on the child's forehead
for good behavior. These may appear to be small matters, but later
in life a parent can pay thousands of dollars for a behavior modification
specialist to tell one to do the same things in support of the child's
education.
    An extended family member can supplement the care provided by

two sound, middle-class parents in a number of ways: being there to relieve loneliness during the parents' working hours; providing supervision, which is critical in this drug- and crime-ridden time; giving immediate, positive feedback for good work and immediate redirection when a mistake has been made; and reinforcing a warm, predictable environment from which a child can emerge when he or she is ready to explore the world.

For many of those Black middle-class parents with teenage or adult children, or those parents who no longer have extended family members available, the opportunity to involve a relative from one's family of origin in the rearing process is lost. For many parents, it has become necessary to make use of paid helpers, surrogates, and institutional alternatives. However, the young members of our group may be able to redirect this process in the interests of their children. Perhaps the older members can help the grandchildren in changing this course for generations to come.

SUMMARY

The education of Black middle-class children can be enhanced in several ways. First, Black parents must search for an educational system that they can trust, and to which they are willing to turn over the education of their children. Parents must be very alert to signs of possible failure, lack of interest in school, or disrespect for teachers, as well as sad and withdrawn or aggressive behavior. They must not ignore these problems or expect them to go away. They must be willing to admit that the child may have psychological or educational problems that require special help.

Efforts should be directed to involve or reinvolve extended family members in the care of the children. When this cannot be done, every effort should be made to duplicate these functions through employed help or through institutional settings.

A decision to change schools should not be made without a careful exploration of the entire situation. It may be indicated for the parents to become more involved with the school.

Finally, if it is too late to do these things for our own children, we can be of considerable assistance in providing extended family supports for our grandchildren, or for some of the large number of needy youngsters in the foster care and other public assistance programs.

REFERENCES

Bloom, B. S., Davis, A., & Hess, R. D. (1965). *Compensatory education for cultural deprivation.* New York: Holt, Rinehart & Winston.

Boykin, A. W. (1980). *Reading achievement and the social cultural frame of reference of White American culture: Issues in urban reading.* Roundtable discussion at the Meeting of the National Institute of Education, Washington, DC.

Coleman, J. S. (1966). *Equality of educational opportunity.* Washington, DC: US Government Printing Office.

Gibson, M. A. (1976). Approaches to multicultural education in the United States. *Anthropology and Education Quarterly, 7,* 7–18.

Guthrie, J. W., Kleindorfer, G. B., Levin, H. M., & Stout, R. T. (1971). *Schools and inequality.* Cambridge, MA: MIT Press.

Jensen, A. R. (1969). How much can we boost IQ and scholastic achievement? *Harvard Educational Review, 39,* 1–123.

Ogbu, J. U. (1981). Black education: A cultural ecological perspective. In H. P. McAdoo (Ed.), *Black families* (pp. 139–154). Beverly Hills, CA: Sage Publications.

12

The Role of the Mental Health Practitioner in Child Advocacy in the School System

Marilyn B. Benoit

CHILD ADVOCACY

Child advocacy is not new to the mental health arena. In fact, the Child Guidance Movement, founded in 1910 by William Healy, was a child advocacy movement to aid juvenile delinquents (Knitzer, 1976; Goldsmith, 1979). The Child Welfare League of America has an outstanding history of service to children and families. Foundations such as the Children's Defense Fund, For Love of Children, and the National Black Child Development Institute maintain a strong presence in our community and are unrelenting in their advocacy work on behalf of children. Indeed, it is extremely important that child advocacy be maintained on the highest political levels, where advocates can be involved in information dissemination, program development, and legislation.

There are national organizations that advocate for society's less fortunate children — the mentally handicapped, physically handicapped, poverty stricken, neglected, abandoned, or victimized. Too often, however, it is only the more severely impaired children who receive state or federal services. Until 1975, when Public Law 94–142 (Federal Register, 1977) was enacted by the 94th Congress, children

The author wishes to thank Ms. Liz Stoff, special education advocate at Children's Hospital National Medical Center, Washington, D.C., for her assistance in preparing this chapter.

with moderate to severe handicapping conditions had no legal right of access to special education that took into consideration the special needs of their specific handicapping condition. For example, it is estimated that from 10 to 20% of elementary-school-age children are afflicted with attention deficit hyperactivity disorder, with or without specific learning disabilities. These children are generally without obvious physical handicap. They are the ones who are difficult in school — they fidget, disrupt the class, daydream, are overly active, and tend to be distractible and impulsive. Such children tend to be labeled as behavior problems and often do not perform well academically. Many of them have concomitant learning disabilities. Attention deficit hyperactivity disorder is a single example, and perhaps the most common, of a childhood psychiatric disorder. Childhood psychosis, autism, pervasive development disorder, Gilles de la Tourette syndrome, child physical and sexual abuse, identity disorder, and obsessive-compulsive disorder are some of the more disabling conditions that may warrant special education placement. When children are identified as problem children, a referral is made to a mental health clinic or a private practitioner.

The advocacy issues discussed in this chapter are by no means exclusive to any racial or ethnic segment of the population. These issues, however, must be addressed in any book targeted to the needs of the Black middle-class population. Black middle-class children have been underrepresented in the children I have treated or whose treatment I have supervised in two community mental health clinics, in private practice, and in a hospital-based pediatric outpatient psychiatry clinic during the twelve years I have practiced child psychiatry in the Washington, D.C., area and its suburbs. This geographical area is one with a high density of professional, middle-class Blacks. Whether the perceived underrepresentation is due to a reluctance on the part of middle-class Blacks to "expose" their "flawed" children is a question that needs to be pursued with well-designed research. My experience has led me to speculate that middle-class Blacks whose foothold in mainstream society feels tenuous may be more vulnerable to the narcissistic wounding that all parents experience when deficits are discovered in their children's cognitive, emotional, behavioral, or physical development. I recall a Black teenaged girl, the daughter of two professional parents, who was having significant emotional problems. She sought her parents' assistance in obtaining psychiatric help, but this was denied her because of their anticipated humiliation of exposure. The girl was able to obtain treatment because of the District of Columbia law that allows teenagers to obtain mental health services regardless of parental knowledge. When mental health providers have occasion to recommend special education services for Black middle-class children, they may need to do so with a special awareness of the sensitivity of the parents.

THE MENTAL HEALTH
PRACTITIONER AS ADVOCATE

One might ask why a mental health practitioner should take up the cause of a child's educational needs. After all, there are educators, their teachers, who should champion that cause. It is important to pause and review what this business of mental health really encompasses. Those of us who have chosen to make our careers in the mental health field have taken on one of the most comprehensive and demanding ways of being involved with people. It is because mental health speaks to the total functioning of an individual — the biological, the psychological, and the social — that every aspect of the individual's life becomes our business. If we should detect evidence of physical illness, we should refer to a physician. We address the issue of self-esteem. This self-esteem relates to how a person functions in the world, how others perceive that functioning, and how that person rates himself or herself on such functioning. Because we are indeed not created (from a biopsychosocial perspective) equal, each one of us brings different constitutional, psychological, and genetic assets and liabilities to the task of coping with the demands of daily life. When our assets are minimal and do not permit us to compensate for our liabilities, the result is a handicap and our ego functioning suffers.

In the case of a child who suffers from an emotional problem, a constitutional deficit, or developmental delay, it is often in the school milieu that problems emerge and prompt a referral for a mental health consultation. In school, from the teacher's vantage point, the child may merely be perceived as a behavior problem or an emotionally withdrawn or troubled child. The teacher's and parents' expectation is that the mental health practitioner will attend to the psychological problem and fix it, so that the child will return to class unencumbered and ready to learn. However, when the child's evaluation indicates that he or she has a significant handicapping condition — be it emotional, behavioral, or developmental — which is a major contributor to his poor school performance, the mental health practitioner, in addition to prescribing remediating psychological ser-

vices (individual and/or family therapy, psychopharmacological intervention, behavioral management), should address the question of
the child's possible need for special education services.

In order to do so, mental health practitioners need to be familiar
with the federal mandate of PL 94–142, enacted in 1975. It is this
Education for all Handicapped Children's Act that mandates federal
funds if states and their school districts comply with the law. The
basic components of the law are as follows (Ballard, 1977; Ballard,
Nazzaro, and Weintraub, 1976; Federal Register, 1977; Yohalem and
Dinsmore, 1978):

- The right to a free, appropriate education at public expense
- Nondiscriminatory and multidisciplinary evaluations in the child's
  primary language
- Development of an individualized education plan
- Provision of necessary related services, such as transportation or
  physical therapy
- Safeguards such as written notice to parents of any program
  changes, permission from parents prior to any assessments, and
  parental access to all school records
- Due process with an impartial hearing if the parent challenges
  the decisions of the school

The related Rehabilitation Act of 1973, referred to as Section 504
(Yohalem and Dinsmore, 1978), is a Civil Rights law which prohibits
discrimination against any handicapped person in programs receiving
federal funds. In addition, it provides for program accessibility and
availability of nonacademic services, such as recreational services, to
handicapped students. More detailed information can be obtained
from the National Information Center for Handicapped Children and
Youth, a clearinghouse headquartered in Washington, D.C.

It is necessary here to refocus on the question "Why must the
mental health practitioner act as advocate?" Consider that the educational system is a bureaucracy and that as in all bureaucracies,
there is a limited operating budget. If one can imagine what school
systems are up against as they attempt to meet normal budgetary
demands, one can appreciate that the education system will not be
too willing to allocate additional funds for children identified with
special needs. To some extent, the educational system is put into a
position of conflict of interests as it must function as gatekeeper in
apportioning special education services. To identify a child as a
possible candidate for special education services, and then to evaluate
the child comprehensively before even making a determination, is in

itself a relatively costly undertaking. Neuropsychological testing is often done to assess for specific learning problems and costs approximately six hundred dollars per child. Psychiatric evaluation, educational assessment, occupational therapy assessment, and medical/ neurological evaluation are often necessary. The school system also finances many hours of professional time for the hearings that are part of the process in accessing special education services. It is not that the educational system is deliberately malevolent; rather, because many systems have limited special education resources, the index of suspicion, and hence identification, of exceptional children may be unconsciously low. Given this possibility, one can understand why someone outside of the educational system — in this case, the mental health practitioner — is in a less conflicted, more objective position to function as the child advocate.

PERSONAL EXPERIENCE

I have had experience with five different school districts. For the most part, the school systems have been responsive and cooperative. They have all had significant limitations, most often because the jurisdiction has failed to provide adequate placement resources within its geographical confines. In the Washington, D.C., greater metropolitan area, which includes suburban Maryland and Virginia, it is a too-frequent occurrence that emotionally disturbed or severely behavior disordered children have to ride for long hours before and after school, on buses which often are erratic in their schedule. It is these very children, who may be impulsive, psychotic, or unpredictable, who should not be transported in large groups over long distances with only a single aide on the bus. This type of situation provides a fertile ground for acting out of deviant behaviors. The complaint of problem behaviors on the bus resulting in suspension is all too familiar with exceptional children.

When one assumes the role of advocate, one must be prepared to make a commitment of effort and time. It is advisable to be in direct verbal communication with the school representative — pupil personnel offices — in addition to submitting written documents. If at all possible, attending a hearing on site at the school or school district's office can go a long way toward convincing the school personnel of how seriously you take the need for special education services for the youngster you represent. Some parents feel intimidated by the school system. This may be especially true for Black middle-class parents, who live in White school districts where racist and prejudicial attitudes may prevail. These parents welcome the encouragement and support of the mental health professional in negotiating their way through the hearing process. In one of the Washington, D.C., suburban jurisdictions, I had to become very aggressive in a case in which a Black principal in a White jurisdiction apparently felt a need to disidentify with a Black student who had significant behavior problems that interfered with his learning. The single parent was offered no assistance by the school. Appropriate placements were not made until psychiatric evaluation took place and placement in a good county resource special education school was strongly recommended.

A particularly difficult case involved Johnny, who was attending public elementary school. He was a gifted and challenging student who was disruptive in class and was referred for a psychiatric evaluation. He was diagnosed as having an attention deficit hyperactivity disorder and a specific learning disability. Although stimulant medication was helpful, Johnny needed a highly structured placement out of the regular classroom. Unfortunately, the only placement available locally was inadequate to meet his academic needs for a gifted placement. As a result Johnny got bored, and the boredom, in turn, led to disruptive behavior in class — behavior which resulted in a suspension. It was after this suspension that I took a more active advocacy role, pushing for placement to meet Johnny's need for academic challenge. I attended a few meetings with the family and school representatives on Johnny's behalf. Using language that was not filled with psychiatric jargon, I was able to impress upon the educators that Johnny's behavior would actually deteriorate if he remained inappropriately placed. Johnny delighted in challenge, which led to a sense of accomplishment and mastery. Appropriate placement would best afford him an opportunity to experience such challenge and enhance ego functioning. The teachers were also helped with some behavior management recommendations. For example, they were advised that Johnny's "smart-aleky" behavior should not be rewarded by their getting into arguments with him. Johnny was subsequently placed in an appropriate private out-of-state day school that had a specialized program for the gifted learning disabled child. The one unavoidable drawback to this placement was that he spent long hours commuting by bus twice daily.

Bobby was a 6-year-old boy who required a special school placement because of his autism. This was a particularly difficult case because Bobby's parents resisted the diagnosis of autism and were therefore reluctant to pursue appropriate placement. Father perceived Bobby as being "hard-headed" and wanted to know when Bobby would "grow out of this stage." As Bobby's advocate, I first had to invest time in educating his parents and helping them to accept his diagnosis and grim prognosis. Only then could they in turn become aggressive about pursuing the emotionally disabled placement he needed. Bobby's first placement was in a school for the mentally retarded — he indeed was retarded, as two-thirds of autistic children are — but he had other needs that were not being addressed in that setting. It took a tremendous amount of advocacy activity before Bobby was transferred to a more appropriate day placement where the educators and therapists were skilled in interacting with autistic children.

Jimmy, an autistic child who was 5 years old, could not be managed at home in a day treatment center. Mother, a Black professional woman, was abandoned by the father when he learned of Jimmy's severe mentally handicapped condition. She was unable to care for him alone even when she tried giving up her job and staying at home with Jimmy. Because school systems must adhere to the "least restrictive environment" mandate of the federal government, it is necessary that the most benign levels of intervention are tried first. As a child fails at each successive level, he is tried at the next restrictive one in the hierarchy. Jimmy had to be placed in a residential treatment center out of state because of the severity of his autistic condition.

CONCLUSIONS

A mental health clinician evaluating a child who needs special placement is advised to carefully itemize the specific modalities of intervention the child would need to maximize his learning potential. For example, a severely hyperactive, learning disabled child may need a prescription for special reading services, a language therapist, a structured classroom with 1 : 1 instruction, a behavioral milieu, and on-site psychotherapeutic and pharmacologic intervention. It is then up to the school system, once a placement is approved, to locate an educational setting that provides such adjunctive services. Such places do exist, but unfortunately not enough of them in local jurisdictions to meet the needs of the youngsters requiring special services.

It appears that the demand for all levels of special education placement is on the rise. As more and more children who are born significantly prematurely, small for gestational age, or with congenital problems are saved by the technological advances of neonatology (newborn medicine), a larger population of children with developmental delays, learning difficulties, and behavioral problems secondary to organic insults is emerging. Some educators outside of the school systems are developing an expertise in advocacy for these special children. Developmental pediatrics is a relatively new subspecialty within pediatrics that is attempting to advocate for these children. Because they and their families often have significant problems in living, they also present themselves to the mental health profession. We in this field must be prepared to address their needs for advocacy with the school system because our business is to attend to all the psychosocial needs of those who seek our help. It is only by advocating for and facilitating comprehensive intervention that we will assist these special youngsters in attaining the highest possible level of functioning.

REFERENCES

Ballard, J. (1977). *Public Law 94-142 and Section 504: Understanding what they are and are not.* Reston, VA: Council for Exceptional Children.

Ballard, J., Nazzaro, J. N., & Weintraub, F. J. (1976). *Public Law 94-142: The Education of All Handicapped Children Act of 1975.* Reston, VA: Council for Exceptional Children.

Federal Register. (1977, August 23). Vol. 42, No. 163. Washington, DC: US Government Printing Office.

Federal Register. (1981, January 19). Vol. 46, No. 12. Washington, DC: US Government Printing Office.

Goldsmith, J. M. (1979). The private agency, children and child psychiatry. In I. N. Berlin & L. A. Stone (Eds.), *Basic handbook of child psychiatry. Vol. IV* (p. 525). New York: Basic Books.

Knitzer, J. E. (1976). Child advocacy: A perspective. *American Journal of Orthopsychiatry, 46,* 200–216.

Yohalem, D., & Dinsmore, J. (1978, March). *Public Law 94-142 and 504: Numbers that Add Up to Educational Rights for Handicapped Children. A Guide for Parents and Advocates.* Washington, DC: Children's Defense Fund. Washington Research Project.

Introduction to Part V

HEALTH AND ILLNESS

Alice F. Coner-Edwards

Benoit, Rankin, and Johnson provide convincing evidence of the interrelationship of the psychological and physiological aspects of illness and the importance of a careful and thorough diagnostic assessment. Their respective messages should be as useful to primary care physicians and other medical specialists as they will be for providers of mental health services.

Wright and Phillips present valuable information about the psychosocial aspects of sickle cell anemia (SCA). Like the preceding contributors, these authors emphasize the relatedness of the "psyche" and the "soma." Key issues of concern, as well as some important consequences that must be reckoned with, are highlighted in the clinical vignettes.

Smith and Espy underscore the need for the obstetrician-gynecologist to be sensitive to the psychological repercussions of patients' life cycle changes and pathological conditions, as well as their physical state. Anticipatory guidance and counseling can serve as effective preventive measures in the care of obstetrical and gynecological patients. The authors do not address the fact that recent changes in the delivery of health services are likely to make for frequent rotations of the physician, and that these rotations may make for difficulties in the development of good rapport. Ideally, in any health service system patients should be scheduled to see the same physician at each visit and provisions made for a complete review of the care, and consultation as needed.

Lonesome notes that drug use among the Black middle-class is often a symptom of an underlying mental health problem. The abuse of alcohol is used as a frame of reference for a detailed discussion of substance abuse. A broad range of consequences is addressed. Lonesome places his analysis within a broader social and political perspective, and suggests strategies for prevention, intervention, and treatment.

13

Physical Illnesses Presenting with Psychological Symptoms

Marilyn B. Benoit

Although the history of medicine reveals repeated attempts to illustrate that the "psyche" and the "soma" have a significant inter-relationship, until recently mainstream medicine had succeeded in establishing a position of separating illnesses into either functional or organic categories. The functional illnesses were unambiguously bi-ological in etiology. Recent advances in medicine that permit us to examine certain illnesses on the neurobiochemical level have given an exciting direction to medical research. With the new insights provided by this research there has been a shift in thinking to the integrative approach of psychosomatic medicine, which has its roots in medicine's earliest history. Psychosomatic medicine has gained new vitality, has the imprimatur of "true science," and has thereby gained new respectability and credibility. With vigorous application of the scientific method, now made possible by state-of-the-art biomedical technology, the future of psychosomatic medicine will undoubtedly define the future of medicine.

The history of psychosomatic medicine begins with the Ancient Greeks, who developed the concept of the four humors (blood, black bile, yellow bile, and phlegm) and believed that personality traits were related to these humors. The Middle Ages brought a shift to a more religious society, providing a backdrop for the emergence of demonology, which attempted to explain illness in terms of demonic possession. Striking evidence of this belief system persists in many contemporary cultures. Examples of this phenomenon can be found in the "espiritismo" of Hispanic cultures, "voodoo" of Haiti, and "obeah" of the Caribbean. The belief exists that a person's mind can be possessed and affected in such a manner that significant and perhaps even fatal physical illness can ensue (Barrett, 1976). With the application of more rigorous scientific investigation of illness in the early 1900s, there was little scientific evidence to support the mind-body interaction. A disease was diagnosable by demonstrating "significant findings" — a positive stain from the pathologist's tissue slide, growth of bacteria or viruses in the microbiology laboratory from a sample of the patient's tissue or body fluids, a positive x-ray film for pneumonia or tuberculosis, or measurable (by relatively unrefined methods) changes in the then-known products or by-products of the body's metabolism.

In his paper on the history of psychosomatic medicine, Schwab (1985) stated that "Francis Bacon advocated investigation of the mental facilities and of the interactions of body and mind by case studies and by study of the relationships between the individual and society. He stated there were two types of knowledge — one of the body and one of the mind." This reflects the shift to the more "scientific" era of medicine, which focused on the understanding of the body's physiology and inevitably caused a chasm in our thinking.

With the separatist thinking that viewed illness as either "physical" (organic) or "mental" (functional), the field of psychiatry suffered a painful estrangement from mainstream medicine. Many are the stories about departments of psychiatry being relegated to the basement or to some free-standing warehouse apart from the general hospital. Psychiatrists were not "real doctors." The "real doctors" were perceived by psychiatrists as insensitive and as caring about their patients not as persons, but rather as disease entities — "the diabetic," "the leukemic."

This destructive separatist trend saw a welcome reversal in the 1970s with a strong resurgence of interest in psychosomatic medicine. The 1980s have brought well disseminated, indisputable scientific evidence for the biological basis of the major psychiatric illnesses. Autism, the schizophrenias, the affective disorders, and anxiety and panic disorders have been and continue to be carefully researched. That these disorders have a biological substrate is no longer even controversial. It is indeed encouraging to note the remarkable movement toward psychosomatic thinking in medicine demonstrated by Henker's (1984) presidential address to the 30th Annual Meeting of the Academy of Psychosomatic Medicine. That address, entitled, "Psychosomatic Illness: Biochemical and Physiologic Foundations," is highly recommended for further reading. It is also no longer controversial that some major physical illnesses cause mental changes — diabetes, thyrotoxicosis, mononucleosis, multiple sclerosis, and pheochromo-cytoma, to name a few. Common anemia is known to cause lassitude of body and mind. It is this latter somatopsychic relationship, which focuses on the effect of physical illness on the mind or "psyche," that will be addressed here and illustrated with several clinical vignettes.

Medical literature provides more than adequate documentation substantiating various physical illnesses that may present with psychiatric symptomatology. In his book *Physical Illness in the Psychiatric Patient,* Koranyi (1982) underscored "the inherent danger of mis-interpreting physical symptoms in psychiatric patients and dismissing them as psychogenic." Here, of course, he is referring to the tendency for professionals to dismiss, as inconsequential, physical illness in patients with previously diagnosed psychiatric disorders. Even neurotic, anxious patients can have chest pain indicative of a myocardial infarct rather than simple hyperventilation. People affected with schizophrenia can have headaches secondary to a brain tumor, and histrionic patients can indeed have seizure disorders. In a study of 658 psychiatric outpatients (Hall et al., 1978), 9.1% were found to have a physical illness presenting as primary psychiatric disease. Hoffman and Koran (1984) stated, "from 9% to 42% of psychiatric clinic outpatients have serious medical illnesses, causing or exacerbating their mental disorder. For 9% to 18% of these patients, a physical disease was the direct cause of the psychiatric symptom." In Hall's study, the criteria used for determining physical illness to be the cause of psychiatric symptoms were as follows: "If 1) psychiatric symptoms abated significantly with medical treatment, 2) medical symptoms seemed clearly related to the onset of psychiatric symptoms, or 3) the presence of a medical disorder, even though untreatable (i.e., progressive arterosclerosis, cardiovascular disease with cerebral impairment), explained the patient's symptom pattern" (p. 1318). If one considers that the psychosocial stressors experienced by the Black middle class in the United States are significantly higher than those of their White cohorts, and it is understood that any disease state represents a summation of both organic and psychosocial "disease," the Black middle class appears to be at a higher risk for presenting with psychiatric symptoms secondary to organic illness. *Psychosomatics,* a contemporary scientific monthly publication, provides scholarly articles that focus on illnesses that illustrate the mind-body interaction in rather poignant fashion. The interested reader is strongly advised to become acquainted with this publication.

CLINICAL REPORTS

An 11-year-old Black boy was referred for psychiatric consultation two days prior to his being discharged from an inpatient pediatric service. He had been admitted for a second diagnostic work-up of a persistent sore throat. The first work-up, at another hospital, had revealed no abnormalities. However, not only had the sore throat persisted, but this young boy, who by psychiatric history had had an excellent psychological premorbid adjustment, had become depressed, socially withdrawn, and anergic, and was losing weight. Although psychiatric assessment supported a diagnosis of a depressive disorder, the depression was not considered to be primary. Developmental, family, medical, and social history offered no data to support a primary psychiatric diagnosis. Additionally, I was struck by the "toxic" appearance of the child on the first encounter with him. The psychiatric assessment was suspicion of an occult malignancy with a depression secondary to the illness and the limitations it imposed on a previously healthy, active, and well-adjusted youngster. This assessment prompted the pediatric service to do a more aggressive work-up, which resulted in a diagnosis of Hodgkin's disease in this patient.

A man in his mid-forties presented with difficulty modulating his moods, an explosive temper, chaotic interpersonal relationships, and a poor job history. He was divorced, estranged from his children, and chronically unhappy. He was argumentative and irritable. He described himself as a "complete lunatic at times." He described occasional feelings of detachment (fugue states) and complained of sometimes awakening with headaches and myalgia (nocturnal seizures?). Given the history and personality style of the patient, it would be tempting to make the diagnosis of a severe borderline personality disorder, pursue no further investigation, and prescribe long-term individual psychotherapy as the treatment of the diagnosed psychiatric disorder. This patient's mood and behavior problems dated (by his recall, only) back to his latency period. All the elements of the chief complaint raised the author's suspicions about complex partial seizures, and referral was made for a neurological evaluation. The patient did indeed have a seizure disorder (epilepsy) with a medial temporal lobe epileptogenic focus. The seizure disorder was treated successfully with carbamazepine. Although this biological treatment was essential to this patient's therapy and resulted in mood stabilization and a remission of his fugue states, psychotherapy was also necessary because the patient had developed a core sense of self that was a direct precipitateof an erratic, unpredictable, dysfunctional neurological system. When one considers that the body ego is the first to emerge in our psychological history and that it becomes a powerful organizer for the nuclear self, one can appreciate what a difficult therapeutic endeavor it was to help this patient in his forties shed disorganized, unpredictable self and (with the combined biological and psychological treatments) restructure and integrate a higher-functioning, healthier self.

A 35-year-old woman presented for an emergency assessment because of extreme anxiety bordering on a full-blown panic attack. Acute marital problems as well as concurrent job stresses were offered by the patient as the cause of the anxiety. However, review of systems and medical history revealed that she had a grand mal seizure disorder for which she had been treated with phenobarbital; carbamazepine had recently been substituted and phenobarbital administration abruptly discontinued. This led us to consider acute barbiturate withdrawal reaction as the primary reason for her anxiety. Phenobarbital treatment was immediately reinstituted in consultation with the neurologist, and a tapered withdrawal of the medication was then undertaken. There was a marked abatement of anxiety after this intervention was made. In addition to drug withdrawal as a cause of acute anxiety reaction, the clinician may consider other physical causes of such a presentation. Mitral valve prolapse, a relatively benign condition suspected to be present in as much as 15% of the population, may be the cause of transient anxiety episodes. The decision to treat this condition medically is made on an individual basis. Premenstrual syndrome, thyroid dysfunction, pheochromocytoma, and substance abuse are other conditions that may be suspected.

A woman in her sixties, a refugee from a war-torn country, presented for emergency psychiatric consultation. Because of apathy, withdrawal, and poor appetite, she had recently been diagnosed as having a major depression. A course of antidepressants did not lead to amelioration of symptoms. On the contrary, she was becoming progressively worse. Mental status examination revealed that this woman was semistuporous. That observation, combined with a history of recent falling and self-injury, raised the suspicion of an acute central nervous system problem. Immediate referral was made to the adjacent general hospital emergency room, where the patient was hospitalized with a diagnosis of meningitis. The meningitis had caused the behavioral changes that were attributed to the "major depression."

A middle-aged woman was brought to the emergency room in a state initially diagnosed as catatonic schizophrenia. Further psychiatric evaluation revealed problems in cognitive function and led to the suspicion of some organic brain dysfunction. On neurological consultation the patient produced an electroencephalogram demonstrating temporal lobe status epilepticus — a condition which mimicked catatonic schizophrenia on presentation.

CONCLUSION

In 1955 Dr. Kenneth Walker in the *Story of Medicine* stated that "illness is a disturbance of the equilibrium of the whole man." At that time, our knowledge of how the "disturbance" actually took place in the organism as a whole was limited by the scientific tools then available for investigation. The advances in biomedical technologies, such as highly sensitive biochemical assays, computer assisted tomography, positron emission tomography, nuclear magnetic resonance imaging, evoked response, and laser technology, allow us heretofore unimagined glimpses into the microscopic, molecular, and biochemical inner workings of the human body. Neuroscience is beginning to unravel the relationships between neurotransmitters and mood and behavior. Much research activity is going on to examine the impact of nutrition on both physical and mental health and illness. One can only speculate that future technological advances and the discoveries they bring will be exponential in scope.

This is all very exciting. However, the technology is only as good as the uses to which it is put by clinicians. As Hoffman and Koran (1984) state, "The primary physician retains the responsibility to formulate a broad differential diagnosis incorporating physical etiologies for the behavioral disturbance, and to ensure that the evaluation is thorough." In the mental health field, with both nonphysician and physician providers of care, it is incumbent upon all clinicians to consider that a primary physical illness may be contributing to the patient's symptomatology. Most patients, particularly in urban settings, receive medical care from specialists who, unfortunately, may service only that body part related to their specialization. Patients are often quite sophisticated and predecide what specialist they should see depending on a given symptom or symptom complex. Psychological symptoms may prompt patients to go directly to a mental health clinician. To collude with these patients and not consider a broad diagnostic scope is to deprive them of a thorough diagnostic work-up, and also to ignore the complexity of the intricate interactions of the human "psyche" and "soma."

Disease states of all kinds (infectious, neoplastic, traumatic, metabolic, endocrine, or intoxications) may present with psychological symptoms. No organ system is exempt from being the "culprit" in causing patients' mental symptoms. For example, it is known that patients with chronic renal disease with secondary uremia can present with an organic brain syndrome. Liver disease secondary to alcoholism may present similarly. According to Hall et al. (1978), "cardiovascular, endocrine, infectious, and pulmonary disorders are the most frequent medical causes for psychiatric symptoms." Hypertension, atherosclerosis, diabetes, cancer, and alcoholism are more prevalent in Blacks than in Whites. These are diseases with significant psychological morbidity. Patients may display the full spectrum of psychological conditions or organic brain syndromes in response to or as a part of their medical illness. It cannot be too strongly emphasized that medical evaluation with methodical and comprehensive review of all organ systems should be an integral part of all psychiatric patients' assessments.

Mental health providers must maintain an index of suspicion that prompts them to request medical consultations for patients. However, they should not be discouraged when physicians do not seem enthusiastic about exploring a suspected physical basis for a patient's psychiatric symptom. Inevitably, the "yield" of positives will be low, but a single positive finding of physical illness far outweighs many more negative findings. Prompt attention to a physical problem will return the patient to psychosomatic equilibrium and avoid the unfortunate experience of unproductive psychotherapeutic intervention. The increasing popularity of holistic medicine in the 1980s is a direct result of the new credibility of psychosomatic medicine and attests to the delicate and exquisite interrelationship between the "psyche" and the "soma" — a relationship that fortunately no longer has to be "proved."

REFERENCES

Barrett, L. (1976). *The sun and the drum: African roots in Jamaican folk traditions*. Kingston, Jamaica: Sangster Bookstores.

Hall, R. C. W., Popkin, M. K., Devaul, R. A., Faillce, L. A., &

156   *Black Families in Crisis*

Stickney, S. K. (1978). Physical illness presenting as psychiatric disease. *Archives of General Psychiatry, 35,* 1315–1320.

Hall, R. C. W., Gardner, E. R., Stickney, S. K., LaCann, A. F., & Popkin, M. K. (1980). Physical illness manifesting as psychiatric disease II. *Archives of General Psychiatry, 37,* 989–995.

Henker, F. O. (1984). Psychosomatic illness: Biochemical and physiological foundations. *Psychosomatics, 25*(1), 19–24.

Hoffman, R. S., and Koran, L. M. (1984). Detecting physical illness in patients with mental disorders. *Psychosomatics, 25,* 655–660.

Koranyi, E. K. (Ed.). (1982). *Physical illness in the psychiatric patient.* Springfield, IL: Charles C Thomas.

Lishman, W. A. (1983, August). The apparatus of mind: Brain structure and function in mental disorder. *Psychosomatics, 24,* 669–720.

McCartney, T. O. (1971). *Neuroses in the sun.* Nassau, Bahamas: Executive Ideas of the Bahamas.

Schwab, J. J. (1985, July). Psychosomatic medicine: Its past and present. *Psychosomatics, 26,* 583–593.

Walker, K. (1955). *The story of medicine.* New York: Oxford University Press.

Walker, S. (1967). *Psychiatric signs and symptoms due to medical problems.* Springfield, IL: Charles C Thomas.

14

Identification of
Responses to Emotional Stress

Frances E. Rankin

Emotional stress can be a critical factor in both psychiatric and somatic illness. Both an external or environmental component and an internal or intrapsychic component are present when an experience is stressful. The internal factors in stress are unique to each person's intrapsychic issues. Among the most stressful external stimuli are novel situations, times of change, and frustrations that cannot be resolved (Kaplan and Sadock, 1985).

PARTICULAR VULNERABILITIES OF BLACKS

The Black family is particularly vulnerable to stress. Racism and its inherent frustrations are part of the fabric of American life. For many Blacks, emerging from poverty remains a difficult or futile struggle. This is also a time of change for some Black Americans; with integration may come new neighborhoods, schools, and job opportunities, coupled with the loss of a supportive network. Increasingly, Black women are heads of households and must bear the tremendous responsibility of maintaining a family alone.

Some illnesses that can be exacerbated by stress have a higher prevalence among Blacks than in the general population. Examples of these illnesses are hypertension, lupus, and sarcoidosis. Twenty to 30% of Black adults have primary hypertension. The incidence of systemic lupus erythematosus is highest in Black women. Sarcoidosis is fourteen times greater in Blacks than in others (Krupp and Chatton, 1979). Stress can also be a factor in the crisis of sickle cell anemia,

157

a hemolytic anemia seen almost exclusively in Blacks. Alexithymia, a difficulty recognizing or verbalizing one's emotional feelings, is thought to predispose a person to psychosomatic illness (Kaplan and Sadock, 1985). As a consequence, physical illnesses in which emotional stress can have a strong effect, such as migraine headaches or gastric ulcers, may occur. It has been suggested that alexithymia is higher among Blacks than Whites. At times, however, poor communication of feelings in a therapeutic setting may be attributed to cultural differences between the patient and the therapist (Jones and Gray, 1986).

MIND-BODY CONCEPT

Throughout history man has struggled to understand the mind-body relationship. The historical perspective is highlighted in the previous chapter. Current research is increasingly sophisticated in probing the mind-body relationship. Although the exact mechanisms are still unclear, emotional stress can trigger changes in the hypo-thalamic-pituitary axis of the brain (Kaplan and Sadock, 1985; Reiser, 1984). External stimuli are processed in the cerebral cortex, which, in turn, activates electrical pathways that reach the axis. This vital center regulates much of the activity of the entire body, exerting its influence on the autonomic nervous system, endocrine glands, and immune system. Stress may also affect the voluntary nervous system, as in conversion reactions. The response to stress may also be anxiety, depression, or other purely emotional symptoms.

CLINICAL VIGNETTES

The clinical illustrations which follow will demonstrate both psychiatric and somatic responses to emotional stress.

Ms. A, a 35-year-old Black divorced female accountant, had made several visits to her family physician with complaints of fatigue. Her hypertension was also poorly controlled. When referred for psychiatric consultation she initially appeared calm but became very tearful as she spoke of her guilt about the divorce. She felt that she had denied her children a complete family within which to grow up. Her parents had divorced when she was a child, and she recalled the loneliness and hardship she had experienced afterward.

At work, other co-workers received promotions while she was told she should be patient when she sought advancement. She was the only Black person in her division. The atmosphere reminded her of the high school she attended; she was one of the few Blacks enrolled in a school within a community that had resisted integration.

In her psychotherapy she was able to make linkages between external stimuli and her internal issues. Raising her children after the divorce rekindled her feelings of abandonment by her father and feelings that her mother was to blame.

The discomfort she experienced at work with unsupportive colleagues and supervisors was similar to childhood unresolved feelings of being an unwanted outsider. Unlike her experiences in high school, where her scholastic achievements won her academic recognition, she was able to make few strides professionally, despite her best efforts. Both the symptoms of depression and the exacerbation of her hypertension were triggered by emotional stress.

Ms. B was a 42-year-old Black woman with poorly controlled adult-onset diabetes who was referred for evaluation by her internist. Her husband received a job promotion that made it necessary to move to another city, away from the support system of their families and former neighborhood. After the move, the difficulties in her marriage came into sharper focus. She had viewed herself as her father's favorite child and was angry that her husband was increasingly withdrawn and unavailable to her. When angry, she felt hopeless about change occurring in the relationship. She did not confront her husband, having incorporated her mother's style of not directly verbalizing angry feelings. She would, however, feel enraged within. Particularly at those times, she would be unable to resist eating voraciously.

The patient's wish for a male figure who viewed her as special, and her difficulty in openly expressing feelings, were intensified within the social isolation of a community far removed from her supportive network. Within this stressful setting, management of Ms. B's diabetes became increasingly difficult.

Mr. C was a 32-year-old Black man who became unable to work because of recurrent urticaria. The swelling and itching occurred initially while he was at work, but it subsequently reappeared even when he entered the vicinity of the workplace. After an extensive medical evaluation, he was not found sensitive to any allergen which would cause his severe physical reactions. In psychiatric evaluation, his struggle with his work supervisor became apparent quite early. He said that he was chosen for difficult assignments because of the high quality of his work, but he was not chosen for the advanced training program he wanted.

In addition, another employee recently had been selected for a performance award he believed he deserved. He often felt there was racial discrimination at work, and it was his style to confront supervisors when he sensed he was being treated unfairly. Early in his career he changed jobs after an adversarial relationship developed with a supervisor. He had continued the pattern of angry confrontations in his current job, but felt he couldn't leave because he hadn't received training in the new skills which would allow him to easily obtain another job. He felt very angry and powerless in his relationship with his supervisor. This situation was reminiscent of his relationship with his father as he grew up. As a child, he had seen his father as distant, rigid, and difficult to please; they had grown close, however, in his adult years. His father also had spoken to the patient of his own feelings of powerlessness, which he felt were related to the racial discrimination encountered in his places of work during the years of overt segregation.

The external component in the stressful situation for this patient was his unsupportive relationship with his supervisor. From within, this patient relived both his father's feelings of powerlessness about perceived racial discrimination and his childhood feelings toward an ungiving and demanding authority figure. He reacted with distressing physical symptoms, which reappeared in association with the work place.

The onset of physical illness is stressful (Guggenheim and Weiner, 1984; Kimball, 1981). When a person develops life-threatening or chronic illness, often with pain, disfigurement, or disability, the emotional reaction can be intense. Some degree of emotional reaction is normal, but prolonged or severe reactions may need psychiatric consultation. Suicidal ideation, denial of the illness, or psychosis may occur; even less catastrophic reactions can be emotionally traumatic. Monitoring a patient's mental status during the course of the illness is, therefore, imperative.

A patient may experience a sense of loss. Feelings of loss of identity in the family or in the community may be present if the patient is unable to fulfill responsibilities to others. Loss of self-esteem may occur if there are physical or cognitive changes brought on by the illness. The loss of autonomy in assuming the dependent patient role can also be difficult. As demonstrated in the case that follows, depression can arise in response to the experiences of loss.

Mr. D was a 47-year-old Black unmarried skilled laborer who developed arthritis in multiple joints. He enjoyed his current job, at which he had worked for many years. He was an avid golfer and had always seen himself as an active person. The arthritis became symptomatic over the course of a few months. He was placed on light duty tasks at work, but requested to return to his regular responsibilities because he felt bored. He also participated in a golf tournament despite the joint pain and swelling. He had not evidenced a good response to any of the trials of medication, and he was increasingly resentful of having an illness that required his daily attention. When seen in psychiatric consultation he appeared angry and depressed. His uncertainty about the future weighed heavily upon him. He was unhappy about the prospect of change at work, and concerned about the fate of relationships with physically active friends. He admitted to feeling self-consciously like an old man when climbing stairs or arising from a chair. As a result he increasingly spent time at home alone. He acutely felt the loss of youth, and the loss of identity at work and with friends. His depression was significantly related to that sense of loss.

Powerless feelings can cause overwhelming anxiety in life-threatening disorders or diseases with an erratic course. In the following case, anxiety is one of the prominent emotions the patient experiences in response to illness.

Ms. E, a 28-year-old Black married woman, had frequent crises of sickle cell anemia. She had had an older brother who had died from the disease in recent years. She stated that she felt powerless and frightened when the crises occurred. She also related having episodes of almost unbearable pain. Despite her illness she continued to work. Her performance, though adequate, was punctuated with frequent absences. Co-workers at times doubted her illness because she always appeared quite healthy; supervisors were frustrated with her unpredictability. Her illness had also begun to cause stress in her marriage. She presented with anger, anxiety, and depression in the psychiatric interview. The death of her brother heightened her anxiety about her own illness and the recurrent crises she felt powerless to control. She was also anxious because she believed her marriage and her job were in jeopardy because of the illness. There was intense anger toward her co-workers, who, seeing no stigmata of disability, offered skepticism instead of concern. Depressive feelings were associated with hopelessness about the future and guilt that she had survived and her brother had not.

SUMMARY

Clinical cases demonstrate how intrapsychic, somatic, and environmental factors may be interwoven in reaction to stress. To facilitate recovery from physical illness, it is important to evaluate the patient's mental status to determine if psychopathology exists. If a patient understands the impact emotional stress can have on physical health, psychiatric consultation, when needed, will be viewed as a natural extension of thorough medical care. Conversely, a patient in psychotherapy who has persistent physical symptoms may warrant medical reevaluation.

For Black Americans the environmental stressors are often great. Further, the incidence of certain illnesses sensitive to stress is higher among Blacks. The mind-body relationship must be addressed in evaluating and treating patients to ensure the best response in both psychiatric and somatic disorders.

REFERENCES

Guggenheim, F. G., & Weiner, M. F. (1984). *Manual of psychiatric consultation and emergency care*. New York: Jason Aronson.

Jones, B. E., & Gray, B. A. (1986). Problems in diagnosing schizophrenia and affective disorders among Blacks. *Hospital and Community Psychiatry, 37*(1), 61–65.

Kaplan, H. I., & Sadock, B. J. (1985). *Comprehensive textbook of psychiatry, Vol. IV*. Baltimore: Williams & Wilkins.

Kimball, C. P. (1981). *The biopsychosocial approach to the patient*. Baltimore: Williams & Wilkins.

Krupp, M. A., & Chatton, M. (1979). *Current medical diagnosis and treatment*. Los Altos, CA: Lange Medical Publications.

Reiser, M. F. (1984). *Mind, brain, body: Toward a convergence of psychoanalysis and neurobiology*. New York: Basic Books.

15

Psychological Aspects of Some Major Physical Disorders: The Role of Physicians in Treatment

Clarion E. Johnson

There are many references in the medical and psychiatric literature to the interrelationship of the mind and body (Deutsch, 1959; Oken, 1967; Selye, 1970; Perlman, Ferguson, Bergum, Isenberg, and Hammarsten, 1971). This chapter will examine the manifestations of emotional problems in physical disorders of Black middle-class patients seen by primary care physicians and medical specialists. Particular attention will be directed to race-related factors that provoke stress, which, in turn, generate physical symptoms in a sizable number of individuals. We will also emphasize the importance of the physician's alertness to the patient's psychological state during assessment and treatment of a physical disorder.

Three major questions will be addressed: (1) Are Black middle-class patients in any way different from their White counterparts? (2) Are there differences between lower-socioeconomic-level and middle-class Blacks as related to illness? (3) How can Black middle-class patients maximize their own interest and that of their physicians in obtaining the utmost in health care?

BACKGROUND

We live in a health-conscious society, with the airways and tabloids filled daily with health-related data. In much of the existing data

Blacks are described as a homogeneous lot. However, the reality is that Blacks vary tremendously in geographical location, housing, density of population, dietary patterns, social habits, and religious beliefs. The heterogeneity continues within the middle-class grouping, although the economic advantage is a common characteristic. The economic advantages of the Black middle class do provide certain benefits, one of which is access to health care. However, as noted in a report generated by the U.S. Department of Health and Human Services (1985), certain potentially fatal illnesses affect Blacks disproportionately. Stroke, heart disease, cancer, cirrhosis, and diabetes were included in the list. The overrepresentation of Blacks among those who die from homicide, suicide, or unintentional injuries, and in the infant mortality figures, also was underscored.

The problems for health care professionals who do not see Blacks as a homogeneous lot is finding and extracting pertinent data on Black middle-class patients. How does the privilege of health care access manifest itself? The significance of dissecting out the Black middle class from the existing information is twofold. First, the health care community needs to know there is a difference in subpopulations; second, the Black middle class itself should know that the diseases ascribed to the community as a whole are not necessarily a sentence under which they must toil. The reality that there exists a subgrouping with health care statistics that vary can begin to serve as a model and standard for health care strategists.

COLORING AND DIAGNOSIS

Physicians are not immune to prejudicial thinking. My wife, an obstetrician-gynecologist, early in her training noted on chart review that Black female patients presenting with lower abdominal pain had often the presumptive diagnosis of pelvic inflammatory disease, whereas their White counterparts were diagnosed presumptively as having endometriosis. The former diagnosis indicates a sexual etiology, whereas the latter represents a hormonal imbalance.

Findings published in a report by the American Cancer Society (The Subcommittee on Cancer, 1986) make a related point.

> . . . Ethnic differences in cancer are secondary to socioeconomic factors and associated processes . . . . [There is a] consistent excess of cancer mortality overall and cancer mortality for many specific sites for patients of lower socioeconomic status

compared to higher socioeconomic status. The economically disadvantaged have a higher incidence for seven sites and lower survival ratios for all sites combined.

Estimates suggest that at least 50% of the survival differential is due to late diagnosis in the economically disadvantaged. If the late diagnosis relates to the inaccessibility of health care services, it is likely that middle-class Blacks are in a better position to benefit from an early diagnosis of cancer.

Behavior patterns, dietary practices and occupational exposure are other risk factors that must be considered across class lines. Another study of two cancers (The Subcommittee on Cancer, 1986), colon and breast, showed a relationship to income; that is, there was a better survival rate for those of means. More recently, bladder carcinoma was discovered to have economics as a discriminant of survival among Blacks (Hackey and Myers, 1987).

STRESSES OF SUCCESS

The many stresses of success can be manifested in a wide range of somatic disorders (Spurlock, 1985). Probably every reader can recall experiences of gastrointestinal symptoms or heart palpitations associated with anxiety about an examination or some other stressful event. For those upwardly mobile Black persons who have a strong sense of responsibility to succeed "for our race," the stresses experienced in the workplace may be compounded. An exacerbation of a preexisting physical problem is a common sequela. Thus, success in the world of work may be associated with an alarming increase in blood pressure, or difficulties in the maintenance of a normal blood sugar level, or a flare-up of a gastric ulcer. It is important that the medical specialist be aware of the role that stress can play in physical illness.

The experiences and observations of former tennis champion Arthur Ashe (1986) vividly illustrate the particular stresses that befall Black men in their early middle years. He called attention to the fact that many of his male peers were among the first generation of Blacks who benefitted from the Civil Rights laws of the mid-1960s, and to the subsequent gains and losses.

. . . My 39- to 45-year-old buddies have paid a very heavy emotional toll. Divorce is the norm rather than the exception.

Nearly everyone is hypertense. The stress is barely bearable most of the time, but it is hidden behind ingenious subterfuges. I am not the only one to have had a heart attack before age 40 — and I was in excellent physical condition.

Ashe emphasizes racial prejudices to be a major factor in the triggering of many stresses. He calls attention to the fact that few of his peers were comfortable with the new privileges afforded by the Civil Rights laws, and refers to the conditioning for "life as a zero-sum game" that took place in their early years. Ashe recalled:

Early on, I learned that white society would tolerate only so many of us in one group at any one time; only so many — or none in some places — "nice Negro families" in a previously all-white suburban neighborhood; only so many in certain public schools; only so many in white colleges. When I got in any of these, I was supposed to feel lucky. My self-confidence was constantly being tested. . . .

The psychological stresses that members of the Black middle class experience have been addressed in each of the chapters in this volume. Many of the examples have been familiar to me and have been observed to be an integral component of many patients' presenting complaints of a physical disorder. However, the general practitioner or medical specialist is likely to overlook the interrelationship between the physical symptoms and the psychological stresses if she or he does not have a detailed referral statement and if time is not set aside that will allow the patient to elaborate about symptoms.

THE IMPACT OF STRESS ON
THE CARDIOVASCULAR SYSTEM

As one laces one's sneakers for a run, walk, or exercise class for that "life-prolonging" jaunt, certain questions may arise pertaining to heart disease. Several excellent references on cardiac disease can provide a depth that is beyond the scope of this chapter (Hurst and Rackely, 1985; Gordon, Kannel, Castelli, and Dauber, 1981; National Heart, Lung, and Blood Institute, 1982; National Center for Health Statistics, 1983).

As a cardiologist, I find the fact that heart disease is the number one killer of Blacks hauntingly real. Prevention of cardiac disease, and of atherosclerosis in particular, is approached by control of risk factors. The major risk factors are hypertension, cigarette smoking, and an increased serum cholesterol level. When stratified by social class, reduction in these risk factors showed no difference between Blacks and Whites for coronary artery disease (National Center for Health Statistics, 1983). The data on the White-versus-Black incidence of coronary artery disease show mixed results. Another study (Gillum and Grant, 1982) noted an association between hypertension and residence in a lower socioeconomic area. Stress from the environment was felt to emanate from poverty, crime, and housing density. However, there are growing numbers of case reports of hypertension in the middle-class Black population of business executives and professionals who experience stresses emanating from their places of work "downtown."

The control of cholesterol level through diet and exercise plays a beneficial role in cardiac disease. There are several other risk factors associated with coronary artery disease, including gender and Type A personality (hard driving, aggressive, compulsive). Considering these latter risk factors, the upwardly mobile Black male, who must be more driven in the workplace if he is to succeed, is especially vulnerable. Cigarette smoking increases the vulnerability. A favorite ploy I use upon discovering that a Black middle-class patient smokes is to remark casually, "I thought only poor, downtrodden people still smoked." Not infrequently, this has been a significant measure leading to cessation. I believe that risk factor modulation can be of most benefit to the middle class.

THE ROLE OF THE PRIMARY
CARE PHYSICIAN OR SPECIALIST

The importance of allowing patients to respond to questions in their own style is illustrated by a family practitioner (Hilfiker, 1985):

An encounter that began with the patient complaining of a persistent cough might easily develop into a lengthy discussion of smoking habits, a drinking problem or job stress. . . . One does not need more than a modicum of interviewing skills to elicit discussion of many problems of immense importance, all discovered during the course of dealing with quite routine physical ailments.

A systems review is incomplete unless the practitioner includes questions about personal or social problems.

As noted previously, the Black middle-class person who "made it" in business, civil service, academe, or another profession may experience stress-related physical disorders. It is not enough to treat the physical symptoms. In fact, it may be a disservice to the patient to ameliorate the symptoms of anxiety by prescribing tranquilizers.

Engel (1980) emphasized the importance of making use of the biopsychosocial model if there is to be accurate assessment and treatment of physically ill patients. In a description of the diagnosis and treatment of a patient who suffered a second myocardial infarction, Engel provides a classic illustration of the interrelationship between the psyche and the soma. In this particular case, the patient's need to be in control and viewed as a responsible person, as well as his emotional reactions (unstated) to the initial efforts of the emergency room medical team, played a significant role in the development of his physical symptoms.

The utilization of the biopsychosocial model in the diagnostic process will certainly assist the medical specialist or generalist in determining the extent to which emotional factors are involved in the development of the physical disorder. It follows that the information obtained from the use of this model will be of considerable value in planning and implementing a course of treatment.

SUMMARY

Black people are not homogeneous. Variations in disease incidence are but one manifestation of their heterogeneity. They, like other groups, suffer stresses that may be manifested as psychiatric, physical, or psychosomatic disorders. Regardless of their station in life, they, unlike most other groups, are likely to experience stresses that are induced by racial prejudices. It is incumbent upon the medical specialist to consider the possible impact of psychosocial stresses on the soma.

There are groups of people who are afforded certain privileges because they are differentially allowed to realize fundamental biological and social goals (Davis, 1942). Middle-class Blacks are one of these groups. Access to health care services is a significant privilege that provides middle-class Blacks continuity of care with the same provider(s), who can, in turn, be instrumental in promoting the physical and mental health of their patients.

REFERENCES

Ashe, A. (1986, August 31). No more zero-sum game. *New York Times Magazine*, p. 26.

Davis, A. (1942). *Social class influence upon learning*. Boston: Harvard University Press.

Deutsch, F. (1959). *On the mysterious leap from the mind to the body*. New York: International Universities Press.

Engel, G. L. (1980). The clinical application of the biopsychosocial model. *American Journal of Psychiatry, 135*, 535–544.

Gillum, R. F., & Grant, C. T. (1982). Coronary heart disease in Black populations: mortality and morbidity. *American Heart Journal, 104*, 839–851.

Gordon, T., Kannel, W. B., Castelli, W. P., & Dauber, T. R. (1981). Lipoproteins, cardiovascular disease and death: The Framingham study. *Archives of Internal Medicine, 141*, 1128–1131.

Hackey, B. F., & Myers, M. H. (1987). Black/white differences in bladder cancer patients. *Journal of Chronic Diseases, 40*(1), 65–73.

Hilfiker, D. (1985). *Healing the wounds: A physician looks at his work*. New York: Pantheon Books.

Hurst, J. W., & Rackely, C. (1985). *The heart*. New York: McGraw-Hill.

National Center for Health Statistics. (1983). *Monthly vital statistics report, 13*(13).

National Heart, Lung, and Blood Institute. (1982, October). *Heart and vascular diseases: II: Magnitude of the problem*. Washington, D.C.: U.S. Government Printing Office.

Oken, D. (1967). The psychophysiology and psychoendocrinology of stress. In M. H. Appley & R. Trumbull (Eds.), *Psychological Stress*. New York: Appleton-Century-Crofts.

Perlman, L. V., Ferguson, S., Bergum, K., Isenberg, E. L., & Hammarsten, J. F. (1971). Precipitation of congestive heart failure: Social and emotional factors. *Annals of Internal Medicine, 75*, 1.

Selye, H. (1970). *The physiology and pathology of exposure to stress*. Montreal: Acta.

Spurlock, J. (1985). Survival guilt and the Afro-American of achievement. *Journal of the National Medical Association, 77*(1), 29–32.

The Subcommittee on Cancer in the Economically Disadvantaged. (1986, June). *Cancer in the economically disadvantaged: A special report*. New York: American Cancer Society.

US Department of Health and Human Services. (1985). *Report of the secretary's task force on Black and minority health: Vol. 1. Executive Summary*. Washington, DC: US Government Printing Office.

16

Psychosocial Issues in Sickle Cell Disease

Harry H. Wright and Laura G. Phillips

Sickle cell anemia (SCA), first described in 1910 by Dr. James B. Herrick, is a common and serious genetic disorder occurring primarily in the Black population. The disease results from the substitution of the amino acid valine by glutamic acid on the beta globin chain of hemoglobin. There is no cure for this disease, but significant advances, particularly in general medical care, have been made in the treatment of the disease within the last fifteen years. Not too long ago, the average life expectancy for persons with SCA was in the range of 20 years. Today, many persons with SCA live into their eighth decade. However, an average life span has not yet been determined. Many patients with SCA experience numerous complications of the disease; others are in relatively healthy states (Williams, Earles, and Pack, 1983). Probably because most reports were based on seriously ill patients, the literature contains little about those who are relatively free of severe complications.

BACKGROUND

Sickle cell anemia has a history studded with misunderstanding and confusion. For many years, SCA was thought of as a condition similar to syphilis and sometimes referred to as "bad blood" (Battle, 1984). Some people still mistakenly consider the trait to be the disease. Some life insurance companies have charged a 25 to 50% higher rate for carriers of the sickle cell gene (Phillips, 1973). There are other accounts of employers, schools, and airline companies who have discriminated against sickle cell carriers.

Although "most patients with SCA have severe psychosocial problems and dealing with these is an essential part of effective management" (Conley, 1979), relatively few studies have focused on these issues. Numerous factors may contribute to the adjustment of SCA patients to their disease. The course of the disease itself is extremely uneven. Once the disease reaches the second decade, the prognosis is dependent on many variables (Powars, Gilani, and Haywood, 1974). This irregularity in clinical expression of SCA suggests that psychological factors are involved in its course (Leavell and Ford, 1983). This chapter addresses these issues and the current literature concerning them.

DIAGNOSIS

Sickle cell anemia patients are usually diagnosed between the ages of 6 months and 2 years, when their fetal hemoglobin is replaced by sickled hemoglobin. The sickling of the red blood cells causes them to clump together and impedes the normal passage of red blood cells through the circulatory system, hence causing the painful vaso-occlusive crises of sickle cell anemia. These unpredictable crises are the most common clinical characteristic of SCA. Psychosocial stress has been shown to precipitate them (Nadel and Portadin, 1977; Leavell and Ford, 1983).

Clinically, children with SCA present with slow growth, lethargy, poor feeding, anemia, jaundice, and "pot belly" caused by enlargement of the liver and spleen (Reindorf, 1980). Strokes have been experienced by school-age children and adolescents (Battle, 1984). In addition, adolescents experience delays in physical and sexual maturation.

Because SCA affects primarily Blacks in the United States, it is laden with racial connotations. It has been called the Black man's disease and may affect the Black child's concept of self-esteem and racial pride (Whitten and Fischhoff, 1974). It can arouse many untoward emotional reactions in the SCA patient. As one researcher wrote, "it is as if the Black population is singled out by the injustices of a hereditary disease that affects them with more frequency than any other hereditary disorder found in other racial and ethnic groups" (Williams et al., 1983). Sickle cell trait occurs in about 8% of the Black population in the United States.

MASS SCREENING

The racist implications growing out of the disease are particularly evident in the mass screening and genetic counseling programs for the disease. Although screening was originally promoted by the Black Panther Party, it was eventually taken over by health agencies (Hampton, Anderson, Lavizo, and Bergman, 1974). The National Sickle Cell Control Act, passed in 1972, established mass screening of the Black population for SCA (Rutkow and Lipton, 1974). Unfortunately, these early screening efforts may have caused more harm than good, because follow-up and counseling were not always provided.

Many Blacks see SCA mass screening programs as discriminatory. They have been referred to as "reverse racism," the "product of compensatory guilt-ridden excess" (Rutkow and Lipton, 1974). Others argue for the screening programs (Francis, 1974; Whitten and Nishiura, 1985) and note that screening allows for the detection of SCA and can save lives in the emergency room, especially for the asymptomatic individual; furthermore, screening will help in controlling morbidity and mortality by providing better care for those at high risk. In addition, screening is one of the best methods of educating the public.

GENETIC COUNSELING

Conflicts also surround genetic counseling for SCA. Several studies have tested the effectiveness of genetic counseling for SCA families, with effectiveness being defined as the retention of knowledge. Grossman, Holtzmann, Charney, and Schwartz (1985) found that families who were counseled and then tested four to eight months later had retained their knowledge of SCA.

Learning that one has sickle cell trait can be anxiety provoking. Novick, Mustalish, and Erdsvild (1973) reported that 61% of the persons whom they studied reported anxiety upon discovery of sickle cell trait either for themselves or for their children. Anxiety and level of knowledge were also found to be inversely related. Another study showed that genetic counseling helped to reduce the anxiety of the carrier state (Whitten, Thomas, and Nishiura, 1981). A comparison of feelings expressed before and after counseling showed that 71% of the people were free of anxiety about having sickle cell trait after completion of counseling. Those counselees who still expressed anxiety seemed to be most concerned about marriage and reproduction issues.

Except in extreme conditions, the carriers have no evidence of disease, but they do have the possibility of having a SCA infant should they marry another carrier.

Children and adults with sickle cell trait were found to exhibit more hostility, anxiety, and depression, and a lower self-concept, than those in a control group (Antley, 1973). This same author reported that genetic counseling actually made counselees more upset. When they learned of their child's carrier status, some parents of Hampton's study (Hampton et al., 1974) responded with guilt, confusion of the trait with the disease, concern about the child's future marriage, and special diets and restricted play for their children. All of these reactions could have adverse effects on the child's psychological development. Woodridge and Murray (1984) studied the effects on self-image of learning that one is a carrier of the sickle cell gene. This research showed no evidence that carriers feel they are stigmatized, either before or after counseling. In addition, it appeared that noncarriers were more likely to have a negative attitude about the carrier status than carriers have about themselves.

Another area of concern is premarital screening and counseling. Stamatoyannopoulous (1974) found in an evaluation of the results of a large sickle cell screening program that knowledge of the carrier status by individuals in no way altered their mating behavior. Premarital screening is controversial because, although it provides a systematic method of detecting carriers and preventing the birth of SCA babies, it may occur too late to be effective. The question of whether or not two carriers should have children may raise a great deal of hostility within the couple. Many Black couples resent being told by White genetic counselors that they should consider not having a child. Some counselors report that the problem could perhaps be alleviated by having more Black genetic counselors work with sickle cell families, but there are no data to support this contention. Furthermore, many couples feel guilty after they do give birth to a SCA infant after having been advised not to have children. Preferably, counselors should provide couples with information, not directives.

Whether or not to have children at risk for SCA is a complex decision. Parents must decide whether or not to have a chronically ill child who will have the potential for a fairly well-adjusted life (Francis, 1974). These issues are also faced by parents who through amniocentesis have found that the mother is carrying a SCA child. Unfortunately, fetal detection cannot prevent the consequences of SCA. However, early identification of SCA can lead to earlier genetic counseling and perhaps a better adjustment for the parents of the child.

Whitten and Nishiura (1985) addressed public issues concerning SCA and offered the following recommendations: (1) individuals with sickle cell trait who are of childbearing age should have the opportunity to be identified and counseled; (2) the goal of sickle cell trait counseling of individuals in their reproductive years should be to enable them to make informed marital and reproductive decisions that they believe are in their best interest; (3) counseling should be nondirective; (4) the goal of mass sickle cell screening should be to detect sickle cell trait in people in their reproductive years; and (5) pregnant women who have sickle cell trait should have an opportunity to know whether the fetus has SCA, and if so, to terminate pregnancy if they elect that option.

It remains to be seen whether these recommendations are accepted by the appropriate medical professionals and whether the controversial issues of SCA mass screening and genetic counseling are resolved.

FAMILY ADJUSTMENT

The family plays a major role in the life of the child with SCA. The family's adjustment to the disease will determine the child's adjustment to the disease (Battle, 1984). Parents who see their child as defective become "high-risk" parents and their child becomes a "high-risk" child (Williams et al., 1983). Likewise, parental attitudes can help to counteract the negative effects of the illness itself and play an important role in the adjustment processes by enhancing self-concept and reducing anxiety (Kumar, Powars, Allen, and Haywood, 1976). The diagnosis of SCA in a child should be reported in a family conference setting, with several members of the health team present to provide a comprehensive intervention plan to the family (Vavasseur, 1977). Unfortunately, in the past, parents of children with SCA have not always received adequate follow-up counseling after their child's diagnosis. Flanagan (1980) pointed out that these families, often with limited scientific background, are forced to assimilate a great deal of information in a short period and at a time of extreme emotional distress. The information needs to be paced as it is delivered to the family, and it may need to be repeated several times.

The family can be a tremendous support to the children by helping them to assess the realities of their condition, and promoting the development of a positive self-image. When an affected child is not in a state of crisis, he or she needs to be treated as much like a "normal" child as possible. Battle (1984) reports that families often become self-sufficient and rely on other family members for support more than friends and more distant family members. Sickle cell patients in this study saw themselves as significant members of the family, who participated in family decisions and provided moral support to the family (Battle, 1984).

When the family initially learns of its child's disease, members may experience feelings of shock, anger, denial, guilt, helplessness, or fear. The bonding between a child and his or her parents may be adversely affected by the diagnosis of SCA in the child. Spouses may blame each other for the child's illness. If the parents are tested and the father is found to be negative for the trait, questions of paternity can throw discord into the marriage. Later in the child's life, the family may have concerns about the child's future success in school, the possibility of an early death, anger over economic concerns, and resentment at the inconvenience of the child's illness. Many families cope with the early phases of the illness through denial, until the symptoms and painful crises become too obvious to ignore. Missed doctor's appointments may be a sign that families do not consider the disease as seriously as they should.

The family maintains responsibility for the child's care by making sure the child sees the doctor regularly, keeping the child's immunizations updated, and keeping a daily record of the child's conditions so that a baseline can be established (Flanagan, 1980). Many parents overly protect or indulge their children, perhaps in an effort to relieve their guilt for "giving" the disease to their child. Overindulgent parents can possibly retard the emotional and social development of their children.

Having a sickle cell child can provoke stress in the marriage (Graham, Reeb, Levitt, Fine, and Medalie, 1982). As in other childhood chronic illnesses, the mother is usually the primary caretaker for the child. The father may tend to remove himself from the illness, spending more hours at his job. The parent who is the primary caretaker may experience severe depression and feelings of isolation from her or his spouse. The mother who shows no outward signs of maladjustment may still be under extreme emotional stress (Tropouer, Franz, and Dilgard, 1970) and in great need of a support system. Community-based family support groups can be helpful in parents' adjustment to their child's illness.

Frequently, siblings of the sickle cell child will be jealous because of the attention parents given to the sick child. Parents may compare their ill child with their unaffected child. Both siblings and parents may be "hidden patients" who also need the physicians' assistance (Graham et al., 1982).

Several studies have focused on the adjustment of families to SCA in their child. Kumar and colleagues (1976) found that SCA adolescents with consistent family support and health care were no different from a matched peer group in personal, social, and total adjustment. The SCA children did appear to test lower in self-concept than their peers. However, a 1976 study (Anonwu and Beattie, 1981) of fifty parents of SCA children and fifty SCA adults found that they had little knowledge of the disease and poor coping skills. Many had a history of disastrous marital, work, and job-seeking experiences.

Nishiura and Whitten (1980) reported that families with SCA children were most likely to report financial strains because of the expense of medical care (expense also related to taking time off from work to accompany the child for medical appointments). A few married couples felt the illness of their child had adversely affected their relationship.

THE CHILD WITH SCA

The common physical manifestations of SCA in the infant have already been discussed. The pain experienced by infants is a significant factor in their development. If their basic needs are not met, they are likely to develop mistrust in caretakers (Williams et al., 1983). Many crises must be managed in the hospital because the infant will not eat enough during periods of pain. Hospitalization may interfere with parental-child bonding, and the mother or primary caretaker may feel displaced by the hospital staff (Williams et al., 1983). In addition, children may feel that they are abandoned when they experience a painful crisis. Hospitalization may trigger or heighten feelings of abandonment. Parents need to support children as much as possible during these painful crises and encourage them to talk about their feelings of abandonment. Because they are at the preoperational stage of cognitive development, preschool age children may have a difficult time understanding their disease, and explanations of the disease may not be comprehensible to them. Consistent support from parents and the medical staff is needed to protect against future psychological problems.

The preschool child struggles with developing a sense of autonomy.

"Normal" toddlers separate from their mothers, becoming more independent, adventuresome, and egocentric. Because of their egocentricity, children with SCA they may feel that they caused their disease, and that the pain is a punishment for misbehavior. They may feel that if they are good, their painful attacks will occur less often or be less severe (Williams et al., 1983). They may restrict themselves more than necessary and not develop the independence that they need for "normal" development. More likely, the child's parents may restrict them unnecessarily, and may outdo themselves in caring for and protecting their child. This only sets such children up for frustration in their efforts to develop autonomy.

The school-age child needs to develop a sense of mastery. A "healthy" self-image at this stage is partially dependent on the successful completion of mastery tasks. Unfortunately, the child with SCA frequently wants to, but cannot, master his or her disease. Even though the course of the disease is unpredictable, for the most part, and the child cannot influence most aspects of the disease (Whitten and Fischhoff, 1974), a child can develop a sense of mastery by learning not to fear the disease and by being aware of the possible things that may precipitate a painful crisis.

The child can also learn mastery by becoming involved with hobbies, games, and other nondemanding physical activities. Because he or she tires easily, the child may not be able to compete as others in some sports. However, this is not to say that SCA children cannot be active at all. Because school-age children are at the concrete stage of cognitive development, they can more reliably assess their illness and are probably in the best position to decide just how active they can be. The child may also be shorter in stature than his or her peers, and this frequently leads to teasing. Mastery in hobbies and sedentary activities can help to compensate for some of these problems.

Frequent crises may interfere with a child's schooling and necessitate the repeating of a grade. It is important that the child's teacher has an accurate understanding of the disease and that homebound instruction be provided for the child when it is needed (Vaughn and Cooke, 1979). School-age children may be labeled as "different" by many people (Williams et al., 1983). The medical profession refers to them as a "sicklers," and parents treat them as sick children. Teachers may see them as "different" because of frequent absences and the need for special bathroom privileges when they are required to drink extra fluids during periods of increased exercise and heat. Some SCA children may not be able to spend the night at a friend's house because of bedwetting. Because of their small size, SCA children may not be readily accepted into their peer group. All of these problems potentially threaten the child's self-worth and may cause him or her to withdraw. SCA children may become angry and depressed, feeling that no one loves them because of their disease. Frequently, these children are overly dependent on their parents and experience separation anxiety when they are separated from their parents for a significant period of time (St. Clair, Rosner, and Karayalcin, 1979).

The family of M. A., a 4-year-old daughter of professional parents, moved to a new community because the parents obtained new jobs and wanted to move closer to their extended families. M. A. had visited the new community, her parents' hometown, three to four times a year throughout her life. On nearly all of the visits, M. A. had experienced major difficulties with her SCA, frequently requiring a visit to the emergency room. When the parents told M. A. that the family was moving to the new community, she became extremely agitated, to her parents' surprise, and also started having temper tantrums. After moving, M. A. began to have SCA-related problems that required an average of one emergency room visit per week. There were also two hospital admissions in the first six months in the new community. M. A. continued to have temper tantrums, although less frequent and less intense than before the move.

M. A.'s parents brought her for a psychiatric evaluation because of the increasing behavior problems. During the evaluation, it was discovered that M. A. had decided and believed that the new community caused her to get "sick" with SCA, because she had had problems on all of her visits to the community prior to the move. She also felt she had to keep her parents close by to care for her if she became ill. After working with a therapist for four or five sessions over the course of six weeks, M. A. stopped requiring trips to the emergency room. The temper tantrums had decreased considerably in frequency and intensity. A year after the initial evaluation, the improvement in behavior problems and in the medical complications of SCA remained.

THE ADOLESCENT WITH SCA

Several authors have addressed the psychosocial dimensions of adolescent SCA (Williams et al., 1983; Whitten and Fischhoff, 1974;

Battle, 1984; Hurtig, 1986; Morgan and Jackson, 1986; LePontois, 1986). For the teenager who has gained a sense of mastery over the disease, adolescence may not be a time of turmoil. However, for many adolescents with SCA, the normal tasks of adolescent coping may jeopardize the management of the disease.

For the normal teenager, adolescence marks a period of physical maturing, sexual development, and a growing independence from one's parents. The SCA teenagers may become particularly stressed over the slow physical development of their bodies compared with those of their peers. They felt "different" from their peers in the latency years, so they may continue to feel "different" from their peers because of delayed puberty. Peer support and acceptance is particularly significant to the adolescent's developing sense of independence. Phillips (1973) has discussed the significance of body imagery to the SCA patient, which is particularly crucial in the adolescent years.

The child who has been dependent on his parents will find it hard to break from their protective nurturing. Because the adolescent may have fallen behind in school, time in school and thus the period of dependence on parents may be longer than normal. Many parents may be fearful of their adolescent's growing independence, but they should help to foster this independence as much as possible. When adolescents encounter the acute phases of their illness, they may regress to earlier states of near-total dependency on their parents. As much as possible, adolescents with SCA should be encouraged to be independent.

Adolescents with SCA may experience a number of negative emotions as a consequence of coping with the illness. They have been described as limited in motivation to succeed, as having poor self-esteem, and as hypochondriacal or depressed. Some may withdraw from peer groups, as well as the family. Embarrassment about the physical signs of disease (such as jaundice, dental deformities, surgical scars, and a small, sexually immature body) may be profound. Because some adolescents experience an increase in the frequency of their painful crises, they may become fearful. By adolescence, heightened awareness of the unpredictable nature of the disease may intensify the fear.

As adolescents finish school, they will begin to think about and plan for the future. Many set goals for themselves that are not realistic. Others place themselves in stressful situations to prove that they are like their peers. Depression often follows the realization of the limitations imposed by the illness. Vocational counseling can help the youth to choose realistic career objectives.

A special concern for the physician should be the vulnerability of the SCA adolescent to drug dependence (Charache and Moyer, 1982). The physician should be alert to this potential problem when evaluating the need for medication for pain. Adolescents will need help in dealing with their limitations as well as identifying and accentuating their strengths. The physician is in a position to provide considerable help in both areas.

In a study of 21 adolescents with SCA, Conyard, Kirshnamurthy, and Dosik (1980) confirmed the similarity of the psychosocial aspects of SCA and other chronic illnesses. Neel (1972), who also studied the psychological effects of SCA in comparison with other diseases, stated that SCA does not create any special problems aside from those inherent in the symptoms. The psychosocial dimensions of the disease were found to be complicated by socioeconomic conditions. In a series of weekly meeting with nine girls, there were frequent expressions of being prevented from making progress toward maturity (LePontois, 1975). The girls were anxious about their pubertal changes because they had learned from earliest childhood to associate bodily change with pain and physical incapacitation. Gradually, through these group therapy sessions the girls achieved a more positive sense of self.

Like other teenagers, those with SCA will need appropriate sex education before and as they experience the changes associated with puberty. Girls, especially, will need to know the risks and complications of a possible pregnancy. Twenty to 40% of pregnancies in the SCA female end in fetal wastage (Sheehy and Plumb, 1977). With careful monitoring, however, the woman with SCA can have a healthy pregnancy with a successful outcome. Samuels-Reid, Scott, and Brown (1984) reported on the contraceptive practices of SCA females. Only 38% of the SCA group reported sexual activity, compared to 81% of the control group. Thirty-three percent of the SCA and 66% of the control group used contraceptives, with oral contraceptives being most commonly used. Although it had been suggested that females with SCA were subfertile, this study did not support this contention. It did show, however, that females with SCA were older at the time of their first sexual encounter than those free of the illness. The authors suggested that delays in sexual maturation, the effects of chronic disease on body habitus and function, and psychological impact of the disease on the individual may limit the exposure of the female to the opposite sex.

Alleyen, Wint, and Serjeant (1976) studied the effects of leg ulceration on the psychosocial development of SCA youths in Jamaica. Their study showed that patients with leg ulceration left school at a significantly earlier age than sickle cell patients without leg ulceration. The leg ulceration group had a harder time finding employment. The age at onset of the ulceration was found to be important, with an early onset paralleling more psychosocial problems.

The study of Kumar and colleagues (1976) on anxiety and self-concept in SCA adolescents found no differences between the SCA group and the comparison group on personal, social, and total adjustment scales. The SCA adolescents did show significantly higher tendencies to withdraw and had fewer social skills. The mean score for self-concept was lower than that of the comparison group. However, the comparison group scored higher on the anxiety scale than the SCA youths.

THE YOUNG ADULT WITH SCA

The young adult with SCA may experience tremendous distress about employment. Eighty-four percent of the SCA unemployed patients in one study (Battle, 1982) perceived SCA to be the cause of their unemployment. Employers may discriminate against hiring a chronically ill patient, particularly when the illness is unpredictable.

Another area of concern for the SCA adult is marriage and intimate relationships. A damaged sense of self-worth is often a contributing factor. Those who have not completed the tasks of adolescence may have a strong sense of dependency and will emotionally attach themselves to whoever offers them security. Young adults with SCA may question whether or not they should marry, and ponder the fairness of asking someone to shoulder the burden of living with a chronically ill person. Additional stress occurs with the planning of and providing for a family. Difficulties in finding a health insurance company that will offer reasonable rates and provide adequate coverage may compound stress.

An individual who has successfully completed the tasks of adolescence should cope equally well during the adult years. Battle (1982) observed high levels of family functioning in SCA adults. The respondents in Battle's study coped with their disease through denial, in that they rejected the notion of a sick role; many did not consider their illness to be serious. The SCA adults wanted to appear to be normal individuals, independent of others for their physical care and financial concerns. They were optimistic about their future despite largely negative odds. Family and religion played a major role in the patient's lives. Despite the successful adjustment that many SCA adults make, they will still need an empathic ear, and may need counseling from time to time. Rarely are the issues of coping with their illness settled, and discussion of their problems will be an ongoing process.

Some SCA adults tend to be preoccupied with their physical disease, hypochondriacal, and self-pitying. Slight changes in their environment will provoke anxiety, and patients may experience chronic or intermittent depression (Whitten and Fischhoff, 1974). Leavell and Ford's (1983) study of sixteen SCA adults showed wide variation in the continuum between psychological normality and severe psychopathology. Morin and Waring (1981) reported three cases of SCA adults experiencing depression, noting that the two conditions appear frequently together and that physicians should be alert to this. Adults may be preoccupied with death, and lack interest in the world around them. At least one report states that counseling will not be effective with these individuals because they probably have personality disorders, but efforts at rehabilitation and education may be beneficial (Whitten and Fischhoff, 1974).

CONCLUSIONS

The major goal in the treatment of persons with sickle cell disease is to provide comprehensive care, providing for social, psychological, and medical needs. Despite the number of persons affected by sickle cell disease, there has been little written about the psychosocial issues in sickle cell disease compared with many other chronic childhood illnesses (e.g., cystic fibrosis, diabetes). Additionally, most of the existing studies have focused on viewing the SCA patient as victims and focused on weaknesses instead of strengths. Clearly, we are just beginning to understand the psychosocial issues involved in sickle cell disease.

Mass screening has raised several issues that were not anticipated prior to the legislation mandating such screening. Some of the earlier misguided efforts have been corrected, and the goals for screening as well as genetic counseling have been clarified. The major public policy issues have been elegantly discussed by Whitten and Nishiura (1985) and should be reviewed by everyone interested in caring for persons with SCA and their families.

Different psychosocial issues are of concern to SCA patients at different ages; thus, a range of interventions should be available. Families have generally been underutilized in treatment intervention with SCA patients. Certainly, the sustenance and strength provided by the family is one of the significant areas that warrants more extensive investigation.

REFERENCES

Alleyne, S. I., Wint, E., & Serjeant, G. R. (1976). Psychosocial aspects of sickle cell disease. *Health and Social Work, 1*(4), 105–119.

Anonwu, E., & Beattie, A. (1981). Learning to cope with sickle cell disease: A patient's experience. *Nursing Times, 7,* 1214–1219.

Antley, R. M. (1973). Responses to genetic counseling of positive families after sickle cell screening. *American Journal of Human Genetics, 25,* 12a.

Battle, S. F. (1982). *Psychosocial Perspectives of Sickle Cell Anemia Patients.* Chicago: Eterna Press.

Battle, S. F. (1984). Chronically ill children with sickle cell anemia. In R. W. Blum (Ed.), *Chronic Illness and Disabilities in Childhood and Adolescence,* pp. 265–276. Orlando, FL: Grune & Stratton.

Binder, R., & Jones, S. (1975, November 2). Prevalence and awareness of sickle cell hemoglobin in military population. *Journal of the American Medical Association, 214,* 909–911.

Charache, S., & Moyer, M. A. (1982). Treatment of patients with sickle cell anemia: Another view. In R. B. Scott (Ed.), *Advances in the pathophysiology, diagnosis, and treatment of sickle cell disease,* pp. 73–81. New York: Alan R. Liss.

Conley, C. L. (1979). Hemoglobin, the hemoglobinopathies, and the thalassemias. In P. B. Beeson, W. McDermott, & J. B. Wyngaarden (Eds.), *Cecil Textbook of Medicine* (pp. 1771–1780). Philadelphia: Saunders.

Conyard, S., Kirshnamurthy, M., & Dosik, H. (1980). Psychosocial aspects of sickle cell anemia in adolescents. *Health Social Work, 5,* 20–26.

Damlouji, N. F., Kevess-Cohen, R., Charache, S., Georgopoulos, A., & Folstein, M. F. (1982). Social disability and psychiatric morbidity in sickle cell anemia and diabetes patients. *Psychosomatics, 23,* 925–931.

Desai, P., & Serjeant, G. R. (1976). Awareness of sickle cell disease among high school students in Kingston, Jamaica. *Public Health Reports, 91*(3), 265–267.

Diggs, L. W., & Flowers, E. (1971). Sickle cell anemia in the home environment. *Clinical Pediatrics, 10,* 697–700.

Flanagan, C. (1980). Home management of sickle cell anemia. *Pediatric Nursing, 6*(2), A-D.

Francis, Y. F. (1974). Screening and genetic counseling programs for sickle cell trait and sickle cell anemia. *Journal of the American Medical Women's Association, 29*(9), 406–410.

Graham, A. V., Reeb, K. G., Levitt, C., Fine, M., & Medalie, J. H. (1982). Care of a troubled family and their child with sickle cell anemia. *Journal of Family Practice, 15*(1), 23–32.

Grossman, L. K., Holtzmann, N. A., Charney, E., & Schwartz, A. D. (1985). Neonatal screening and genetic counseling for sickle cell trait. *American Journal of Diseases of Children, 139*, 241–244.

Hampton, M. L., Anderson, J., Lavizo, B. S., & Bergman, A. B. (1974). Sickle cell "nondisease." *American Journal of Diseases of Children, 128*, 58–61.

Hurtig, A. L. (1986). The "invisible" chronic illness in adolescence. In A. L. Hurtig & C. T. Viera (Eds.), *Sickle cell disease: Psychological and psychosocial issues* (pp. 41–61). Chicago: University of Illinois Press.

Kramer, M. S., Rooks, Y., Washington, L. A., & Pearson, H. A. (1980). Pre- and postnatal growth and development in sickle cell anemia. *Journal of Pediatrics, 5*, 857–860.

Kumar, S., Powars, D., Allen, J., & Haywood, L. J. (1976). Anxiety, self-concept and personal and social adjustments in children with sickle cell anemia. *Journal of Pediatrics, 88*, 859–863.

Lane, J., & Scott, R. (1969, November). Awareness of sickle cell anemia among Negroes of Richmond, Virginia. *Public Health Report, 84*, 949–953.

Leavell, S. R., & Ford, C. V. (1983). Psychopathology in patients with sickle cell disease. *Psychosomatics, 24*(1), 23–37.

LePontois, J. (1975). Adolescents with sickle cell anemia deal with life and death. *Social Work in Health Care, 1*(1), 71–80.

LePontois, J. (1986). Adolescents with sickle cell anemia: Developmental issues. In A. L. Hurtig & C. T. Viera (Eds.), *Sickle cell disease: Psychological and psychosocial issues* (pp. 75–83). Chicago: University of Illinois Press.

Morgan, S. A., & Jackson, J. (1986). Psychological and social concomitants of sickle cell anemia in adolescents. *Journal of Pediatric Psychology, 11*, 429–440.

Morin, C., & Waring, E. M. (1981). Depression and sickle cell anemia. *Southern Medical Journal, 74*, 766–768.

Nadel, C., & Portadin, G. (1977). Sickle cell crises. *New York State Journal of Medicine, 6*, 1075–1078.

Neel, A. F. (1972, June). The psychological effects of sickle cell anemia and other chronic illnesses. Paper presented at the National Conference on the Mental Health Aspects of Sickle Cell Anemia, Meharry Medical College, Nashville, Tennessee.

Nishiura, E., & Whitten, C. F. (1980). Psychosocial problems in families of children with sickle cell anemia. *Urban Health, 9*(8), 32–35.

Novick, L., Mustalish, A., & Erdsvild, G. (1973, November). The New York City Department of Health: Establishment of a sickle cell screening program. Paper presented at the 101st Annual Meeting of the American Public Health Association, San Francisco.

Phillips, J. R. (1973). Mental health and SCA: A psycho-social approach. *Urban Health, 2*(6), 36–40.

Powars, D., Gilani, D., & Haywood, J. (1974). Sickle cell disease: Demographic factors influencing morbidity. In *Proceedings of the First National Symposium on Sickle Cell Disease* (Publication No. NIH 75-723, pp. 281–283). Bethesda, MD: US Department of Health, Education and Welfare.

Reindorf, C. A. (1980). Sickle cell anemia: Current concepts. *Pediatric Nursing, 6*(2), E-G.

Rudolph, W. C. (1983). Social issues in perinatal screening for sickle cell anemia. *Urban Health, 12,* 32–34.

Rutkow, I. M., & Lipton, J. M. (1974). Some negative aspects of state health departments' policies related to screening for sickle cell anemia. *American Journal of Public Health, 64*(3), 217–221.

St. Clair, L., Rosner, F., & Karayalcin, G. (1979). Experience of children with sickle cell anemia in a regular summer camp. *Journal of the National Medical Association, 71,* 1144–1146.

Samuels-Reid, J. H., Scott, R. B., & Brown, W. E. (1984). Contraceptive practices and reproduction patterns in sickle cell disease. *Journal of the National Medical Association, 76,* 879–883.

Seeler, R. A. (1972). Deaths in children with sickle cell anemia. *Clinical Pediatrics, 11,* 634–637.

Sheehy, T. W., & Plumb, V. J. (1977). Treatment of sickle cell disease. *Archives of Internal Medicine, 137,* 779–782.

Stamatoyannopoulous, G. (1974). Problems of screening and counseling in the hemoglobinopathies. In A. G. Motulsky & W. Lenz (Eds.), *Birth Defects* (pp. 268–276). Proceedings of the 4th International Convention, Vienna, Austria. Amsterdam: Excerpta Medica.

Tropouer, A., Franz, M. N., & Dilgard, V. W. (1970). Psychological aspects of the care of children with cystic fibrosis. *American Journal of Disabled Children, 119,* 424–432.

Vaughn, W. M., & Cooke, D. R. (1979). Help for students with sickle cell disease. *Journal of School Health, 9,* 414.

Vavasseur, J. (1977). A comprehensive program for meeting psycho-social needs of sickle cell anemia patients. *Journal of the National Medical Association, 69,* 335–339.

Whitten, C. F., & Fischhoff, J. (1974). Psychosocial effects of sickle cell disease. *Archives of Internal Medicine, 133,* 681–689.

Whitten, C. F., & Nishiura, E. N. (1985). Sickle cell anemia (public policy issues). In N. Hobbs & J. M. Perrin (Eds.), *Issues in the Care of Children with Chronic Illness.* San Francisco: Jossey-Bass.

Whitten, C. F., Thomas, J. F., & Nishiura, E. N. (1981). Sickle cell trait counseling: Evaluation of counselors and counselees. *American Journal of Human Genetics, 33,* 802–816.

Williams, I., Earles, A. N., & Pack, B. (1983). Psychological considerations in sickle cell disease. *Nursing Clinics of North America, 18*(1), 215–229.

Woodridge, E. Q., & Murray, R. F. (1984). The psychodynamics associated with sickle cell gene carrier status. *Birth Defects, 20*(6), 169–186.

17

Psychological Responses to "Female Disorders": The Role of the Obstetrician-Gynecologist

Richard E. Smith and M. Jeanette Espy

The obstetrician-gynecologist is the primary care physician for many women during most of their lives. The relationship starts with puberty and continues through adulthood and the climacteric. The role that the obstetrician-gynecologist plays is very important in how women deal with many of the physiological and pathological changes in their lives. Anticipatory guidance and counseling can help the patient adjust to these changes.

The obstetrician-gynecologist not only influences the attitudes of the patient but those of her spouse and other family members as well. It is important to recognize the significant role that the obstetrician-gynecologist has in assisting the Black family through all stages of life, and it is equally important for the obstetrician-gynecologist to recognize the important role he or she has.

ADOLESCENCE

Adolescence begins with the appearance of secondary sex characteristics and ends with the cessation of somatic growth and the completion of maturity. It is also defined as a cognitive growth period that should allow the development of abilities to make decisions and accept social restraints that are a part of the adult world.

187

The stress of adolescence can disrupt the most stable family as adolescents seek to define their individuality. Preparation for this period of development must include an understanding of the physical events of puberty, of increased sexual feelings, and of the need for contraceptive information. The onset of puberty in girls is heralded by the growth spurt that occurs between the ages of 9 and 10 years (Baker, 1985). The earliest event in sexual maturation is breast budding. The entire period of breast development covers approximately four years. Following an orderly sequence, pubic and axillary hair begin to appear. The last event of puberty is menarche. The average age of menarche in the United States is 12.6 years. Girls with higher body weight will menstruate at an earlier age. A delay in menstruation is defined as the absence of menses at age 16 in the presence of secondary sex characteristics, or at age 14 without secondary sex characteristics. The absence of menses may be anxiety provoking to the knowledgeable adolescent, who wants to be "normal."

Primary amenorrhea in many instances may be due to constitutional delay, or may be experienced by extremely athletic girls (gymnasts, runners, or dancers, for example). More serious causes include eating disorders such as anorexia nervosa, pregnancy, and congenital anomalies of the reproductive tract.

The developing self-image is another aspect of adolescence. With the current emphasis on being thin in our society, many adolescents feel compelled to purposefully starve themselves to stay thin. Even in pregnancy, this fear of becoming "fat" may play a role, resulting in an inadequate diet. The loss of 25% of body weight will cause the cessation of menses in most young women. This is an indication for aggressive intervention.

Dysmenorrhea also occurs soon after menarche. It is related primarily to ovulatory menstrual cycles. Rarely does severe menstrual cramping begin with onset of menses. Within the first gynecological year, however, ovulatory cycles begin and are associated with increased production of prostaglandin F_2 alpha. Many families and health care professionals, as well, have described dysmenorrhea as a psychosomatic or conditioned response to menses. Evidence now, however, clearly demonstrates a cause-and-effect relationship to the production of prostaglandins and their effect on the myometrium. Although rare in early adolescence, endometriosis can also be a cause of dysmenorrhea. This is particularly true in late adolescence (ages 18 to 19). Young teenagers who present with a history of chronic pelvic pain must be thoroughly evaluated for endometriosis. When the condition is suspected, a diagnostic laparoscopy can be performed.

It is important to make this diagnosis to identify those patients with organic causes of pelvic pain, and, also, for the prevention of infertility.

An important part of normal adolescence is the increased feelings of sexuality. Adolescents will, at times, complain of irregular menses or pelvic and abdominal pain as a means to open up and discuss a particular feeling or experience. It is, therefore, most important at this sensitive time to provide anticipatory guidance and honest information. Despite the inquisitive nature of adolescents, they do not always ask appropriate questions. The absence of questions by no means indicates an understanding; rather, it all too often indicates a fear of demonstrating ignorance.

Through much of the last two decades, sexual morals have changed dramatically in the United States. This is reflected most obviously in the print media and popular music, as well as television and movies. A great deal of social and peer pressure is placed upon the adolescent to engage in sex. Some will have intercourse; most will not use contraception. Today, four in ten adolescents have had sex by the age of 17. The average age of initiating sexual intercourse among Black young women is 15.5 years.

Young women who feel some control over their future and have a good self-image are more likely to be responsible contraceptive users, or even to delay sex. The more passive adolescent is at increased risk, as is the teen who falls behind in school. The pregnancy rate for Black teenagers is twice that for White adolescents. Anticipatory guidance must be provided through this period and should include sex education, value clarification, and help in developing decision-making skills.

Adolescent pregnancy continues to be a major dilemma for Black families. Pregnancy through the teenage years causes a major upheaval among family members. Often, at times, parents will blame each other; the gravid teen sometimes is put out of the home, threatened with abortion, or may even receive bodily harm. A sense of failure is experienced by family members, and, at times, a feeling of betrayal.

Nearly 80% of all teen pregnancies are unplanned (*Teenage Pregnancy*, 1981). As a result, reactive depression is seen in as many as 25% of all teen pregnancies. Suicidal attempts are not uncommon. Most adolescents, once becoming aware of the pregnancy, become very frightened and feel very alone. It is because of the stress of being pregnant that the adolescent will use the defense mechanism of denial quite effectively. She may wear loose clothing, explain her increased weight gain by saying she "eats a lot," or even report monthly menstrual periods. Guilt is also very strong, and there is a feeling that the pregnancy is a punishment for having sex. Appropriate family counseling is very important with all adolescent pregnancies. Occasionally, there is a punitive parent who experiences a sense of failure and social embarrassment; then, hostile feelings begin to emerge. In these instances, medical services are sometimes withheld. These feelings, too, must be addressed to ensure proper prenatal care for the high-risk adolescent.

The adolescent who is having sexual intercourse is at risk not only for pregnancy, but also for contracting many sexually transmitted diseases (Smith, Thompson, and Betts, 1986). Gonorrhea and *Chlamydia* infection, specifically, can cause chronic pelvic disease and produce life-long chronic pelvic pain, placing the adolescent at increased risk for ectopic pregnancies and infertility. A recent study of pregnant adolescents (average age, 16) disclosed that 60% of them had one or more sexually transmitted diseases. The most common included gonorrhea, *Chlamydia* infection, and condyloma acuminata, which is caused by the human papilloma virus (HPV) ("Human Papilloma Virus," 1987). All these infections may be asymptomatic in the early phase. Although adolescents represent a high-risk group for these infections (the more than one million reported cases of gonorrhea), the highest incidence was in the 20- to 24-year-old age group. *Chlamydia* infection and gonorrhea are common causes of acute salpingitis. After a single episode of salpingitis, 10% of young women become infertile. The inability to conceive in the mid-twenties often leads to depression, guilt, and a lowered self-esteem. The HPV infections have increased 400% in the last two decades. Not only is this infection disfiguring, but evidence now points to a direct association to cervical interepithelial neoplasia. Fear of transmission of disease and a fear of uncleanliness often interfere with the ability to establish healthy adult relationships.

ADULTHOOD

Endometriosis was long thought not to be a disease associated with the Black woman. The socioeconomic profile of the patient with endometriosis was a woman of high economic class, deferred pregnancy, and higher education. Support groups for women with this disease continue to be predominantly White oriented.

With the development of endoscopic examination of the pelvis, accurate diagnosis of this disease in Black women has increased. This disease can result in chronic pelvic pain, dyspareunia, and infertility.

There is a high frequency of multiple surgical procedures and medical therapy. The consequences can be serious, economically and psychologically, in the Black family. This disease, which has not been considered a "Black" disease, can make the family feel isolated. The painful coitus can lead to loss of sexual intimacy. The stress generated by a chronic disease must be addressed by the primary care physician, while medical and surgical therapy are used.

Uterine leiomyomas are the most common tumors of the female pelvis. Approximately 20 to 30% of all women have these tumors. Black women have a much higher incidence of the disease. In addition, the tumors occur at an earlier age in Black women. Uterine leiomyomas are associated with an abnormal menstrual pattern, which can lead to anemia. Lower abdominal pressure and pain can accompany the growth of these tumors. Infertility, increased spontaneous abortions, and premature labor are also associated with uterine leiomyomas.

Because uterine leiomyomas are more prevalent in Black women, the frequency with which the gynecologist must deal with associated problems is increased. The gynecologist may have to deal with a young Black woman in her early twenties with a significant leiomyoma. The impact that this can have on a young woman, when educational and professional responsibilities may be at their greatest, can be overwhelming. The tumor could require conservative surgery, a myomectomy, even during the twenties. The consequences of having to deal with changes in reproductive potential at this age must be addressed to allow the patient to express her fears and concerns. During the late thirties and forties, leiomyomas may become increasingly symptomatic in women, particularly after childbirth. At this point, hysterectomy may at times be the treatment of choice.

Hysterectomy may be required in a number of gynecological pathological conditions (Mattingly and Thompson, 1985). Gynecologists should deal with the significant stress that women experience as a result of having this surgery.

In these cases, the Black couple must adjust to the changes associated with the surgery. Black males and females commonly have misconceptions about a hysterectomy. Just as fear of breast surgery can delay a woman from evaluating a breast lump, concern over a change in body image and function can delay and frighten a woman who faces a hysterectomy.

First, the family must deal with the loss of reproductive function. The loss of the ability to impregnate or become pregnant can be associated with sexual dysfunction. Femininity and masculinity can be tied to the ability to have a child. Some couples experience a loss which they must grieve, particularly in cases where there was some ambivalence as to whether another child was desired.

Fertility rates decrease with advancing age, and Black couples who have deferred childbearing while building careers are becoming a portion of the 15% of couples who are infertile. Infertility is defined as the inability to conceive after one year of regular sexual relations. The problem is considered to be one of the couple, since the male factor is involved in 40% of the cases. The initial evaluation involves semen analysis, the keeping of basal temperature charts, timed intercourse, and some uncomfortable procedures such as endometrial biopsy and hysterosalpingogram. Further evaluation and treatment can involve extensive surgery, artificial insemination, and in vitro fertilization (Wallach and Kempers, 1985).

The treatment and evaluation of infertile couples can result in sexual dysfunction. Now sex becomes associated with the anxiety of not achieving pregnancy. Pressures increase to have sex at the correct time in the cycle. This can be a very difficult time for a couple, with the intimate aspects of their relationship being scrutinized by a physician. The onset of each menstrual period is associated with disappointment and depression. In some cases, Black men resist participating in the infertility evaluation, convinced that infertility is a woman's problem.

The physician must be sensitive to the problem of the infertile patient and her spouse. Besides technical expertise, the physician must have the ability to address the additional stress placed on the couple. The physician's supportive attitude can be helpful to the primary patient and her husband. One, or both, may react with guilt or tend to place blame. The couple should be encouraged to deal with their feelings together. Economic considerations can place additional stress on the family, because technical procedures are expensive.

The number of cancer deaths in Blacks is greater than that in Whites ("Black and Minority Health," 1985). The incidence and mortality rate of cancer of the cervix is two and a half times that in the White population. Risk factors include early onset of sexual activity and multiple sexual partners. The condition can affect women as early as their mid-twenties. Cancer of the ovary has a more insidious course, with few symptoms at the initial stages. It is therefore often diagnosed at a later stage. Endometrial cancer is highest in the postmenopausal patient and is characterized by abnormal uterine bleeding.

It is thought that the number of cancer deaths in Blacks is increased because diagnosis and treatment are delayed. Inadequate insurance or "out-of-pocket" coverage for health care is usually not a problem for the middle class (as compared to the "working poor" or unemployed). However, delay in seeking care is often fostered by denial. It is important that the obstetric-gynecology physician take the responsibility of educating the patient regarding early symptoms of disease and have an encouraging attitude when the diagnosis is made.

Treatment modalities for gynecological cancers include surgery, radiation therapy, and chemotherapy. The morbidity and side effects associated with treatment can result in depression, discouragement, and change in sexual functioning.

The anxiety associated with abnormal findings on a Papanicolaou's smear (Pap test) must be recognized by the obstetric-gynecology physician. The patient frequently associates even the most minimal change with the presence of cancer. Education and reassurance are necessary in treating these minor problems to decrease the associated anxiety.

THE CLIMACTERIC

Climacteric is a transitional period in a woman's life that is often clouded with myths and half truths. It is a normal physiological change brought on primarily by decreased estrogen production. Mood disorders often characterize this period. Sleeplessness, melancholia, and decreased libido also may occur. It also represents a time of osteoporosis, vasomotor instability, and increased cancer risks, specifically breast, uterine, and colon. Menopause, one hallmark of the climacteric, occurs between ages 45 and 55, the average age being 50 years. Fears during this time often include that of late-life pregnancy (and, therefore, also concern regarding contraception) and loss of one's intimate partner as a result of the loss of youth. Sexual dysfunction may at times have an organic cause. For example, lack of estrogen may lead to atrophic vaginitis and dyspareunia. Urinary incontinence may also occur and may result in social embarrassment. Most women, however, maintain an active sexual life well into the eighth decade. Loss of spouse and illness later in life often lead to diminished sexual activity. The patient should be made aware that death rarely occurs during coitus.

Estrogen replacement therapy along with counseling is of tremendous benefit to most women. Estrogen helps to relieve them of anxiety-provoking vasomotor symptoms, corrects atrophic vaginitis, and most important, reduces osteoporosis. Osteoporosis may affect 25% of postmenopausal women. Hip fracture as a result of bone loss causes more deaths than endometrial cancer. Estrogen therapy also has a more favorable impact on cardiovascular disease. Current therapy includes oral and transdermal estrogen administration. The approach of hormonal therapy and counseling can reduce the stress and discomfort of the climacteric period.

SUMMARY

The obstetrician-gynecologist is the primary care physician for many women; the Black middle-class woman is no exception to this pattern. The obstetrician-gynecologist is trained to be alert to the various psychological ramifications of obstetrical and gynecological disorders, both for the primary patient and for her family; also, to be alert to the possibility of stress-generating gynecological symptoms. Thus, the physician is in a position to provide medical services that are specifically related to the physical symptoms, but also to evaluate the patient's psychological picture and to provide proper counseling or serve as a referral source.

Problems that are of particular concern to or prominent in Black families were addressed, but many of the psychological repercussions of obstetrical-gynecological disorders are not race related. "Female disorders" can result in a change in self-image, fear, sexual dysfunction, guilt, anger, and depression regardless of the patient's ethnic or racial identity (or that of her partner, who may also be psychologically affected by the primary patient's gynecological disorder). Early recognition, treatment, and counseling can help the patient and her family adjust to those changes associated with gynecological disease.

REFERENCES

Baker, E. (1985, September). Body weight and initiation of puberty. *Clinical Obstetrics and Gynecology, 28*(3), 573–579.
Black and Minority Health. (1985). US Department of Health and Human Services. Washington, DC: US Government Printing Office.
Human papilloma virus. (1987, June). *American College of Obstetrics and Gynecology Technical Bulletin,* No. 105.

Mattingly, R., & Thompson, J. D. (1985). *Operative gynecology,* 6th ed. Philadelphia: Lippincott.

Smith, R., Thompson, Y., & Betts, J. (1986). The impact of a comprehensive prenatal care program on adolescent pregnancy. Paper presented at the meeting of the World Symposium on Adolescent and Pediatric Gynecology, Washington, DC.

Teenage pregnancy: The problem hasn't gone away. (1981). New York: Alan Guttmacher Institute.

Wallach, E. E., & Kempers, R. D. (1985). *Modern trends in infertility and conception control.* Philadelphia: Lippincott.

Worley, R. (1981, March). Age, estrogen and bone density. *Clinical Obstetrics and Gynecology, 24*(1), 203–218.

18

Substance Abuse: Impact on the Black Middle Class

Ronald B. Lonesome

Substance abuse or chemical dependency represents a major threat to Black Americans in general, and this surely includes the Black middle class. When the term *substance abuse* is used, we tend to think of illegal drugs such as heroin, cocaine, and PCP (angel dust). Yet our health, longevity, and socioeconomic life are even more affected by other chemical use. Alcohol use and abuse and cigarette smoking are more pervasive and more devastating to the health of the Black community. Excessive use of minor tranquilizers, especially among women, also represents frequent chemical dependency problems for Black Americans. In this chapter we will review the limited data available on the prevalence of chemical use and dependence among Blacks, with a special emphasis on data that seem especially relevant to the middle class. Then we will review some theories about the etiology of alcoholism and abuse of other substances, again with possible special factors for middle-class Blacks. Finally, we will look at some larger issues that relate to treatment, prevention, and politicosocial issues for an effective response to the impact of alcoholism and substance abuse on individuals, families, and our communities.

DEFINITIONS

The terms *use, abuse,* and *dependency* will be used throughout this chapter. *Use* implies that a person will use a drug at some point.

196

The term does not, in and of itself, tell us if there is a "problem," although use of an illegal substance does raise questions of law breaking. Alcohol use is widespread, involving 80 to 90% of Americans at some point in their lives. Drinking practices tell us something about patterns of use, whether it is rare, occasional, frequent, heavy, or compulsive.

The term *abuse* has a judgmental ring to it and is often unclear. It has been defined in DSM-III (American Psychiatric Association, 1980) as a pattern of use that is continued over a period of time and results in significant problems for the user: social, medical, emotional, and so forth. Persons who abuse a substance may not necessarily have a "loss of control" or lack of ability to exercise some conscious, rational choice about stopping or changing their patterns. Young people, or people in some life crisis, may slip into abuse. With some appropriate intervention they may be able to interrupt this pattern, with or without formal treatment. Others with an abuse problem may, in fact, be out of control and require extensive professional help. Certainly, whether or not there is loss of control, real disaster can occur during episodes of abuse — accidents, violence, crimes, and even death.

Dependence implies that the user has all of the problems of the abuser, and in addition physiological and psychological addiction. There is a change in tolerance, a presence of craving, and withdrawal symptoms if the person attempts to stop or cut down significantly on use of the substance.

ALCOHOL

History of Drinking Patterns of Black Americans

An exhaustive review of drinking practices among Black Americans is presented by Herd (1985 and 1986) in several publications. She notes that West Africans who were brought to this country as slaves had a long tradition of using fermented grains and palm sap. The non-Islamic groups brewed beer, and others made palm wines. Beer and wine were used in ancestral ceremonies and at weddings, funerals, births, and legal agreements. In precolonial times the consumption of these beverages did not yield high rates of social problems (Cherrington, 1929). Value was placed on moderate drinking. These rituals and restraints were continued into the 18th and early 19th centuries.

After the American Revolution, concern about drinking, especially among lower-class Whites and among Native Americans, increased (Rorabaugh, 1979). Blacks were very active in this temperance movement, in part out of their own traditions, but also because of the close relationship between the anti-slavery and anti-liquor movements (Herd, 1985).

The Black church was at the forefront in promoting anti-alcohol sentiments among Blacks. Also, abolitionists such as Frederick Douglass were quick to draw the parallel between enslavement to drink and slavery as an institution. "It was the sober, thinking slave who was dangerous, and needed the vigilance of his master to keep him a slave" (Douglass, 1967). Formal groups (e.g., the Colored American Temperance Society, organized in the early 1830s, and the Daughters of Temperance Unions) were organized by Blacks to raise the consciousness of their fellow Blacks as to the linkage between political freedom and freedom from alcohol (Herd, 1985).

Even after the Civil War, Blacks, through church and benevolence organizations, actively supported temperance in order to concentrate on building their new homes, advancing education, and furthering economic progress. One study expressed the view that Blacks were physiologically protected from alcoholism because of the absence of chronic drunkenness (Koren, 1899).

There was a significant change in the direction of the temperance movement after Reconstruction and in the early 20th century. Southern White politicians in particular began to blame alcohol problems on Blacks and on their voting habits. They portrayed Blacks as "crazed" by alcohol and willing to vote for "wet" rather than "dry" legislative measures. The anti-alcohol movement had become anti-Black. These developments undercut Black political and community support for temperance, except in the Black church. In the early decades of this century, liquor for Blacks "lost its power as a symbol of social oppression and instead became associated with urbanity, sophistication and freedom from oppressive Southern norms" (Herd, 1985, p. 161).

There were factors that contributed to a shift away from the temperance movement. In the early 20th century and especially after the First World War, thousands of Blacks migrated to the cities in the South and in the North. This meant a break with traditional ties to the land, the community and its mores, and even with the centrality of the church in their lives. Bootlegging gained in popularity and economic importance among Blacks in the South. In the North, a new nightclub subculture began to flourish. Entertainers were new role models and were associated with the free flow of alcohol. Even

Prohibition seemed to work against sobriety for Blacks, as Black-American communities became the target for wide sale and distribution of illegal alcohol. Some Blacks saw this trade as a source of much-needed income and entrepreneurship. During this period there was a disproportionate increase in death from alcoholism among Blacks, as well as increased hospital admissions for alcoholic psychosis (Herd, 1985). By 1950 and afterward, the cirrhosis mortality rates of Blacks rose above those for Whites for the first time.

Contemporary Drinking Patterns

The ambiguity in drinking patterns in the Black communities has been noted (Herd, 1985). There is a persistence of traditional temperance values, as reflected in the high rates of abstention among Blacks, especially women, and especially in Southern and rural areas. But there is also the role alcohol plays as a socializing agent, and a luxury or status commodity in the Black community.

According to the findings of a 1979 survey of American drinking practices, Black men and Black women were more likely than Whites to classify themselves as "abstainers." A higher percentage of Black men (14%) than Black women (7%) were identified as "heavy drinkers." Rates of drinking among Blacks vary greatly by geographic region (more in urban, Northern, and Central areas) and by religious background (less in Fundamentalist Protestant denominations) (U.S. Department of Health and Human Services, 1986).

Morbidity and Mortality

The rates of death from liver cirrhosis are twice as high for Blacks (21.1 per 100,000) as for Whites (11.1 per 100,000) (Herd, 1985). Alcohol is also a factor in the high incidence of esophageal cancer (ten times that of Whites) (National Cancer Institute, 1985). Likewise, the high hypertension rates for Blacks are made higher by excessive alcohol consumption. The Department of Health and Human Services report also cites some studies pointing to higher incidences of fetal alcohol syndrome (damage to the fetus from pregnant mother's drinking) and fetal alcohol effects among children of Black women who drink, though the data are "inconclusive" (p. 311).

A study by Babor and Mendelson (1986) of 8,155 male admissions to 13 private hospitals in the western part of the United States may shed some light on alcoholism issues for middle-class or at least middle-income Blacks. Three hundred (3.85%) of the total sample were

Blacks, who represented a high percentage of bachelors (12.3%) and the highest rate of divorce (35.7%). Blacks also had a high rate of current unemployment (40.5%) and significant percentage of skilled (50%) and unskilled (25.7%) laborers. Professional positions were represented by 12.2% of the Black patients; 7.4% held white collar jobs or were employed in small businesses.

Of the Blacks, 66.2% (the highest level of any group) learned about the treatment program through media advertising, especially television. Physician referrals (6.3%) and self-referrals (7.2%) were low. Some social network (friends, family, etc.) were the source of 20.3% of referrals, but Blacks were the lowest of any of the groups using this method of referral. Blacks had the highest rate of dependence on third-party insurance (81.4%) for payment (private or job insurance, Medicare, Medicaid, etc.), and the lowest rate of use of personal resources (3.4%) to pay their bill, though 15.2% used a combination of personal funds and insurance.

In terms of daily alcohol consumption, Blacks were in the middle of the range, at an average of 10.2 oz of absolute alcohol per day. However, Blacks were quite low in the incidence of drinking and driving arrests as compared with most other groups.

Studies from the 1950s and 1960s reported that Black and White male college students exhibited similar drinking patterns (Straus and Bacon, 1953) or that Blacks were more likely to be heavy drinkers than Whites (Maddox and Williams, 1968). In another study of students at thirteen colleges (including two predominantly Black colleges), it was found that more Whites (84%) than Blacks (60%) drank, and about three times as many Whites were heavy drinkers. The difference in heavy drinking was more marked in men. More Black women college students (48%) than White women (18%) were nondrinkers, but approximately the same percentage of White (5%) and Black (4%) women were reported to be heavy drinkers (Engs, 1977). In a study of a large southeastern university system, Stimbu, Schoenfeldt, and Sims (1973) found that Blacks in predominantly White schools were more likely to be drinkers than those in Black schools.

Fletcher (1987), in a limited but informative study, described drinking practices among 113 lower-middle-class Black women residing in four rural, predominantly Black counties in Mississippi. He reported that the onset of drinking was two years later than the national average (16 to 18 years of age), and that these women drank in social settings rather than to combat loneliness or because they were depressed. Women in the higher educational categories tended to drink more (as noted in other ethnic groups).

"HARD DRUGS"

Turning to the wider issues of drug use dependence among Blacks, we see again a disturbing picture of wide-ranging impact on this community.

The 1980 census indicates that Blacks constitute 11.7% of the U.S. population and 22.5% of the population of the inner cities. Given the prevalence of drug abuse in the urban areas, Blacks are, at least geographically, at greater risk. A 1982 national survey of public and private treatment programs found that Blacks are three times more likely to be in treatment for drug abuse–related problems than are Whites (National Institute on Drug Abuse, 1983).

Significant findings are noted in the report on Black and minority health of the United States Department of Health and Human Services (1986). Of the 180,002 patients admitted to drug treatment facilities in 1983, Blacks were represented at a level equivalent to twice their percentage in the general United States population. They were generally older than other groups at admission for abuse of each of the four drugs: heroin, cocaine, marijuana, and phencyclidine (PCP, angel dust). The majority of Black patients had multidrug problems; 31% had a primary heroin problem, as well as a cocaine problem; 27% used smoking (or freebasing) of cocaine as their route of administration; most had a higher level of intravenous use of cocaine than other groups; and, along with Puerto Ricans, they constituted 76% of the clients who were "speedballing" (intravenous shooting of combined heroin and cocaine).

Of 96,047 nationally surveyed emergency room visits in 1984, Blacks (males and females) sought help for heroin, cocaine, marijuana, or PCP ingestion more often than Whites (National Institute on Drug Abuse, personal communication, March 1985). Although Black males sought help in greater numbers, 18% of the total number of individuals seeking emergency care were Black females. Alcohol was one of the agents in 80% of emergency room visits involving a combination of drugs. Cocaine and heroin were the second most frequently reported drug combinations. Between 1982 and 1984, cocaine-related cases more than doubled, whereas the number of heroin-related cases remained fairly stable. Blacks and other minorities showed increased visits for PCP-related problems in emergency rooms. In drug-related deaths, Blacks represented 45.3% of the cases related to heroin. Although the actual numbers were much smaller, the percentage of deaths in Black females related to heroin, PCP, and cocaine was greater than for Black males. In fact, between 1982 and 1984, cocaine-related deaths among Blacks tripled. Finally, given the association between drug use and homicide, it was reported in 1982 that 42% of drug-related homicides in New York City involved a Black victim and a Black perpetrator (New York City Police Department, 1982).

Turning to some social class issues, Schnoll, Daghestani, and Hansen (1984) reviewed 150 patients who were treated for cocaine dependence in a university-affiliated, Chicago-based chemical dependence program. Almost one-half (48%) of the patients were Black. Note was made of the high level of education and employment in the entire group. At the time of admission, most of the patients denied use of other drugs. However, the staff noted many patients showed signs of sedative-hypnotic and/or alcohol withdrawal. After closer questioning, they estimated that a high percentage of these cocaine users had a history of multiple substance abuse, which they tended to overlook or deny or minimize. Weekly costs of the habit ranged from $200 to $3,000, with the average user spending $800 a week for cocaine. Those who injected or smoked cocaine generally consumed larger quantities than those who snorted.

Because cocaine is frequently mentioned as a drug with special attraction for the middle class, it may be illuminating to take a closer look at a 1982 national survey of drug abuse (Clayton, 1985). Findings indicated that cocaine use is related to educational attainment. The two groups with the largest percentage of "users" are those with some college education and those who are college graduates or at higher levels of educational attainment (19% and 18.8%, respectively). The two lowest groups are individuals with an elementary school education or less (1.3%) and some high school (7.6%). Respondents in managerial positions had the largest percentage of users (26.6%), followed by skilled workers (19.6%), service workers (18.3%), and then professionals (17.1%).

The largest percentage of cocaine users are those making $50,000 or more (15.7%) and those making between $10,000 and $20,000 (15.3%). Clayton concluded that the rather small overall differences in the rates of use from one income category to another suggest that "too much has been made of the association of cocaine use with various indices of success."

PATHOGENESIS

Some interpretations and conclusions can be drawn from data that have been cited. It is clear that Black Americans are deeply affected by alcohol and substance use and dependence. However, as the United States Department of Health and Human Services report (1986) makes clear, cigarettes, by far, cause more illness and premature deaths for Black Americans. Alcohol is clearly the second most destructive drug, causing not only medical and other health consequences, but also social and economic disruption that affects individuals, families, and communities.

It is only in the last sixty years or so that alcohol and drug use have become a significant problem in increasing segments of the Black community. This raises the question of why these developments occurred, and makes it clear that we are not talking about any inherent tendency in Black Americans to fall prey to chemical dependency.

In order to respond to this question of etiology, it is necessary to make clear certain definitions. It is simplest to use alcohol as our model, although other substances may fit the model as well, albeit with some important differences. In order to make an accurate assessment of the statistics of heavy drinking or heavy drug use among Black Americans, it is important to understand the nature of this use and to consider that there are probably many subgroups in this population of users. The concept of alcoholism as a disease implies a special condition. In the most "pure" and classical form, it is a disease with social, physiological, and psychological (and some would say spiritual) components. On this more strict definition, there seems strong evidence that there is a genetic component as well (Goodwin, 1986).

King (1983) has proposed a useful model for understanding etiological factors in alcoholism and human behavior in general, on both the individual and group levels. He calls the model "irreducible subsystems of human action" and describes four areas of influence: biological, cultural, socioeconomic, and psychological. If we use this model to arrive at an understanding of the etiology of alcoholism, then we can readily apply the data that have been presented in this chapter.

For instance, we could apply this model to understanding the causes for the drinking patterns of a Black middle-class person who has been labeled "alcoholic." The biological aspects could include the physiological responses of his or her body to the drug ethyl alcohol. How do the cells and the body systems respond to this drug? Does the person have a hereditary vulnerability to alcohol that allows for increased tolerance? Perhaps enzymes (inherited) responsible for metabolism in this person are of such a nature that he or she can drink larger amounts of alcohol than the next person. Drinking larger amounts over time may lead to other changes in the system that may affect substances such as epinephrine, norepinephrine, dopamine, and endorphins. These are all natural substances affecting central nervous system activity. A cycle could develop that perpetuates alcohol use and eventual dependence.

A look at the cultural history of this same person brings to light the fact that a Black middle-class American is a product of at least two cultures. As described previously, there is a historical African influence that viewed alcohol as a substance to be used for limited and specific purposes, and imposed sanctions against excessive use and loss of control. With cultural and social changes, geographic migration, changes in values, and especially influences from other ethnic groups, drinking practices can be altered. With easy availability of alcohol and heavy advertising, often targeted at Blacks, changes can occur in how alcohol is seen. For middle-class Blacks, the new cultural view and values put a premium on being able to "hold your liquor." Alcohol use can become a rite of passage. Being able to afford "top shelf" brands can be a symbol of success. Blacks purchase more than 30% of the scotch sold in the United States and more than half the cognac (Harper, 1976). An urban existence, with less connectedness to the fundamentalist Black church and its spiritual, ethical, and communal supports, can pave the way for a person to become alienated and vulnerable to being swept up by other mainstream currents.

If we turn to socioeconomic factors, we see that our Black alcoholic is surely going to be affected by racism — whether it is the historical legacy in our country or the day-to-day minor and major assaults on one's ego that say that in a competitive, status conscious, individualistic society, persons of color cannot just be different, they have to have a hierarchical order. In America, that means a lower position, less valued and further away from the dominant culture's view of what is beautiful, intelligent, and valuable. The social and economic expression of this attitude leads to exploitation, repression, and discrimination, as well as economic vulnerability, unemployment, and dependency. Politically, it can even lead to the use of alcohol and drugs as agents of oppression and social control. Supplies of alcohol and drugs, whether by conscious design or not, since slavery times have been made available to distract and narcotize Black Americans. For those who fall prey, the resultant deviant behavior and social chaos can then be pointed to; the victim can be blamed for this sorry state, and further controls and oppression can be applied — "for their own good" and to "save the community."

The economic factors of profit can not be overlooked in the alcohol and drug industries. Blacks can be seduced into becoming entrepreneurs in this business. In the mid-1970s, middle-class Blacks received Small Business Administration loans to start liquor businesses more often than for any other business venture. Inner city youth can be, and are, mesmerized by "big bucks" to be gained in selling drugs. With over 50% unemployment among Black teenagers, falling prey to such a temptation is all too predictable.

Finally, we can appreciate that, in spite of these external influences, individual psychological factors must also play a role. Theories about underlying psychological conflicts (anxiety, oral dependency needs, sexual conflicts, low self-esteem, and depression) abound in the literature. It seems clear that many roads lead to alcoholism, and certainly there is no consistent profile of personality in alcoholics, and no way of predicting, based on such profiles, who will become alcoholics, though there certainly are risk factors that seem to increase vulnerability.

For Black middle-class alcoholics and substance abusers one can point to many sources of stress. The whole issue of upward mobility has frequently been mentioned. Feelings of conflict about identity are certainly common. Moving up the ladder can mean alienation from family, parents, friends, and one's roots. The larger culture can symbolize material success, power, and escape from poverty and from the association with oppression and discrimination. Yet that same person may long for his or her roots in the Black community, for intimacy, love, spiritual connectedness, and emotional expression. For some, a successful bicultural balance may be struck; for others, confusion, conflict and despair can result. The need for escape and even self-medication for stress reduction can lead to the search for chemical solutions.

Even success itself can be a mood changer and lead to a sense of "survival guilt" in the Black who is an achiever (Spurlock, 1985). Not unlike some survivors of the Nazi concentration camps, Blacks who escape poor schools, unemployment, and the ghetto may feel deeply conflicted, unworthy, alienated, and guilty about leaving brothers and sisters "behind." A self-destructive process can be initiated. Again, drugs can be the agent of this negative process.

It is important to acknowledge that there is a subgroup of alcoholics whose primary problem is another psychiatric diagnosis: schizophrenia, major affective disorder, or personality disorder. Schuckit (1983) gives a good review of national studies of persons in treatment for alcoholism in whom the alcoholism appears to be a second diagnosis and for whom the use of alcohol may represent an attempt at self-medication. The incidence of these conditions has been reported (Schuckit, 1983) at various levels ranging from 1 to 5% in schizophrenia, 5 to 20% in major affective disorders, and 5 to 30% in personality disorders. Certainly, Black alcoholics are also affected by these conditions, and these patients obviously require specific psychiatric interventions in addition to effective treatment for their alcohol and/or substance abuse problems.

TREATMENT

The issue of treatment for the Black middle-class person is crucial if the aforementioned problems are to be addressed and resolved. Several basic factors warrant emphasis:

- There is hope. While the modalities and settings are varied, persons do change, and also stop their use of alcohol and drugs.
- There are useful and effective steps to follow in treating the Black alcoholic and substance abuser (Brisbane and Womble, 1985). Black middle-class persons may present with extremely strong denial about the scope and impact of their problem, a result of their relatively strong social and economic position. As with any alcoholic, this denial has to be confronted firmly and directly. Family, friends, and co-workers may be useful in this process.
- The goal of total abstinence is the safest and most rational objective in treatment, in spite of some studies suggesting that controlled drinking is possible for an ill-defined subgroup of alcoholics. Neither alcohol nor mood-altering drugs are necessary for a full and satisfying life.
- Specific guidelines are outlined in a review of the work of several researchers, who stress the importance of culturally sensitive and relevant treatment of alcoholic and chemically dependent Black patients (Lonesome, 1985). The treatment staff must raise its consciousness and those of the patients about racism, ethnic influences, and cultural diversity. Black middle-class patients must have a chance to explore their own life histories to determine the impact of their ethnicity on their lives. Issues of their self-image, self-esteem, identity, and values should be explored. The goal is to understand how their use of substance is related to these issues, and how their recovery can be assisted by using a positive and confident self-image. An Afri-centric model of treatment that recognizes the African influences in our culture has

been proposed (Akbar, 1979). This approach allows for sensitivity to differences in world view, with a stress on the central roles of person-to-person relationships, differences in the style and use of language, and the strong emotional expressiveness and the deeply spiritual orientation of many Black Americans. Recognition of the latter may lead to awareness of the differences in belief systems that may, in turn, lead to the utilization of an alternative form of healing.

- Self-help groups, such as Alcoholics Anonymous and Narcotics Anonymous, are essential, and *do* work for Black folks (Caldwell, 1983).

- Insurance issues are especially relevant for middle-class patients. The availability of a plan that covers the full range of alcohol and drug treatment services is crucial. Middle-class patients may be more prone to avoid clinic settings and other publicly funded programs for treatment. In some cases this may be understandable and inevitable. However, the need for confrontation, self-help groups, and culturally sensitive treatment should still be recognized. Seeing a private psychotherapist may be a step in the recovery process, but without some open, direct lifestyle changes and some positive association with other recovering people, the therapist can be pulled into a collusion with the patient's denial, and thus become an enabler for the patient's continued chemical dependency.

As an example of working with a segment of the Black middle-class, Bell (1986) describes issues in treating impaired Black health professionals. Noting the racist aspects of our society, he states that the impaired Black health professional may want to avoid being identified lest he or she give "ammunition for those who would say, 'See, I told you Blacks were incapable of professional training and status; look at how the stress of professional status impaired this one. . . .' "

CONCLUSIONS

It is too simplistic to say that drug and alcohol problems in the Black community are just the reflection of socioeconomic conditions of poverty, unemployment, and ghetto lifestyles. If these were the only or even the major factors, then one would expect the Black middle class to be more insulated from drug and alcohol problems. It is not. In fact, we have seen that with higher levels of education and income, there may be a more accepting attitude toward alcohol use. For most, this, in and of itself, is not a problem. But for a disturbing subgroup this use can progress to abuse and even dependence, especially if issues of personal vulnerability are present, along with alienation from roots (family, church, and self).

There seems little doubt, however, that racism, poverty, unemployment, poor schools, and limited access to quality health care all add additional risk factors, both for getting into chemical dependency and for having difficulty getting the proper, effective treatment.

With the loss of many of our family, church, and community supports, the Black middle class seems ambivalent in its attitudes toward the use of drugs, especially cocaine and marijuana. There are conflicting views and values on the proper use of alcohol. There seems to be little agreement on what are acceptable uses of alcohol, and how much drinking and behavior change are too much. Views run the gamut from judgmental religious proscriptions of any drinking to "do your own thing" liberal attitudes. The attraction of "fads" and the wish to prove "we have arrived" often get intertwined with the use of alcohol or drugs as a statement of who we are and what we can afford.

There is great danger in the "utilitarian" use of alcohol or drugs — that is, using these substances as a way of "coping," of feeling better, or of dealing with stress. Even the concept of "recreational" use of drugs and alcohol can lead to a loss of confidence in our ability to have warm, intimate and joyous times and relationships without the use of these chemical facilitators or "crutches."

Blacks are strongly affected by all forms of media. In one study (Babor and Mendelson, 1986) we saw that it was television that was the treatment referral agent for the largest number of Black middle-class patients. This observation has obvious implications for prevention and outreach. But it also shows the special danger of the impact of target advertising that saturates Black communities and urges the purchase of alcohol and tobacco. The skillful exploitation of our desire for signs of success, acceptance, and glamour is being used destructively. Frequently, the Black-oriented media themselves are used as a vehicle. This last point has often led to disproportionate dependence on liquor and cigarette advertising dollars by Black media, and even community and national organizations.

Prevention and education efforts are woefully inadequate in the Black community. Gary and Gary (1985) point out that those Blacks with religious (spiritual) involvement and strong racial consciousness and pride are least likely to have an accepting attitude toward alcohol and drug abuse. This observation gives a useful avenue to explore for prevention as well as treatment strategies for Black folks.

Finally, it is essential to keep in mind that alcohol and substance abuse do not occur in a vacuum. The political, social, and historical factors that affect Black people in America also affect attitudes, values, and behaviors. The destructive use of alcohol and drugs evolves from this complex of contextual issues. Thus, the move toward greater group strength, self-sufficiency, and cohesion must be an integral part of any rational program or strategy to resolve chemical dependency problems in the Black community.

REFERENCES

Akbar, N. (1979). Awareness: The key to Black mental health. In W. D. Smith, K. H. Burlew, M. H. Mosely, & W. M. Whitney (Eds.), *Reflections on Black psychology.* Washington, DC: University Press of America.

American Psychiatric Association. (1980). *Diagnostic and statistical manual of mental disorders* (3rd ed.). Washington, DC: American Psychiatric Association.

Babor, T. F., & Mendelson, J. H. (1986). Ethnic/religious differences in the manifestation and treatment of alcoholism. In T. F. Babor (Ed.), *Alcohol and culture: Comparative perspectives from Europe and America. Annals of the New York Academy of Sciences, 472,* 45–59.

Bell, C. C. (1986). Impaired Black health professionals: Vulnerabilities and treatment approaches. *Journal of the National Medical Association, 78,* 925–930.

Brisbane, F. L., & Womble, M. (Eds.). (1985). *Treatment of Black alcoholics.* New York: Haworth Press.

Caldwell, F. J. (1983). Alcoholics Anonymous as a viable treatment resource for Black alcoholics. In T. D. Watts & R. Wright (Eds.), *Black alcoholism.* Springfield, IL: Charles C Thomas.

Cherrington, E. H. (1929). *Standard encyclopedia of the alcohol problem: Vol. 5.* Westerville, OH: American Issue Publishing Company.

Clayton, R. R. (1985). Cocaine use in the United States: In a blizzard or just being snowed? In N. J. Kozel & E. H. Adams (Eds.), *Cocaine use in America: Epidemiologic and clinical perspectives* (Research Monograph No. 61). Rockville, MD: National Institute on Drug Abuse.

Douglass, F. (1967). *Life and times of Frederick Douglass.* New York: Collier Books.

Engs, R. (1977). Drinking patterns and drinking problems of college students. *Journal of Studies on Alcohol, 38,* 2144–2156.

Fletcher, B. (1987). Sociocultural correlates of normative drinking behavior among 113 Black southern females. *National News and Views: The National Black Alcoholism Council Newsletter,* No. 11.

Gary, L. E., & Gary, R. B. (1985). Treatment needs of Black alcoholic women. In F. L. Brisbane & M. Womble (Eds.), *Treatment of Black alcoholics.* New York: Haworth Press.

Goodwin, D. W. (1986). Genetic factors in the development of alcoholism. In S. M. Mirin (Ed.), *Substance Abuse. The Psychiatric Clinics of North America, 9,* 427–434.

Harper, F. D. (1976). *Alcohol abuse and Black America.* Alexandria, VA: Douglass Publishers.

Herd, D. (1985). Ambiguity in Black drinking norms. In L. A. Bennett & G. M. Ames (Eds.), *The American Experience with Alcohol.* New York: Plenum Press.

Herd, D. (1986). A review of drinking patterns and alcohol problems among U.S. Blacks. In *Report of the Secretary's Task Force on Black and Minority Health: Vol. 7* (pp. 75–140). Washington, DC: U.S. Government Printing Office.

King, L. M. (1983). Alcoholism studies regarding Black Americans: 1977–1980. In T. D. Watts & R. Wright (Eds.), *Black Alcoholism.* Springfield, IL: Charles C Thomas.

Koren, J. (1899). *Economic aspects of the liquor problem.* Boston, MA: Houghton Mifflin.

Lonesome, R. B. (1985). In-patient rehabilitation for the Black alcoholic. In F. Brisbane & M. Womble (Eds.), *Treatment of Black alcoholics.* New York: Haworth Press.

Maddox, G., & Williams, J. (1968). Drinking behavior of Negro collegians. *Quarterly Journal of Studies on Alcohol, 29,* 117–129.

National Institute on Drug Abuse (1986). Drug abuse among minorities. *Report of the Secretary's Task Force on Black and Minority Health: Vol. 7* (p. 14). Washington, DC: U.S. Government Printing Office.

National Institute on Drug Abuse (1983). *Main findings for drug abuse treatment units.* Rockville, MD: U.S. Government Printing Office.

National Cancer Institute (1985, January). *Cancer Incidence and Mortality in the United States, 1973–81* (NIH Publication No. 85–1837). *Vol. 2: Black, White, and Other Group Comparisons.* Bethesda, MD: US Department of Health and Human Services.

New York City Police Department (1982). *Homicide analysis.* New York: Crime Analysis Unit.

Rorabaugh, W. J. (1979). *The alcoholic republic.* New York: Oxford University Press.

Schnoll, S. H., Daghestani, A. N., & Hansen, T. R. (1984). Cocaine dependence. *Resident and Staff Physician, 30*(11), 24–31.

Schuckit, M. A. (1983). Alcoholism and other psychiatric disorders. *Hospital and Community Psychiatry, 34,* 1022–1027.

Spurlock, J. (1985). Survival guilt and the Afro-American of achievement. *Journal of the National Medical Association, 77*(1), 29–32.

Stimbu, J., Schoenfeldt, L., & Sims, S. (1973). Drug usage in college students as a function of racial classification and minority group status. *Research in Higher Education, 1,* 263–272.

Straus, R., & Bacon, S. (1953). *Drinking in college.* New Haven: Yale University Press.

U.S. Department of Health and Human Services. (1986). *Report of the Secretary's Task Force on Black and Minority Health: Vol. 7.* Washington, DC: U.S. Government Printing Office.

Introduction to Part VI

TREATMENT

Alice F. Coner-Edwards

This section focuses attention on some of the critical treatment issues facing select middle-class groups, including children, couples, and individuals with interpersonal conflicts that require group treatment. Wright's work on therapeutic interventions with troubled children begins with a discussion of the epidemiology of developmental, emotional, and behavioral disorders in children. Major treatment issues, including therapist and patient attitude and interactions, continuation in treatment, and psychiatric diagnosis of Black children, are delineated. Therapeutic interventions that involve the family are suggested. Special attention is given to the biracial child. Finally, an analysis is made of the use and misuse of psychopharmacotherapeutic intervention with Black children.

Henry Edwards's work on long-term psychotherapy with Black patients provides a comprehensive analysis of salient issues that emerge between Black therapists and Black patients. Major obstacles reported by Edwards include initiating and sustaining treatment in the face of internal patient resistances and external criticisms of the efficacy of analytically oriented treatment for Black people; and such counter-transference issues as denial of racial issues, overidentification, and Black prejudices. Summarily, Edwards highlights the advantages of Black therapists working with Black patients and points out the benefits of long-term analytically oriented psychotherapy for Black people.

Cunningham and Edwards provide an analysis of the group as a teaching, training, and treatment modality within a large psychiatric teaching hospital setting. These authors, along with the late Walter Bradshaw, to whom this volume is dedicated, designed this highly

213

structured group psychotherapy program over ten years ago. Through the years the program has been so well refined that issues associated with case selection, group cohesiveness, tasks and techniques of the therapists, and dynamics can be vividly illustrated. The efficacy of group therapy as a treatment and training vehicle is delineated and illustrated through vignettes. Emphasis is placed on the experience of Blacks as patients in the group process. Attention also is called to the experience of Blacks as therapists, teachers, and students of the group process.

Pinderhughes's focus is family therapy. She emphasizes the precarious position of Black families in the context of the broader social system that negatively affects the individual family members. Note is made of the fact that Black middle-class families have erroneously assumed a nodal position of anxiety reliever and tension reducer for the conflicts experienced by individuals within the broader society. Therefore, a critical aspect of treatment is to help families understand this unique position and to utilize specific adaptive modes for managing the stress that emanates from it.

Coner-Edwards and Edwards shift from a focus on troubled children and adult individuals to the relationship issues and treatment dilemmas of Black middle-class couples. They explore selected factors that are critical to relationship development, maintenance, and satisfaction over time, including liking and loving, intimacy, self-disclosure, empathy, and sharing at a deeper level. The Edwards suggest a model for more severe, long-standing, chronically disabling conditions, rather than short-term task-specific activities or pattern-specific interactions. Case vignettes illustrate specific conceptualizations related to psychotherapy.

19

Treatment with Black Middle-Class Families: A Systemic Perspective

Elaine B. Pinderhughes

The nodal role of Black families in the American social system entraps them in positions of great vulnerability. The concept of the societal projection process helps explain this entrapment and suggests that one group in a society uses projection upon another to relieve anxiety and reduce tension in itself, thereby improving its own functioning (Bowen, 1978).

Using this conceptualization to expand understanding about Black families and their realities, I have suggested that they, as minorities and among groups identified as victims of this societal process, have been trapped in positions of relative powerlessness. Confined and prevented from full participation in the mainstream of American society, they have been the recipients and circuit-breakers for much of the tension, conflict, contradiction, and confusion that has existed within it (Pinderhughes, 1983).

The validity of this hypothesis is borne out in several ways. It may be seen in the existence of ghetto inner-city communities, where large numbers of Black Americans (and other minorities) live among poverty, drugs, crime and system inadequacy (i.e., services that are disorganized, inadequate, or absent). In addition, a number of social policies, though developed to help Blacks (and others disadvantaged by the social system), in reality entrap them further.

Black families become trapped in spatial conditions that make them vulnerable to the anxiety and tension belonging to the entire society, and trapped in stereotypical images and roles that seem to justify the social structures and policies erected to deal with their problems. In such positions, Black families relieve anxiety and tension for Whites, and, at the same time, are forced to deal with intense stress, ambivalence, contradiction, and even paradox. This chapter will focus on the effects of this nodal role for Blacks in general, on the differences for middle-class families, and on treatment strategies with the latter group. In the discussion, there will be an emphasis on the contradictions and conflicts inherent in the role, on the adaptational responses that have resulted, and on treatment strategies that enable coping.

The stresses that confront all Black families exist on many levels. Slavery, which undermined African cultural practices and made for intensely oppressive conditions, left them without the unified, cohesive culture necessary as a phase to successfully change their predicament. Although there is disagreement among experts about what constitutes Black culture, how much African values and practices remain a part, the severity of the cultural cut-off remains clear. In a dramatic demonstration of this situation, Charles Pinderhughes conducted an experiment at a conference on cross-cultural training in psychiatry.* Everyone in the group was asked to rise. He asked the 30 Blacks who were present to go to one side of the room, the 30 Whites to the other, and the 9 Asians to the rear. He then asked all who knew the country, language, and religion of their ancestors to sit down. All 9 Asians, 28 Whites, and 4 Blacks sat down. He then hypothesized that (1) the Blacks who sat down were from Africa or the Caribbean or were members of the Vaughn or Haley families (who have traced their ancestry back to Africa) and (2) the Whites who remained standing were orphans. These hypotheses were largely validated. Two of the Blacks who sat down were members of the Vaughn family, and two were from the West Indies. Both of the Whites who remained standing knew the nationality, language, and religion of their mothers but not of the fathers; one had been born out of wedlock, and the other had lost his father as an infant.

Culture has been defined as a response to people's economic, political, and social realities (Navarro, 1980). Thus, the responses that Afro-Americans developed to manage the cut-off we have so dramatically demonstrated, along with the subsequent realities related to their nodal position in the society, have become critical factors in the culture that has evolved. Because the effects of this cut-off and

---

* Conference on Training in Mental Health Services for Black Populations, Port Chester, New York, March 2–5, 1980.

subsequent conditions have differed greatly, having been dependent on many factors including the severity and harshness of the immediate social environment, these adaptations also have varied. They, along with emphasis on values and practices from African and American culture, have constituted the three sources of Black culture. Each of these cultural systems has different value orientations and is embraced in differing combinations by Blacks. This accounts for the diversity and complexity found among them and for the conflict in values that has plagued them, becoming one major source of stress. Value conflict, but one manifestation of the conflict and contradiction with which Blacks have had to cope, cannot be resolved by the solution that experts recommend. Integration of values (Spiegel, 1976) is not an option for them, as it is for White ethnics, because of their excluded position in society. Biculturality, a mechanism that can create amazing strength or take an extensive toll, is the best alternative, but it means living perpetually with conflicting values and never integrating them as Whites can. For middle-class Black families, this conflict is compounded by (1) their greater involvement in the non-Black world and (2) the distance created between them and their non–upwardly mobile kin. Such a situation requires the ability to live in two worlds, managing dual sets of values, expectations, and roles.

HEALTHY BLACK FAMILIES

Numerous experts have described healthy Black families even though there has been little agreement on the definition of Black culture. According to Hill (1972) Black families are characterized by strong work orientation, high achievement orientation, strong kinship bonds, strong religious orientation, and flexibility in roles. Placing these attributes in the context of family theory, it can be said the healthy Black families function with strong, flexible boundaries; values that support cooperation, facilitating at the same time toughness and strength; structure and process that is marked by a high degree of organization and self-differentiation in members; effective leadership; ability to communicate clearly; ability to tolerate differences in values and perceptions among members; ability to negotiate conflicts; ability to function biculturally; and the capacity to build and use strong support systems (Pinderhughes, in press). Goals for treatment with Black families would, thus, be based on the aforementioned factors. Many families have been able to acquire such structure for themselves, securing the necessary external and internal resources. However, it is clear that such functioning is in constant jeopardy of being undermined, since its existence is largely dependent upon managing successfully their nodal position, for which so few supports exist.

A vital resource for the family's survival in this nodal position has been the extended family, historically viewed as the basic family unit. Roles within the nuclear family — provider, protector, nurturer, enhancer — have been supported by the network and the values of the extended family, which, in turn, has been critical in the integrity of the community and the survival of the group. However, for upwardly mobile middle-class families, connection with the extended family can prove stressful as well as beneficial. A sense of responsibility for non–upwardly mobile family members, obligation toward those who have assisted them in their move up the ladder, is compelling for many.

Extended family and community support may be absent for middle-class families for several reasons. Some, who over time have managed to stay connected to a well-functioning extended family and/or a cohesive ethnic community, are pushed to move away from these supports in pursuit of educational and economic opportunities. Others have identified with the dominant American culture, emphasizing values of individualism and autonomy, and are isolated from or have very loose connections with the extended family.

Without the support of the extended family and community, families are not only isolated and cut off from nutritive supplies but also experience increased vulnerability to societal forces of racism and oppression that make replacement of these supports and extraction of supplies from other systems in society more difficult. The societal institutions, normally regarded as substitute supports, reflect the destructive, stereotypical, paradoxical stance of the larger social system.

THE ENTRAPMENT: EFFECTS ON FAMILY ROLES

Adaptive attempts to manage the stress emanating from the nodal role can threaten the cohesive and flexible functioning so necessary for coping with this role. The conflict and contradiction to be managed, and the strain that results, can push the flexibility, mutuality, and adaptive compensation that marks healthy functioning into rigidity marked by overly tight boundaries, inflexible rules and relationships, exaggerated over- or underfunctioning in roles, disorganization, conflict, and confusion. When the family must engage in extensive protective maneuvers, having to close off frequently to protect itself from noxious, external influences, it risks becoming isolated and rigid in structure. This risk is very high for Black families who must exert energy to protect against the destructive systems erected by the societal projection process.

Shervington (1985, p. 5) discusses the consequences of isolation for Black children who grow up with a "narrow understanding of the Black self" that relies on societal stereotypes and embraces little knowledge of the rich heritage of Black Americans which can negate these stereotypes. On the other hand, the struggle to secure resources in the face of threat from the larger social system can prompt some families to become overly connected to certain external supports. Their boundaries become too open, causing distancing between family members, conflict in roles, and, like isolation, problems in other aspects of functioning.

At risk, even for middle-class families, are the family roles of provider, protector (traditionally male), and nurturer, supporter, enhancer (traditionally female). Threat of inadequacy or failure in these roles leads to exaggerated efforts to be overly protective or overly demanding of other family members, or to withdrawal. The protector role can be a special trap. The expectation of pain and recognition that hard work may not necessarily bring rewards, which are considered realistic preparation for managing inevitable road blocks, may also dull ambition and create tolerance for low expectations. The expectation that one will suppress the anger and frustration encountered in the workplace as a result of the aforementioned factors, means channeling these emotions elsewhere. The receptacle of the emotional overload can become the self or the family, in particular the mate or children.

MALE-FEMALE RELATIONSHIPS

The pervasive problems in relationships between Black males and females, which are outlined in other chapters in this volume, can be understood in this context. The flexibility and cohesion that characterize the supportive family functioning necessary to cope with the existing contradiction and conflict embodies caring, sharing, cohesion, and relatively harmonious relationships. Such attributes require the ability to be vulnerable, to negotiate conflicts, to use reciprocity, and to manage effectively high emotional overload. But, as we have noted, this functioning is jeopardized by the severity of the stresses the families face and by adaptive attempts to cope.

A central issue in the achievement of such relationships is the management of power in Black families. It is commonly suggested that egalitarianism has traditionally been characteristic of Black husbands and wives. This practice, which is based on African culture and did not "denigrate the independence of women nor define a man by the dependency of his woman" (Mullins, 1985, p. 18), is at the same time a residual of slavery and later oppression which forced Black women into the job market. It has meant that within the family, neither male nor female was dominant. White experts have misinterpreted that to mean that the Black male, having less power in his family than the White male in his, was dominated, castrated, dependent, and passive, the female overly powerful, and the family a dysfunctional matriarchy. Thus, the female was labeled the castrator.

Others, however, have noted the tendency for the male role to be undermined (Staples, 1978; Harris, 1980), making power conflicts and relationship struggles a hazard. A number of factors contribute to making power conflicts such a hazard for Black families: (1) the undermining of African values and cultural patterns of affiliation and collaterality, which, as noted earlier, had variable effects and which also left Black Americans without unified cultural guidelines for managing conflict; (2) the adaptive values of strength and toughness, which, under stress, can slip into behaviors calculated to defend against powerlessness;* such behaviors are reactive and conflict producing; (3) high tolerance for conflict, contradiction and confusion; and (4) American middle-class values that emphasize power, money, possession, ownership, and mastery.

Many Black families remain together, trapped in these multilayered conflicts. Traditional middle-class injunctions against separation and divorce have held together many families whose members have been frustrated with unsatisfactory relationships full of conflict and abuse. Another factor discouraging marital dissolution may be the tolerance for pain and expectation of frustration that by consensus validates avoidance of responsibility for ending an unsatisfactory relationship (Hines and Boyd-Franklin, 1983). However, the power of these injunctions is decreasing, as evidenced by the growing number of separations and divorces among higher status Black families than among comparable White couples (Bagarozzi, 1980). It is not un-

---

* Such behaviors are reactive and aim to bring a sense of power. Among those which may produce conflict are manipulation and identifying with the aggressor. The latter is characterized by a power-over stance and is manifested in domination, aggression, entitlement, arrogance, and supposed superiority.

common for a therapist to find a woman intensely angry and miserable as she resists efforts to act on her dissatisfaction. Her immobilization also can stem from empathy for the entrapment of the man, so that the resolution of separation or divorce is seen as "collusion with the system."

CLINICAL IMPLICATIONS

Treatment requires understanding the realities of Black middle-class families in all their varied forms and consideration of the interaction of all the factors that entrap them in their nodal position. Treatment, in this context, is best conceptualized as freedom from these entrapping roles, which, while balancing the larger social system, can keep them stuck, frustrated, and exhausted. It means facilitating their ability to manage the duality and conflict besetting them so that they can fulfill their family and work roles competently. Theirs is the task of maintaining family solidarity and cohesion in the face of conflicts and contradiction, managing rage and frustration to function competently and with organization, raising children to be cautious and strong in a hostile environment, and maintaining loving, caring relationships marked by sensitivity and the ability to be vulnerable in the face of stress that evokes rigidity and power behavior as a defense. A simple educational approach that clarifies the ambivalence, ambiguity, polarity, conflict, and contradiction of the context is the first step. When families understand their nodal position and the way in which coping responses can create further problems, they can sort out what belongs to the system and what belongs to them, beginning to take responsibility for any collusion in their predicament.

Because Black families are vulnerable when isolated from extended families and community supports, assistance must be offered to create and maintain the supports necessary for execution of their provider, protector, nurturer, supporter, enhancer roles. Particularly must this be considered for one-parent families, in which isolation and stress on the executive role may be excessive. If the extended family is unavailable or functioning inadequately, this may require linkage with substitute supports. If working to enhance the supportive function of the extended family is not an option, encouraging a link or repairing a severed connection with other ongoing supportive networks can be critical, especially for isolated one-parent families. Such a focus is vital to modulate the stress that can overwhelm them. This can mean supportive groups of any kind — cultural groups, church groups, activity groups, therapy groups. Gary (1978, p. 38) cites research showing the extensive use of voluntary organizations such as service centers, fraternal organizations, job and business organizations, and other informal networks by Black men "to solve personal and community problems." When the family, as often happens, has affiliation with a church, Hines and Boyd-Franklin (1983) suggest enlisting the support of the minister. Linking with a network and undoing isolation are strategies that are consistent with cultural expectations.

Because biculturality is a cultural imperative for these families, they must be able to live in two worlds while holding onto their cultural heritage. Preserving cultural identity and connectedness is vital for connection to the emotional and material support needed to execute their tasks. Conflicted, fragmented, and negative identity must be identified in family members, and strategies used to change it. The importance of a search for strengths should not be underestimated. A focus on the family's strengths is a demonstration by the clinician of appreciation for the struggle involved in that nodal position.

Behaviors that appear extreme or pathological can be relabeled as manifestations of the individual's determination to cope and do a good job. As noted, overfunctioning and underfunctioning are behaviors that stem from the stress produced by the nodal role. Such a strategy validates the person's struggle and views that behavior as a symbol of love and sense of responsibility. Relabeling is a technique that deals very effectively with contradiction and ambivalence. But the relabeling must be consistent with cultural practices. Thus, when a mother appears extremely controlling, she can be told that she is trying too hard to organize the family or she is taking too much responsibility for everyone's happiness. A father who overworks to exhaustion is trying extra hard to be a good provider, to be loyal to his father role. And this "overfunctioning" can be placed in the context of the family's nodal role. Underfunctioning, too, can be relabeled an attempt to keep peace, reduce stress, protect family members, and so forth.

It is important to convey the idea that it is not necessarily the family members or their adaptive strategies that are at fault, but rather the degree to which they have been exaggerated or the inflexibility with which they are used. For example, hard work, toughness, struggle, strength, persistence, determination, adaptability, creativity, and caution have been critical strategies for managing the nodal position. Under stress, however, adaptability can too easily slip into inconsistency, toughness and strength into abuse and power behavior, persistence into stubbornness, caution into immobilization, and hard work into driven dedication. Treatment strategies, therefore, do not aim to eradicate those behaviors but to moderate their rigid or exaggerated aspects. An overinvolved mother can learn to back off some if the goal is set to teach the child responsibility through letting him or her execute more tasks. In assisting a person functioning in an exaggeratedly dominant or passive mode to moderate his or her stance, it is important to remember that withdrawal or passive behavior by one partner can play just as strong a part in pushing the other toward dominant behavior. In this situation, the "dominant" one may feel more trapped.

Because of the frequency of power conflicts and the use of dominant-submissive behavior as responses to the nodal role, strategies based on power concepts may be useful. Goals would focus not only on recognizing the adaptability of the maneuvers families use, but also on helping them see that their problems are due, in part, to the natural wish of everyone to get a sense of power and be strong. As noted earlier, being strong is a valued attribute that needs validation. The strength and resilience must be acknowledged. People can be helped to see that their determination to have a sense of power° by using reaction formation or by being oppositional, passive aggressive, stubborn, manipulative, attacking, or even abusive is a way to cope with a sense of powerlessness. Although these behaviors make them feel strong, they also make for problems: they keep power struggles going, maintain a stance in which one always wants the power position in order to win or to put others down. Most important, we can help individuals see that while these behaviors do bring a sense of power, they also mean that one is always reacting instead of acting and therefore cannot make decisions, make choices, assume leadership or real responsibility. When one is preoccupied with reacting to another's initiative, one cannot behave in accordance with one's own goals and beliefs. In this way, family members are respected for their struggle and attempts to cope but warned of the price they pay. They can be taught there are other ways to be strong — that taking the initiative in not escalating the battle, in deciding to allow oneself to be vulnerable and take a one-down position requires strength. In family

---

° A sense of power is critical to mental health. Therefore, people engage in a variety of behaviors to defend against being powerless, using reaction formation, opposition, passive aggression, manipulation, striking out, and identification with the aggressor (Pinderhughes, 1983). Even dependency can be seen as an attempt to gain a sense of power by being close to its source.

work, as in individual work, the capacity to tolerate vulnerability can be a major issue. And for Black families whose nodal position has pushed them into adaptive behaviors that defend heavily against vulnerability, such a strategy is critical. Patton (1981) and Braithwaite (1981) discuss the importance of Black men learning to tolerate feelings and recognizing that kindness and gentleness are not weakness.

With persons who are intensely enmeshed (and again I repeat my belief that their nodal position reinforces such behavior), relabeling, and teaching about these dynamics may not be enough. For instance in one case, after repeated relabeling sequences, family members continued to defend oppositional behavior in battles with one another by focusing on others as attacking, unreasonable, and the like. The therapist finally insisted that the discussion be limited so that each person focused on his or her own behavior. Whenever another's behavior became the focus, the speaker was immediately interrupted. Without others to focus on, it became obvious that members were unclear about themselves, their own wishes, beliefs, and goals. There were long silences and an atmosphere of depression before family members were able to begin to make statements about individual perceptions and feelings.

Strategies that enable family members to share perspectives, to look clearly at how each perceives a given situation, and to identify the values that guide their behaviors and the beliefs they hold, focus attention on issues of sameness and differences within a family. When people are able to process their beliefs in the presence of one another, they can be helped to see that agreement or sameness in perspective may not be realistic or even desirable given the contradiction and paradox with which Blacks live. There can be agreements on the way in which the perspectives differ and acceptance of the ambiguity and contradictions that are a part of their realities. This may be the most that can be expected (Harris, 1980).

Developing tolerance for conflicting values and perspectives in oneself and within the family is a must, being part and parcel of the equipment needed to cope with the nodal role. Such a capacity enhances the ability to manage conflict, negotiate, compromise, and work together, cutting down on the conflict that stems from the need for sameness. It is the mark of high self-differentiation.

SUMMARY AND CONCLUSIONS

The nodal role as anxiety reliever and tension reducer in the larger social system embodies conflict and contradiction in a number of areas, creating intense frustration and anger. Stereotypical expectations, irreconcilable conflict leading to a duality in values and roles, and increasing nonavailability of the extended family as resource with consequent degrees of isolation from nourishing supports creates, in turn, intensification of emotional processes and stress on family roles. Responses to these stresses can take the form of a rigidified and exaggerated under- and overfunctioning in roles and individual behaviors calculated to defend against the sense of powerlessness. However, these behaviors, adaptive for dealing with stress and bringing a sense of power, too often create other problems. Treatment based on this understanding uses strategies that focus on strengths, builds links to supports, and moderates exaggerated and rigid roles; these strategies counter psychological fusion and enmeshment by enhancing self-differentiation and positive identity, and help the family develop a sense of meaning that will facilitate structure and cohesiveness.

REFERENCES

Asante, A. (1981). *Black male and female relationships: An Afrocentric context.* In L. Gary (Ed.), *Black men.* Beverly Hills, CA: Sage Publications.
Bagarozzi, D. (1980, April). Family therapy and the Black middle-class: A neglected area of study. *Journal of Mental and Family Therapy, 6*(2), 159–166.
Bowen, M. (1978). *Family therapy in clinical practice.* New York: Jason Aronson.
Braithwaite, P. (1981). Interpersonal relations between Black males and Black females. In L. Gary (Ed.), *Black men.* Beverly Hills, CA: Sage Publications.
Gary, L. E. (Ed.). (1978). *Mental health: A challenge to the Black community.* Philadelphia: Dorrance.
Gary, L. (1981). *Black men.* Beverly Hills, CA: Sage Publications.
Harris, O. (1980). Intervening with the Black family. In C. Janzen & O. Harris (Eds.), *Family treatment and social work.* Itasca, IL: F. E. Peacock.
Hill, R. (1972). *Strengths in Black families.* New York: Emerson Hall.
Hines, P., & Boyd-Franklin, N. (1983). Black families. In M. McGoldrick, J. Pearce, & J. Giordano (Eds.), *Ethnicity and family therapy.* New York: Guilford Press.
MacAdoo, H. (1978). The impact on upward mobility of kin-help patterns and reciprocal obligations in Black families. *Journal of Marriage and the Family, 40*(4), 761–776.
McClelland, D. (1975). *Power: The inner experience.* New York: John Wiley and Sons.

Mullins, L. (1985). Anthropological perspectives on Afro-American families. In M. Thompson-Fullilove (Ed.), *The Black family: Mental health perspectives.* San Francisco: UCSF School of Medicine.

Navarro, U. (1980, November 8). Cross-cultural and transcultural issues in family health care. Panel on Culture and Health symposium conducted at the University of California, San Francisco.

Papajohn, J., & Spiegel, J. (1975). *Transactionism in families.* San Francisco: Jossey-Bass.

Patton, J. (1981). The Black male's struggle for an education. In L. Gary (Ed.), *Black men.* Beverly Hills, CA: Sage Publications.

Pinderhughes, E. (1982). Family functioning of Afro-Americans. *Social Work, 27*(1), 91–96.

Pinderhughes, E. (1983). Empowerment for our clients and for ourselves. *Social Casework, 64,* 331–338.

Pinderhughes, E. (1986). Minority women: A nodal role. In M. Aultroche (Ed.), *The Functioning of the Social System.* Rockville, MD: Aspen Systems.

Pinderhughes, E. (in press). *Teaching cultural sensitivity: Ethnicity, race and power at the cross-cultural treatment interface.* New York: Free Press.

Rodgers-Rose, L. F. (1980). *The Black woman.* Beverly Hills, CA: Sage Publications.

Shervington, W. W. (1985). The Black family: Clinical overview. In M. Thompson-Fullilove (Ed.), *The Black family: Mental health perspectives.* San Francisco: UCSF School of Medicine.

Spiegel, J. (1976). Cultural aspects of transference and countertransference revisited. *Journal of the American Academy of Psychoanalysis, 4,* 447–467.

Staples, R. (1978). Black family life and development. In L. Gary (Ed.), *Mental health: A challenge to the Black community.* Washington, DC: Institute for Urban Affairs.

20

Relationship Issues and Treatment Dilemmas for Black Middle-Class Couples

Alice F. Coner-Edwards and Henry E. Edwards

This chapter explores some of the basic problems in Black male-female relationships through analysis and case illustration of select operational and in-depth issues that are frequently presented to psychotherapists by Black middle-class couples. The operational or practical issues are associated with parenting, changing sex roles, dual careers, labor market role conflicts, differing lifestyles, and quality of life concerns. Deeper issues relate to marriage at an early age, self-disclosure, intimacy and empathy, and conditional love and the need to deliver, associated with the resurrection of issues from the earliest relationship, defensive individuality, the search for confirmation, and problem solving. Unlike most treatment work with couples, which generally focuses on prevention and intervention and involves the couple in short-term task-specific activities or focuses on pattern-specific interactions, the model presented here offers a treatment approach for more severe, long-standing, or chronically disabling conditions. Emphasis is placed on the creation of a safe and holding environment, problem solving through development of a "couple ego" as arbiter, and the male-female co-therapy approach.

THE COUPLE

Couples are opening up their intimate worlds to psychotherapists, sex therapists, and family therapists in unprecedented numbers. This fact notwithstanding, marriages are continuing to end in separation and divorce in record numbers. Factors that are theorized to be critical to understanding these developments are being examined by researchers and practitioners alike, and many questions are being raised.

Who are these couples who are willing to open up their intimate personal worlds to a total stranger? What do they expect to accomplish or to get from the therapist? What is the nature of the presenting problems and what factors have interfered with their solution? Are these couples generally happy but presenting with specific issues, or are they the neurotic discontents of the world whose existing problems before marriage have been exacerbated by the range of selves and issues that emerge between them within the partner system? What approach is taken by the therapist in identifying the problems to be worked on, and what is the process and nature of the treatment? These and other questions provide the focus of this analysis.

The authors, like many other psychotherapists, are seeing increasing numbers of couples who present with serious marital difficulty, and individuals presenting with relationship difficulties who ultimately bring the partner into treatment. The authors have observed individuals varying in background, place of origin, age group, income level, and educational and occupational background. Although each individual and couple presents differing dynamics, the presenting problems of twenty Black middle-class couples seen during the past five years can be categorized into several broad types. These are presented in the following section.

Presenting Problems

Many couples present with practical or operational issues, and usually one or both partners are experiencing discomfort. Both partners report that something is not right, but very often they are vague or unclear about the reasons. Their discomfort is manifested in statements such as "He works all the time; we never take a vacation or spend time together" or "She is too busy with her career or corporate friends to take time out for us." Other more untenable situations develop when opportunities are presented to one or both members of the middle-class couple in different geographical locations, for example, a female journalist has been offered a dream position with a prominent newspaper in another city while her husband is moving up the corporate ladder with a large local architectural firm.

Some middle-class couples present with differing values, desired lifestyles, or role expectations. The upwardly mobile successful business executive wants an old-fashioned wife to attend corporate luncheons with him, while she would prefer to dress down and spend time hanging out with a friend. The husband, sometimes more fitness and exercise oriented, likes the out-of-doors, whereas the middle-class wife is a depressive who prefers to spend time alone indoors. Some of these concerns are surface issues that mask serious or chronically disabling problems.

Young Marriages and Discontinuity in Development

Couples who marry immediately after graduation from undergraduate school, sometimes with the same majors, may develop along very different paths. These couples come to therapy five or ten years later with the hope that they can return to the matrimonial bliss that they once had, or to achieve a meeting of the minds, or a satisfying life together. Usually, after college, the man has continued his education to achieve the heights in his field. He is respected among his colleagues and is very satisfied with his career and his personal life generally. The wife has generally terminated educational or career pursuits after undergraduate school to rear children, manage the household, and be the pillar of strength for her young struggling husband. She has few outside networks, and as the children reach school age and move into outside activities, she becomes more absorbed and commands increasingly less respect, admiration, and attention from her partner, who in addition to his successful and attractive career is active with outside hobbies. Typically, the husband criticizes the wife as lazy and dull and berates her for failing to professionalize herself or for refusing to accompany him on business trips and to social activities. She complains that he doesn't spend enough time at home with her or doesn't appreciate the importance of her role as homemaker and mother. The criticism triggers defensive behavior rather than compromise or individual development. The two fortify themselves individually, dig in their heels, and get locked into a stance of defensive behavior which brings them into therapy.

Intimacy, Self-Disclosure, and Empathy

Both Edwards and Coner-Edwards have consistently documented elsewhere in this volume, through case study and review of the literature, the importance of intimacy and self-disclosure to satisfying and stable relationships. Some authors have emphasized the importance of the response to intimate disclosure, suggesting that self-disclosure from one partner and a response of empathy by the other promotes intimacy and is the satisfying element in the relationship. Intimacy exists when one is able to expose the innermost self and get a response of intimacy from the other (Scarf, 1987).

Intimacy can exist between any two people; however, there is an equilibrium point beyond which intimacy becomes uncomfortable. We posit that as intimacy tolerance increases and the equilibrium point expands, the couple shares increasingly more of their deeper selves with each other. Many individuals have waited all their lives to share with another charged material that they fear could only be criticized by a partner. When the material is shared and the individual is still accepted and loved, the person can allow the surfacing of underlying conflict associated with the fear and anxiety of the intimate content. Defenses are relaxed and increased closeness with the intimate partner achieved. Subsequently, a stronger emotional bond between the couple develops, one that is less likely to be eroded by external stressors or by one or both of the partners seeking this ongoing intimate relationship elsewhere. Lack of self-disclosure and/or failure of empathy brings the couple to therapy seeking a safe environment that will allow self-disclosure, empathic understanding, and ultimate answers to the question, "Am I OK?"

Reenactment of Early Relationship

Marriage, or a stable relationship, is a vehicle whereby traditional functions are discharged within the supportive arms of the larger society. As these functions are discharged, individual needs are fulfilled. Some of the major needs include companionship, escort to social affairs, acceptable long-term outlet for sexual feelings, appropriate conditions to start and rear a family, and the sharing of economic and operational needs of family life.

Marriage, or a stable relationship, also serves as a vehicle for having deeper needs satisfied or an opportunity to return to earlier unfinished business. The relationship provides the opportunity to have a "mother" or "father" taking care of one's basic needs in a preoedipal or infantile sense. Dependency needs continue to surface throughout life, and these needs are met for the child by the mother or significant caretaker. The adult seeks fulfillment of these needs from the significant object, usually the spouse in a marriage. When the partner complains that the other is acting like a child and refuses to respond to the childlike needs, the other acts out in anger toward the perceived rejecting partner. When the partner can understand the childlike needs and give an empathic response, the other partner can often move back to an adult mode. These couples sometimes present to therapists locked into a seemingly endless parent–child struggle.

The relationship provides a more appropriate and acceptable opportunity to have the mother or father as exclusive "love object." It offers gratification of libidinal longings (pleasure) and the opportunity to effect, through parental surrogates found in the husband or wife, the things that the individual as a child wanted to do for parental figures. The husband who grew up in a stressful family wherein he consistently perceived that he needed to support or protect his mother or to make her happy, may perceive these same needs in his wife. The mother's behavior may have reinforced in the young boy a need to "deliver" for her. If the mother consistently presented conditions for the boy's behavior, such as "If you get good grades, I will buy you a new coat," then the boy learned that if he delivered what his mother wanted, he would get what he wanted and he would be loved. In adult relationships, the boy continues to feel this pressure to deliver even when it is not expected by the wife. The wife, on the other hand, may have felt, as a child, that she needed to be a helpmate to her father. She may have perceived her mother as unable to take care of her father or make him happy. She then plays out the father–daughter role conflictually in the marriage. Because neither is playing out the role that is most consistently desired by the other, they are failing to make each other happy, and neither is feeling "OK."

The role that these partners perceived for themselves as children or their desires to make the opposite-sex parent happy were impossible to fulfill. Thus, in their early youth, neither felt totally successful or validated in his or her efforts. These adult partners are continuously searching for confirmation that they are "OK." Questions around the issue of being "OK" bring them into treatment. One or both present as unsettled, with depression and underlying anxiety usually associated with the earlier parent–child conflict. Statements are made such as "My spouse does not behave in a way that allows me to feel OK about myself." Beyond all the righteous indignation at the behavior of the partner — whether neglect, abuse, rejection, or extramarital relations — is the haunting, disturbing question "Is it because in some way or another, I am not OK?"

Ideally, the question "Am I OK?" should be answered by the individual. However, experience with couples demonstrates that real confirmation comes in the context of an important on-going relation-

ship wherein there is sufficient self-disclosure and intimacy to know
that the significant other's judgment and confirmation are based on
knowing one's best and worst sides. Thus, within the therapy relationship, these individuals must settle the question "Am I OK?" They
must also settle the infantile issue of "conditional love and the need
to deliver." Only then can they respond to each other as themselves
rather than as "parent" or "child" or as "mother" or "father."

Defensive Individuality

The need to become a separate and autonomous individual is as
urgent as the yearning to merge forever in "umbilical bliss." The
two needs are never completely relinquished or reconciled. Originally
manifested as a complete union with the mother in the womb and
as a biological push for differentiation around 5 months of age (Mahler,
1975), these needs can resurface defensively in later relationships.

Development begins with the emergence of one or both of these
needs and the individual's struggle for closeness or individuation.
During the 9-month gestation before the inevitable separation toward
living individually in the world, the infant is at one with the mother.
This need for total insulation from aloneness, known as a state of
bliss, is never completely relinquished. Some students of Freudian
psychology suggest that one's life-long pursuit for union originates
in the yearning to return to the umbilical connection or a symbiotic
union. In poetic chronicles of development, it has been suggested
that, though a necessary loss, the rupture of primary unity remains
an incurable wound that inflicts the destiny of the entire human race
(Viorst, 1986).

Mahler (1975) has defined psychological birth as occurring at
approximately 5 months of age, when the individual enters the stage
of differentiation. This marks the beginning of the movement from
oneness into separateness or social differentiation. It is at this point
of development that ambivalence sets in. As walking, talking, and
other maneuvers are mastered, the child will desire help at times,
at other times electing to do these things alone in a more defiant
manner. There is holding tight and pushing away, insisting on the
separateness while fearing the separation, and simultaneous rage at
one's helplessness. The ultimate in development is the ability to
regulate closeness and distance, to find a distance not too close and
not too far away from the significant other wherein one can psychologically stand alone.

What happens in later relationships to the child reared by an overwhelmed mother who could not help the child move comfortably with the tasks of individuation? The early developmental experiences of the individual are reawakened in subsequent relationships. Many individuals, unable to find a comfortable distance between themselves and their partner, develop a stance that we can call "defensive individualization." "Individuation," as used here, denotes a biological activity wherein the push for separation represents an inner drive. "Defensive individualization" represents a more conscious effort but relates to the degree of success at individuation in earlier life. The defensive stance for individualization develops when one partner feels that the other does not value or respect what he or she does. Those of the middle class speak with pride about their success as individuals, and to have that success threatened by a partner perceived to be insensitive is met with defense. The partners develop a strong need to defend their personal behavior, attitudes, or activities in order to maintain themselves as individuals, of worth, as "OK."

Couples operating in the defensive individualization mode are unable to develop a sense of "we" or of "couple." They operate from the position that the best defense is a strong offense. The partner takes a defiant stance of "I don't need you, I can do it myself." The partner is unable to allow the other to love her or him, or to receive special things. Thus, important aspects of the relationship such as giving, receiving, demonstrating, caring, and mutual sharing are lost. The individual is often cold, unfeeling, and rejecting, and builds a wall between the self and the partner. When both partners are in this mode, they become completely isolated from each other. Without the fulfillment of the basic needs for closeness in the relationship, the couple will present as feeling angry, devalued, depressed, and in an intense emotional entanglement. The couple comes to therapy with each partner seeking an ally, or someone to say he or she is right. Problem solving is impossible, because the defensive stance prevents the achievement of a compromise.

Problem Solving — Ego as Arbiter

These scenarios indicate that couples find themselves locked into conflict situations that they are unable to resolve. The couple comes to therapy seeking help to get unstuck, as evidenced in statements such as "We've tried everything"; "We don't know what else to do"; "We can't go on like this much longer." Such reactions indicate that the couple has exhausted their problem-solving skills. We have repeatedly observed the basic issue that inhibits problem solving to be the absence of a "couple ego." Because of transferences, regression, need, anger, or frustration, the couple has become subjectively overwhelmed and is unable to step back to take an objective look at what is going on.

Although it is sometimes difficult to convince them, the partners are behaving toward one another, from a Freudian perspective, as "id" (feeling) and as "superego" (critical), or, more simply, from the perspective of Berne (1964), as parent–child. Absent, when the "heat is on," is Freud's (1961) observing, objective, problem-solving "ego," or Berne's "adult."

Each partner, feeling frustrated, anxious, and depressed, desires the therapist to be referee, judge, or arbitrator and each is hoping that she or he will be declared right. The therapist(s) will inevitably serve some such function, but generally from a point equidistant between the spouses. The more immediate need of the couple is the therapists' confirmation that they are "OK." This validation allows them to pursue the difficult task of saving the marriage.

TREATMENT

The Co-Therapy Model

The co-therapy model has been used extensively in group psychotherapy. Cunningham and Edwards note its usefulness in a later chapter of this volume. Although this model fails to be financially practical in work with couples, we have observed certain distinct advantages in its use. The co-therapy model has been repeatedly observed to: (1) provide a model of interaction for the couple; (2) provide male and female figures for individual partners to identify with; (3) prevent "triangulation deadlock," which can often block or stymie therapy; (4) provide an additional pair of eyes and ears to attend to the many dynamics in the therapy room; and (5) allow the therapists to model dyadic communications for emulation by the couple.

Problem Assessment

The initial appointment involves one and one-half to two hours of interview time to hear the presenting problem and the couple's expectations or reasons for coming to therapy. The therapists delineate the need for further evaluation and the nature of the evaluation process. The couple's commitment to the evaluation process is also determined. Should the therapists and the couple mutually agree that further evaluation is warranted, a contract is established which details the assessment process, including time, fees, and number of sessions.

During the evaluation phase, each partner is seen individually for two to three sessions by one of the therapists, wherein a detailed individual history is taken with emphasis on early and current relationships. The partners are allowed to select the therapist of their choice for this phase. This selection generally results in the male partner pairing with the male therapist and the female partner with the female therapist.

Information is gathered in the evaluative sessions for clarifying and focusing of the problem; determining the history of the problem and its chronicity or acuteness; determining the prognosis and whether there is hope for problem resolution; developing a therapeutic alliance, and determining whether or not the couple and the therapists can work together.

The final step of the evaluative phase includes the "interpretative" session. The therapists elicit from the couple their response to the process and any conclusions that they may have come to. The therapists then offer their individual observations and joint recommendations. A final decision is made by the couple regarding their continuation in treatment. If further treatment is decided upon, then the treatment process, goals, day and time of treatment, and all pertinent aspects of the "treatment frame" are delineated.

Treatment Process

Treatment is conducted in one or two one-hour sessions per week. The couple is expected to initiate the interaction. At times, the session is an insight-oriented, discovery process wherein the therapists make periodic interventions. At other times, the therapists are more aggressive and directive — for example, utilizing the technique of the "reflective loop," the therapists stop the stymied interaction process and request the partners to reflect on the immediate, preceding interaction in order to understand the pattern and to observe how they get "stuck." Other times, the therapist, in modeling appropriate communication, will stop the couple's stymied interaction to communicate with each other about the process, to raise questions about the dynamics, or to share thoughts openly about the couple's interactions or behavior.

Use of the "directive" technique is also valuable in teaching the couple to talk and listen alternately for a specified period of time. Experience indicates that although couples have been talking "at" each other for years, they may never have completely heard each other out.

Although we consistently make use of the "here-and now," focusing on the therapy hour and the current relationship, we find genetic material to be pertinent. Some patterns of interaction existed before the marriage in previous or even childhood patterns of coping and adaptation. The use of the genetic material or transferences and the couple's reactions to the therapists provide the focus for specific inappropriate interactions in the marriage. Patterns of interactions with others are indicated in interaction and responses toward the therapists. Little attention is given to interpreting the childhood roots, even though the responses may be rooted in childhood.

Many negative transference reactions manifested in psychotherapy impede the treatment process: issues such as competitiveness, envy, resentment, charges that one or both therapists are siding with the other partner, or feeling like an outsider without an ally. This matter needs to be brought to the attention of the couple. Occasionally, the couple will join together and act out hostility and anger against the therapists. All of these responses are illuminated by the therapists to point out destructive or defensive behaviors or patterns that prevent the couple from solving problems and resolving conflicts.

Treatment Objectives

We propose three major treatment objectives for long-term psychotherapy with couples presenting with long-standing, disabling problems. The first objective is to provide a "safe environment" for the emergence of self-disclosure and intimacy. Each member of the couple must come to feel free to express herself or himself openly during the session without being attacked by the partner, either during the hour or outside the session. The development of openness is a gradual process for which the ground rules are established in the initial session. This issue is spoken to continuously, and whenever a partner is attacked during the hour, the use of the reflective loop provides the attacking partner an opportunity to reflect on the need for revenge, the need to attack the other, and other feelings about the situation. A safe environment is one in which an individual feels comfortable about free expression and does not have to be concerned about being rejected. The therapists encourage negative and positive self-disclosure through reinforcement with a positive encouraging response to the material. Thus, self-disclosure is not only encouraged but elicited and reinforced.

A second objective of treatment is to help the couple develop an observing "couple ego" directed toward effective problem solving. All too often the couple is so subjectively involved that neither can get enough distance to objectively observe the problem. The ability to get distance from the problem comes about by observing the therapists as models, developing insight, using the reflective loop, talking and listening alternately, and clarifying the problem focus. A primary indicator of the existence of a "couple ego" is the couple's ability to reenact the therapeutic problem-solving process outside the therapy hour. Initially, the partners will consider the therapists' choice of responses to a particular problem. Later, with an observing ego, the partners will select from their own response repertoires.

A third objective of treatment with couples is to help the partners arrive at a "free and objective choice" about the relationship. Should they choose to remain in the relationship, through the accomplishment of the first two objectives, they will possess the necessary problem-solving tools to promote a long-standing satisfying relationship.

SUMMARY AND CONCLUSIONS

In this chapter, we have identified five major relationship issues that are often presented by Black middle-class couples. The first issue is presented by couples who were married at an early age but developed along different paths. The second issue is a lack of intimate self-disclosure and failure of empathy. A third issue relates to the reenactment of earlier relationships and the return to unfinished business. A fourth issue is defensive individualization; the last is the lack of a couple ego and the inability to problem solve.

We have encouraged the use of the co-therapy model and the development of a safe environment. The safe environment allows the couple to self-disclose, developing awareness and understanding of themselves as individuals and of each other. The process allows them to decide whether or not they wish to continue the relationship. Should the couple desire to continue, they will have developed the necessary problem-solving tools from the treatment experience that will allow them to deal with recurring, subsequent, or on-going relationship difficulties. The type of commitment required by this demanding treatment modality, involving finances, intense emotional effort, and time, can be made more readily by Black couples who have achieved solid middle-class status and economic stability.

REFERENCES

Berne, E. (1964). *Games People Play.* New York: Grove Press.
Freud, A. (1966). *The ego and the mechanisms of defense.* New York: Basic Books.
Freud, S. (1961). The ego and the id. In J. Strachey (Ed. and Trans.), *The standard edition of the complete psychological works of Sigmund Freud* (Vol. 19). London: Hogarth Press. (Original work published 1923)
Mahler, M. (1975). *The psychological birth of the human infant.* New York: Basic Books.
Scarf, M. (1987). *Intimate partners: Patterns in love and marriage.* New York: Random House.
Viorst, J. (1986). *Necessary Losses.* New York: Simon and Schuster.

21

Dynamic Psychotherapy When Both Patient and Therapist Are Black

Henry E. Edwards

The observation that ever-increasing numbers of Blacks are involved as patients and therapists in long-term, insight-oriented psychotherapy and psychoanalysis stimulated interest in the nature of the therapeutic process when both patient and therapist are Black. Material for this chapter is based on a review of the literature, my own experiences as an analyst and psychotherapist, supervision of the treatment of Black patients, and ongoing discussions with Black colleagues doing similar work. Emphasis in this chapter is on experiences using insight-oriented psychotherapy with Black middle-class patients, a group which has been largely neglected. The bulk of research and studies on Black families, Blacks in therapy, and similar topics has tended to focus on lower-class, inner city Blacks (Allen, 1978).

The focus on long-term insight-oriented psychotherapy and psychoanalysis does not mean that these forms of treatment are being advocated as the treatment of choice in every case. There are many forms of psychotherapy. The common ground of all psychotherapy, according to Karasu (1980), is

the treatment of mental and emotional disorders based primarily on verbal (and nonverbal) communication within the context of a special therapeutic relationship between two persons, wherein the one seeking help is the recipient of affective experiences (catharsis, abreaction, etc.), behavioral regulations (advice, control, etc.), and cognitive mastering (insight, explanation, etc.)

in relation to her/his presenting and/or underlying problems. (p. 34)

He divided the psychotherapies into two broad groups based on their hypothetical end points: adaptation to current reality and intrapsychic conflict resolution. Emphasis in this chapter will be on the latter, that is, treatment that emphasizes intrapsychic conflict resolution by means of insight-oriented psychotherapy or psychoanalysis.

There are three critical issues related to the use of this form of treatment when both patient and therapist are Black: giving patients the opportunity to learn of the value of such treatment, establishing a treatment alliance that will help patients remain in treatment despite strong internal and external resistances, and recognizing and handling specific critical transference-countertransference issues that arise in this specific situation.

It is my experience that if these issues can be successfully dealt with, a therapeutic situation can be established and treatment can proceed in an essentially conventional manner.

INITIATING TREATMENT

Although there are more Blacks than ever in psychoanalytically oriented long-term therapies, the numbers are still relatively small. Thomas and Sillen (1972), in their book *Racism and Psychiatry*, attribute this partly to "the establishment, that often limits the number of Blacks entering such treatment by not considering them good cases." Blacks supposedly have too little of the desired ego strengths that make good patients, such as motivation, intelligence, introspective capacity, the ability to delay gratification, and the willingness to repudiate action in favor of thinking. This view was further elaborated by Bradshaw (1978), who pointed out the racist implications that Blacks must be infantilized, that they do not have enough ego capacity to form a therapeutic alliance or to use insight to understand their own dynamics. In essence, this clearly biased view maintains that Blacks simply do not have the capacity to use therapeutic methods designed to offer maximum opportunity for developing ego autonomy and freedom from neurotic conflict. Bradshaw (1978, p. 1522) added that some Black mental health professionals also foster resistance to analysis or therapy by expressing thoughts that "dynamic psychotherapy is not suitable for Black patients because it is too cold and intellectual . . . that the average Black patient's needs are more immediate and that it is not relevant to the patient's struggle in the world." He suggested that many Black therapists have unconsciously adopted some of these myths about supposed Black inferiority.

Dorothy Evans (1985), in a review of the training process for psychotherapeutic work with Black patients, pointed out that traditional approaches, especially insight-oriented psychotherapy, are seriously underutilized and often devalued as treatment for Blacks. The implication is that "Black families may require something uniquely different from families of other races." She identified three issues in the training of psychotherapists that contribute to attitudes and approaches toward psychotherapy of Blacks: (1) a lack of clear understanding of the patient's intrapsychic dynamics, (2) rapid movement toward "activist and supportive therapy approaches because of unconscious fear of and/or identification with the intrapsychic aspects of their patients' problems" (p. 457), and (3) lack of exposure to available data showing the validity of psychodynamically oriented individual therapy with Black patients.

Despite the aforementioned barriers, large numbers of Blacks come to mental health professionals for treatment, but they stop short when the recommendation is for psychoanalysis or long-term intensive psychotherapy. Middle-class Blacks seek mental health treatment motivated by a desire for relief from suffering, bowing to the persistent urging of a relative, spouse, close friend, or physician, or in pursuit of gratification for concealed or thinly veiled wishes for dependence, attention, love, or even masochistic suffering. Most come with some conflict or lack of satisfaction or security in their interpersonal relationships — that is, trouble with their love life or lack thereof. Middle-class Black men most often present as depressed, despondent, and possibly suicidal, often despite professional and economic attainment and outward signs of success. There is a sense that something is missing. Black middle-class women most often present as anxious and often angry, with the focus on the future. Their present sense of dissatisfaction causes them to look with great apprehension to the future, wondering if there is satisfaction and security to come. Both men and women present with feelings of not being understood and of loneliness, and with low self-esteem and sense of worth. Many Black patients will come only if they can see a Black therapist. For this group, Black therapists seem to hold a promise of rapport, of being understood and accepted by someone they imagine has had a similar background and shared their Black experience. This expectation is usually borne out, and as described by Billy Jones and colleagues (1982) in their on-going study on therapeutic relationships between Black patients and Black therapists, "establishing rapport and the therapeutic engagement of the patient was less frequently a problem than most other treatment stages" (p. 1176). The initial consultation is often very pleasant and seems to represent an early positive transference stemming from a positive experience of sitting and talking to a significant person in their past.

Unfortunately, many will drop out after getting some immediate relief from symptoms, after having satisfied their need to appease a significant other, or after finding that the expected gratification of their wishes is frustrated. But many will stay and work in psychotherapy, prove themselves "good cases," and derive a benefit they otherwise may never have had. So the aforementioned motivating factors, coupled with the facilitating availability of a Black therapist, may get many into psychotherapy, but the step into long-term analytically oriented psychotherapy and especially psychoanalysis itself is not easy.

RESISTANCES

What, then, are some specific issues that contribute to the resistance of many Blacks to entering the psychoanalytic therapies? Many are not related to race or ethnic group but are, rather, commonly seen resistances to treatment.

Wariness of Freud and Metapsychological Concepts

A frequent question is, "How can the thoughts and methods of a Jewish analyst who lived and worked with White patients in Vienna 80 years ago help me, an American Black in the 1980s, with my problem?" Also, many patients themselves introduce certain partially or poorly understood concepts such as "unconscious," "ego," "superego," "oral," "anal," "phallic," and "Oedipus complex" and reveal their anxiety about them by defensive denial, rejection, derision, or humor.

Concern with the Reactions of Others

Psychoanalysis and psychotherapy are not always approved of by the Black community, and the Black potential patient is fearful of the probable opposition and criticism of peers and family, who are very likely to call it a waste, a luxury, or self-indulgence. Blacks are therefore more often likely to feel guilty or ashamed than proud for taking this step and tend more often to hide the fact of their analysis or therapy, or come with the desire to get in and get out as quickly as possible. Jones, Gray, and Jospitre (1982) commented, "In our society there is still a stigma attached to individuals who seek psychotherapy and a Black professional may feel he can least afford to have his mental competence or psychological stability questioned." In contrast, analysis is "in" for many White patients. Many proudly speak of "my shrink." However, Black patients tend to be more secretive. Also, many White middle-class educated professionals seek and prefer "analysis" rather than "support" and "someone to talk to."

Concern with the Structure of Analysis

"It just doesn't make any sense that it has to be so expensive, time consuming, rigid, and formal." Blacks appear to have more difficulty with the deprivation of visual contact (as occurs when the couch is used in psychoanalysis) and the lack of immediate and practical feedback. The result can be very intense feelings, loneliness, and in some cases suspiciousness. The anonymity of the analyst is sometimes especially difficult for Black patients coming to a Black analyst. This fact seems related to a custom or ritual widely practiced when middle-class Blacks meet one another — they quickly try to establish some link such as "Where are you from?" "Where did you go to school?" "Do you know . . .?"

Fears of the Consequences of Being in Analysis

- Fear of finding out negative things about oneself — e.g., that one is mentally ill, sexually abnormal, violent, etc.
- Fear of self-disclosure and spontaneity — may result in rejection by the analyst/therapist and others
- Fear of loss of control of one's own feelings — sexual, aggressive, dependent; there may be fear that one's feelings will be consuming or overwhelming
- Fear of loss of control to another — reflective of the fear of dependency in the passive position
- Fear of being changed, brainwashed, or forced to accept and adjust — as one patient put it, "being forced to give up my signature"

THE DEVELOPMENT OF
A THERAPEUTIC RELATIONSHIP

In order to begin and maintain an intensive, long-term, insight-oriented psychotherapy or psychoanalysis in the face of the patient's fears and resistance, both internal and external, it is necessary for the patient and therapist to form something more than instant rapport, positive feelings, or a sense of familiarity. Karasu (1980), for example, points out that psychotherapeutic change invariably occurs within the context of an interpersonal relationship between the patient and therapist and that the unique nature of this relationship is substantially different from the traditional physician–patient relationship in medicine. In psychotherapy the special relationship established may be the critical therapeutic agent. A real object relationship, a therapeutic alliance, and the transference have been identified as the basic forms or levels of relationship between the patient and therapist (Karasu, 1980).

Real Object Relationships

This level of relationship has to do with the actual visual characteristics, facts, and observations of the patient and analyst/therapist. It includes the decor and arrangement of the office, the fee, as well as such cultural characteristics as race, gender, ethnic group, social status, religion, and age. The behavior of the therapist is critical. His or her calm, interested, helpful, and empathic attitude is essential for providing a warm, understanding milieu which enables the patient to establish trust and to undertake the difficult task of treatment. The nature of the relationship at this stage is critical, although in some ways it seems the easiest. In talking about treatment of Black patients, Jones and colleagues (1982) noted that "establishing rapport and the therapist's engagement with the patient was less frequently a problem than most other treatment stages."

Therapeutic Alliance

This relationship level has been variously called therapeutic alliance (Zetzel, 1956), working alliance (Greenson, 1965), or treatment alliance (Sandler, Dare, and Holder, 1973). The therapeutic alliance is a conscious, rational, nonregressive aspect of the relationship between the patient and therapist. It represents an agreement to work together according to the requirements of the therapeutic situation.

Thus, it is essential to the work, and one of the major tasks of the
therapist is to foster its development. It is fostered in the patient by
the therapist's empathy, demonstrated through his or her awareness
of the realities of the external environment and social pressures the
patient is subjected to daily. It is strengthened through interpretations
of the patient's resistances. As Carter (1979) emphasized, Black
patients expect some response to their immediate and current problems. He points out that a frequent early mistake of the therapist is
to fail to deal with the immediate, more distressing problems before
moving on to a more introspective therapy.

Transference

Transference has been defined as "the displacement of patterns of
feelings and behavior, originally experienced with significant figures
of one's childhood, to individuals in one's current relationships"
(Moore and Fine, 1968). Transference has its most important therapeutic use in insight-oriented therapy and its maximum use in psychoanalysis. At the same time, according to Bird (1972), transference
is the most usual stumbling block for doing insight-oriented psychotherapy. He describes it as the greatest obstacle as well as the greatest
ally in the treatment process. Freud, as early as 1905, pointed out
that working with transference was the hardest part of the whole
task of analysis and described how the analyst would be tempted to
attenuate, modify, or even omit it. How well the transference can
be used in the treatment depends in large part on how firmly the
therapeutic alliance has been established.

According to Karasu (1980), the value of using the transference
in therapy is that it allows the patient, through frustration of the
gratification of immediate needs, to reexperience early childhood
wishes, conflicts, and reactions as though they were directly related
to the therapist. Exploration of these feelings, therefore, allows the
opportunity to develop insight and subsequent control of some of the
most deeply seated emotional conflicts and anxieties.

One of the biggest difficulties with the transference is dealing with
negative feelings — criticism, open anger, demands, teasing, and acting out, as well as the much more difficult, subtle, and often silent
ways the patient attempts to undermine and thwart every move by
the therapist and in a sense to destroy the very therapeutic process
he or she claims to want. There is a tendency on the part of the
therapist to avoid confronting and dealing with such negative feelings
and behavior. However, one cannot have a "safe," conflict-free ther-

apy and have much chance of reaching patients where they need to be reached.

Countertransference

Countertransference refers to attitudes and feelings, only partly conscious, of the therapist toward the patient. These responses may reflect the therapist's own unconscious conflicts, a displacement onto the patient of attitudes and feelings derived from earlier situations in the therapist's life. One of the cardinal purposes of analysts' or therapists' own analysis is to make them aware of their own conflicts and derivatives so that they do not distort the therapeutic work with patients by their own countertransference. The therapeutic process may become seriously impaired if the therapist does not attend to his or her own countertransference phenomenon.

The importance of countertransference was clearly expressed by Freud (1957), who noted that "we have become aware of the countertransference which arises in [the analyst] as a result of the patient's influence on his (the analyst's) unconscious feelings, and we are almost inclined to insist that he shall recognize this countertransference in himself and overcome it. . . . No psychoanalyst can go further than his own complexes and internal resistance permit."

As Freud himself advocated, the way to deal with countertransference of any sort is by analysis. The personal training analysis provides the major safeguard against countertransference problems for the analyst, but all too often the unconscious foundation and psychodynamics of basic racial issues are not worked with or worked through in the Black analyst's own analysis, which more often than not is with a White analyst. Supervision, which is another potential opportunity to deal with some of these issues, often falls short for similar reasons. To quote Viola Bernard (1953):

> If, therefore, an analyst has insufficiently analyzed his own unconscious material pertaining to his own group membership . . . he and his patients may be insufficiently protected from the interference of a variety of positive and negative countertransference reactions stimulated by the racial elements that are present in the analytic situation, the patient's personality, and in the specific content of the patient's material." (p. 259)

COUNTERTRANSFERENCE: BLACK THERAPISTS WORKING WITH BLACK PATIENTS

Clearly, therapists must deal successfully with their countertransference feelings. For purposes of this section the focus will be on those countertransference feelings, attitudes, conflicts and behaviors related to the fact that the therapist and the patient are both Black. Therapists working with Black patients have to deal with their own feelings, as well as the feelings that patients have, about being Black. There are some specific countertransference issues that seem to recur in Black therapist–Black patient psychotherapy and psychoanalysis.

Underemphasis or Denial of Racial Issues

Some Black therapists deny or minimize the importance of the racial factor. They attribute little or none of the responsibility for the patient's difficulties in life to racism. In some cases, it is true that the scant attention paid to racial issues per se is a valid expression of their minor importance to the patient at that time in regard to his or her presenting problem, stress, or conflict. But much more often the underemphasis represents a sidestepping of the issue or reflects a personal settlement of the racial issue by denial, suppression, or repression by both patient and therapist. Therapists blinding themselves to racial factors may play into patients' resistances as well as deny some of the social realities of their current existence.

Overemphasis of Racial Issues and Overidentification by Analyst

This tendency is based on a felt bond with another Black person, who is seen as an extension of oneself because of a presumed common racial experience. It is perhaps the primary problem of Blacks who work with Blacks. It may, as Calnek (1970) reports, result in joint griping sessions, or the therapist might, consciously or unconsciously, encourage the patient to gripe about, or act out, racial problems "without giving him much help with his non-racially linked problems" (p. 42).

The analyst may unwittingly become an ally of the patient's resistance in failing to grasp the unconscious defensive uses to which the Black patient may put racial matters. The patient may emphasize racial prejudice and discrimination as the cause of his or her problems. The mutual displacement, in which patient and analyst join forces and blame White society for the patient's ills, also serves to avoid dealing with aggression, competition, and other intrapsychic conflicts within the transference. A therapist who is uncomfortable and insecure with the fears and anxieties associated with his or her own aggression may have difficulty and try to avoid dealing with the usually subtle hostility, projections, competitiveness, and, indirectly, disparaging behavior of Black, especially male, patients. Pinderhughes (1973) outlined some of the indirect, nonadaptive aspects of dealing with aggression by Black patients that often become serious obstacles in the path of psychotherapy: denial, paranoid feelings and distrust, silence, claims of passivity, precipitation of crises, lateness, nonpayment of bills, and missed appointments. Pinderhughes advocated quick identification and interpretation of these resistances in order to engage the patient. These indirect, nonadaptive ways of dealing with aggression thus represent fear of direct assertiveness by the patient and can, if not recognized and dealt with, lead to serious countertransference difficulties, deprive the patient of the opportunity to deal with her or his anger, hostility, and resentments, and ultimately jeopardize the very continuation of the treatment.

Jones, Gray, and Jospitre (1982) found that "aggression/passivity was the most frequent unconscious conflict encountered in the survey. . . . Black men often have unresolved conflicts in this area because society does not allow them healthy expression of aggression [or] self-assertion" (p. 1176). The concern here is that the therapist not also deny the patient the opportunity to express his aggression. Thus, overidentification can be a countertransference form of resistance and serve to direct aggression outside of treatment rather than bringing it inside therapy, into the transference, so that it can be analyzed, understood, and thereby resolved or better integrated for the patient. The therapist must become comfortable and secure enough, within himself or herself, to avoid joining the patient in directing outrage against "those S.O.B.'s out there." In this way, the patient will be helped to direct some of that outrage to the S.O.B. sitting across the consultation room and thereby be given the opportunity to study the anger.

Class Difference and Black Prejudice

A third source of countertransference difficulties for Black therapists working with Black patients has to do with class differences and "Black prejudice." In American society one cannot talk about race without considering the mediating effects of class. In most discussions of Blacks there is little distinction made among the "Black elite," middle-class, lower-class, and the "underclass." However, there are very important differences, including values, cultural lifestyles, historical and current experiences, and extent of interaction with Whites.

Such things as skin color, hair texture, family origins, and educational and occupational status all play important roles in the conflicts and prejudices that exist within the Black communities. A large part of "Black neurosis" relates to how the families of Black patients dealt with these and similar issues. In growing up Black in America, one is likely to have experienced more direct conflict with other Blacks than with other racial groups. Consequences in therapy vary depending on whether patient or therapist belongs to the "higher prestige group" of the Black social hierarchy. The therapist may have to deal with intragroup, racially related feelings such as envy, jealousy, competitiveness, vindictive resentment, superiority, and inferiority.

Calnek (1970) observed that therapeutic work with Black patients is often felt to be low-status work because of the almost universal negative images and myths associated with Blacks. The therapist who already sees herself or himself as having low status may see that status as even lower when working with Black patients. The result could be countertransference feelings of anger at and rejection of Black patients as being unsuitable. On the other hand, Black therapists may be hard on their Black patients if the latter "acts White" because of the countertransference fear of recognizing the therapist's own tendency to deny her or his Blackness. Then again, the Black therapist may in effect insist that their patients "act White" before he or she accepts them, as an aid to help the therapist deny the fact that he or she is working with Black patients. As noted by Samuels (1971):

> The Black leader [therapist] who has achieved middle-class status may have taken over White perceptions and evaluations of the behavior of Blacks in the course of learning to compete successfully within the White system. In the process he may also have lost contact, to some extent, with the lifestyle of Blacks of lower socioeconomic status. In his efforts to keep a protective distance between his present life and his past, he may be prone to misjudge and be offended by certain aspects of Black behavior patterns.
>
> The same may be true for the Black leader who comes from White-oriented, middle-class family background and who has had little first-hand contact with lower-class patterns. This insecurity or ambiguity about his own identity may cause such a leader to insist, in effect, that Black patients act White before he accepts them, rather than accepting them in the context of their own lifestyle. (p. 734)

In other words, Blacks who manage to improve their socioeconomic condition may develop feelings of hatred and revulsion toward characteristics of their own group. Grier and Cobbs (1968) have described how Blacks may develop such hatred and contempt for their own self-image. According to Calnek (1970), Black therapists (and Black middle-class patients) who discourage or disapprove of lower-class Blacks' lifestyles may betray the therapist's desire to avoid remembering his own grueling struggle from lower class to middle class. Bradshaw (1978) pointed out that countertransference feelings and attitudes often are used to ward off feelings of inferiority and negativity in the therapist.

If therapists have not resolved conflicts connected with their own Blackness, they may be unable to help patients deal with theirs. A major prerequisite for Black therapists working with Black patients is a thorough examination of their own feelings, beliefs, and attitudes about being Black, their victimization, and their own racism and prejudice. In defining prejudice from a psychodynamic point of view, Samuels (1971) stated that prejudice often represents a faulty attempt to cope with intolerable feelings of self-contempt by directing the hatred away from the self onto another person or group, who serve as substitutes for the rejected parts of the self. The individual may then enjoy a feeling of superiority as he looks down on others. Black therapists and middle-class Black patients are clearly both victims of this projection, but they must also be willing to examine the extent to which they also use the same mechanisms. Unless therapists are aware of their own feelings about Whites as well as Blacks, they will be unable to help patients to deal with their own. Therapists, therefore, must come to grips with their own stance on racism.

ASSUMPTION OF SAMENESS

It is often a misleading assumption on the part of the Black analyst and Black patient that their bond is based on common experiences and attitudes: "You know what I mean" or "You know what it's like, Doc." Often the analyst does not. It is important for the analyst to remain aware of what was shared and what was not. There is a basic initial tendency on the part of many Black patients to prefer and feel more comfortable with a Black therapist, who they feel will be more understanding and accepting. There is some obvious, at least early, advantage to this arrangement, as Carter (1979) states: "Self disclosure is . . . a by-product of the patients' perception or belief that the helper is similar to himself" (p. 1008). And there is some validity for this in Pinderhughes's (1973) observation that "basically those who perceive themselves as members of the same group understand each other primarily by introjection and identification, while those who perceive themselves as members of different groups understand each other by projection" (p. 101). These dynamics would result in a more comfortable initial encounter, but unless recognized and dealt with could result in serious limitations in helping the patient arrive at an understanding of his or her individuality.

There is little doubt that Blacks of any social class or subgroup have a common bond by virtue of belonging to the same ethnic group and experiencing racism while growing up in America. But because of vastly diverse socialization experiences, based on varying exposure to educational, recreational, geographic, and sociocultural influences, as well as amounts and types of exposure to other racial and ethnic groups, there are marked differences in lifestyle, interests, and attitudes in Blacks.

In addition to different "growing up" experiences, many Black analysts have had most or all of their training in dynamic psychotherapy and psychoanalysis with predominantly White teachers and patients. At times, therefore, the Black analyst does not know what a Black patient "means," or "what it was like," and at times certain Black lifestyles may seem more unfamiliar than certain "White" lifestyles.

CONCLUSIONS

If Black therapists can work through the basic conflicts involving their own Blackness, they will be able to work empathically with Black patients without countertransference defensiveness leading to avoidance, denial, overidentification, rejection, pretense, or attempts to prove their Blackness. They will be able to utilize the feelings of countertransference as a tool rather than an obstacle, as in the description of Heimann (1950) of countertransference as an important phenomenon in helping the analyst to understand the hidden, unconscious meaning of material brought by the patient. Finally, by helping control of countertransference feelings, one is able to retain the professional attitude of a therapist which allows one to maintain a certain distance from the patient and yet remain in touch with one's own and the patient's feelings.

If not interfered with or distorted by countertransference, there are definite advantages that can be utilized when the therapist of the Black patient is also Black:

- Black therapists are not likely to misinterpret characteristic Black folkways and behavior as psychopathology
- Black therapists are better able to see positives and strengths within the context of the Black American lifestyle
- The fuller knowledge of the Black therapist of the patient's ways of life and those of his or her parents helps greatly in the establishment of mutual rapport, effective communication, and comprehension of the social reality in the patient's development and current situation
- Black analysts should be more able to see that not all of the patient's problems revolve around the condition of being Black
- The Black analyst is sometimes in a better position to differentiate the role of reality as reality and reality as defense

It is important for any therapist working with Black patients to keep in mind that not all psychiatric problems of Blacks derive from racial issues. To think otherwise is to dehumanize the Black person, to deny that he or she, like other persons, has conflicts, ambivalences, desires, and frustrations. Many of the difficulties of Black patients are psychoneurotic, arising out of early life experiences in the particular family constellation in which they grew up, as it is with anyone else. Discrimination serves to intensify neurotic problems of Black patients, but not to deform them psychologically. At the same time, to blot out the patient's Blackness serves to deny a significant aspect of his or her identity. So it is an error to ignore the issue of race, and an equally serious error to interpret whatever a patient says about race as defensive. Racial issues must be dealt with forthrightly in order to see the manner in which they have affected the patient's life, how they have affected the issues brought by the patient to therapy in the first place, and the extent to which they may be serving as a source of resistance to prevent the patient from dealing with deeper emotional conflicts. The Black therapist must not allow the fact of a patient's Blackness to obscure the view of the whole person, and thereby deprive the patient of reaching and working through whatever his or her basic difficulties may be. The therapist's goal, therefore, is to reach a point at which the Black patient can be viewed as an individual whose total being and specific life experience, including that of being Black, is the field of therapeutic interest and work.

REFERENCES

Allen, W. (1978). Black family research in the United States: A review, assessment and extension. *Journal of Comparative Family Studies, 9*, 167–189.

Bernard, V. W. (1953). Psychoanalysis and members of minority groups. *Journal of the American Psychoanalytic Association, 1,* 256–267.

Bird, B. (1972). Notes on transference. *Journal of the American Psychoanalytic Association, 20,* 267–301.

Bradshaw, W. H. (1978). Training psychiatrists for working with Blacks in basic residency programs. *American Journal of Psychiatry, 135,* 1520–1524.

Calnek, M. (1970). Racial factors in the countertransference: The Black therapist and the Black client. *American Journal of Orthopsychiatry, 40,* 39–46.

Carter, J. H. (1973). Race and its relevance to transference. *American Journal of Orthopsychiatry, 42,* 865–871.

Carter, J. H. (1979). Frequent mistakes made with Black patients in psychotherapy. *Journal of the National Medical Association, 71,* 1007–1009.

Evans, D. A. (1985). Psychotherapy and Black patients: Problems of training trainees, and trainers. *Psychotherapy, 22*(25), 457–460.

Freud, S. (1957). The future prospects of psycho-analytic therapy. In J. Strachey (Ed. and Trans.), *The standard edition of the complete psychological works of Sigmund Freud, 11,* 141–151. London: Hogarth Press. (Original work published 1910)

Greenson, R. R. (1965). The working alliance and the transference neurosis. *Psychoanalytic Quarterly, 34,* 155–181.

Grier, W. H., & Cobbs, P. M. (1968). *Black rage.* New York: Basic Books.

Heimann, P. (1950). On countertransference. *International Journal of Psychoanalysis, 31,* 81–84.

Jones, B. E., Gray, B. A., & Jospitre, J. (1982). Survey of psychotherapy with Black men. *American Journal of Psychiatry, 139,* 1174–1177.

Jones, B. E., & Gray, B. A. (1985). Black & White psychiatrists: Therapy with Blacks. *Journal of the National Medical Association, 77,* 19–25.

Karasu, T. B. (1980). General principles of psychotherapy. In T. B. Karasu & L. Bellak (Eds.), *Specialized techniques in individual psychotherapy* (pp. 133–144). New York: Brunner/Mazel.

Moore, B. E., & Fine, B. C. (Eds.). (1968). *A glossary of psychoanalytic terms and concepts.* New York: American Psychoanalytic Association.

Pinderhughes, C. (1973). Racism and psychotherapy. In C. V. Wilie, B. M. Kramer, & B. S. Brown (Eds.), *Racism and mental health* (pp. 61–121). Pittsburgh: University of Pittsburgh Press.

Samuels, A. S. (1971). The reductions of interracial prejudice and tension through group therapy. In H. I. Kaplan & B. J. Sadock

(Eds.), *Comprehensive group psychotherapy* (pp. 724–753). Baltimore: Williams & Wilkins.

Sandler, J., Dare, C., & Holder, A. (1973). *The patient and the analyst: The basis of the psychoanalytic process.* New York: International Universities Press.

Thomas, A., & Sillen, S. (1972). *Racism and psychiatry.* New York: Brunner/Mazel.

Zetzel, E. R. (1956). Current concepts of transference. *International Journal of Psychoanalysis, 37,* 369–376.

22

Group Psychotherapy:
An Alternate Form of Treatment

Wayman B. Cunningham and
Henry E. Edwards

The purpose of this chapter is to describe the basic concepts of group psychotherapy and examine its use with Black middle-class patients at Howard University Hospital over a 15-year period. Our discussion is not about race-related issues that are played out between Blacks and Whites in American society, but about treatment of maladaptive behavior that the mental health professional is faced with in treating Black middle-class patients.

A review of the literature on group psychotherapy reveals few articles describing this form of treatment with Black middle-class patients. For the most part, when Black patients are involved, the emphasis is on group therapy or group process with (a) interracial groups, as a means of reducing racial tensions and enhancing self-awareness of racial differences; (b) homogeneous groups, such as alcoholics, drug addicts, or schizophrenics; and (c) groups of adolescents or adults with minor adjustment problems. For resolving intrapersonal and interpersonal conflicts of Black middle-class patients experiencing daily life crises that reduce the effectiveness of coping mechanisms, group psychotherapy, it would seem, is almost nonexistent. We believe, however, the contrary is true, and that Black and White therapists use this modality of treatment with Black middle-class patients more often than is reported in professional literature.

The opinions we offer draw on clinical experience in working with group psychotherapy as a model of treatment for Black patients of all classes and with groups consisting of patients with various ethnicities as well as the Black middle class. The implication is that group psychotherapy has meaning and value for any hospital, clinic, or private practitioner treating Black patients. Our experiences, reflected in this chapter, clearly indicate that the basic principles of group psychotherapy do not have to be altered in working with Black middle-class patients.

DEFINITION AND TYPES

Before defining group psychotherapy, we must define psychotherapy, since group psychotherapy is one form of it. Psychotherapy is a modality that treats persons with emotional difficulties through psychological means, that is, verbal communication rather than chemical or biological intervention (Kolb, 1968). More specifically, psychotherapy is a process established in the relationship between a professionally trained therapist and a person with emotional difficulties. By assuming an empathic, nonjudgmental, accepting attitude, the therapist in this relationship creates a psychological atmosphere in which the patient can explore conflicting thoughts and feelings that are uncomfortable, often confusing, and sometimes frightening.

Group psychotherapy, as defined by Kaplan and Sadock (1971a), is a "form of treatment in which carefully selected emotionally ill persons are placed in a group, guided by a trained therapist, for the purpose of helping one another effect personality change. By means of a variety of technical maneuvers and theoretical constructs, the leader uses the group members' interaction to bring about that change."

Types of group psychotherapy fall into two broad categories: (a) "dynamic" or "uncovering" therapies and (b) the "supportive" therapies (Kolb, 1968). The dynamic therapies are usually long term and seek to effect change in the structure of the personality. The supportive suppressive therapies, however, are frequently short term and seek to suppress or alleviate troubling symptoms.

The dynamic therapies include the psychoanalytic group therapies, which are based on Freud's psychoanalytic theory of personality. Some therapists believe that psychoanalysis can be carried out in a group in which the focus is primarily on the unconscious motivation of the patient's behavior and the interpretation of transference (Kaplan and Sadock, 1971b). On the other hand, there are therapists, dynamic in their thinking, who focus on what goes on among the group members in the "here and now" (Kaplan and Sadock, 1971b). Others use the "transactional approach," which focuses almost exclusively on the "here and now," fosters positive relationships, and analyzes negative feelings (Kaplan and Sadock, 1971a).

Under the supportive group therapies are the "inspirational groups," such as Alcoholics Anonymous, where members share common experiences and support one another; the "discussion groups," where the members engage in decision making and cooperation in order to complete a task; and the "confrontive groups," where the therapist confronts the patient with observed symptoms and provides dynamic explanation for them. The confrontive groups are used frequently to treat psychotic patients (Kaplan and Sadock, 1971b).

HISTORY

Group psychotherapy began in this country in the early 1900s when J. H. Pratt, a Boston physician, started to hold classes in his home for tubercular patients who could not afford to go to a sanatorium (Kaplan and Sadock, 1983). Although Pratt probably did not have group psychotherapy in mind, he noticed that the patients learned how to manage their medical and emotional problems through the sharing of symptoms and feelings.

Group psychotherapy progressed slowly after this unexpected beginning. Major contributions, however, have come from such early practitioners and writers as Adler, Slavson, Schilder, and Moreno (Kaplan and Sadock, 1983). More recent additions to the field have appeared from contributors like Foulkes, Bion, and Yalom (Kaplan and Sadock, 1983; Yalom, 1975).

STRUCTURE

When patients begin dynamic group psychotherapy, they meet regularly in a group with one to two therapists once or twice a week for one to two hours. These groups usually include six to eight members, because fewer than six patients usually does not provide the stimulation necessary for group interaction. More than eight patients limits the time that each patient has for involvement and hinders the therapist's professional guidance of the issues. The number of patients in the inspirational, supportive, and activity groups may be larger, because the purpose of these groups is to support patients and strengthen their healthier defenses as a means of suppressing or alleviating troubling symptoms; this process requires a less intensive focus than that of the dynamic groups.

During group meetings, the therapist, who has a thorough knowledge of each patient's psychiatric history and basic maladaptive pattern, facilitates interaction among the patients. Although the patients focus primarily on the therapist, they become involved with each other and along with the therapist interpret the issues (Kaplan and Sadock, 1971a). Through this process they give feedback to one another.

As a consequence of this interaction, members of the group begin to perceive each other in ways similar to their interactions with siblings and parents. Some of their earlier patterns of behavior, conflicting feelings, and emotions surface and manifest themselves in interaction with the other group members, especially the therapist. Through the development of a cohesive psychological atmosphere, norms are established to encourage the study of behavior and to offer constructive feedback. The group structure, therefore, provides a channel for correcting the maladaptive behavior manifested in the interaction of patients. As the members become more invested in the group, they gain the strength to take risks and to expose their conflicting thoughts and feelings. This lowering of defenses enables the patients to accept feedback from others, to evaluate their behavior, and to begin correcting their maladaptive behavior patterns (Yalom, 1975).

SCREENING PATIENTS

In some circles group psychotherapy is viewed as a lesser form of treatment, one to be used for improving socializing techniques or for patients considered unacceptable for other modes of treatment. However, group psychotherapy can be a viable form of treatment for patients in many diagnostic categories.

Useful for the so-called normal population, the group method contributes to the accomplishment of educational tasks and personal growth. The T-groups and sensitivity groups popular in the early seventies promoted personal development via the group method. By contrast, group psychotherapy is a form of treatment for patients with maladaptive difficulties, that is, neurotic or character disorders. The goals differ with each category of illness (Kaplan and Sadock, 1971a).

Before placing patients into groups, the therapist should screen very carefully. Indispensable are a thorough knowledge of the patient's psychosocial history, level of defenses, basic conflicts — conscious and unconscious — and a dynamic formulation of the patient's problem.

It is often asked whether groups should be homogeneous or heterogeneous in terms of problem, age, race, sex, and socioeconomic level. We endorse the view that the therapist should be selective but that groups should be as heterogeneous as possible to ensure interaction.

The issues involved in the selection process are more related to ego strength than to the type of problem presented. In the university setting where we treated Black patients from different socioeconomic backgrounds, the issue often arose with attending physicians and medical students in training whether patients with different social backgrounds should be placed together in groups. There seemingly was a tendency with the attendings and students, often more implied than expressed overtly, that middle-class Black patients should be treated in a group more homogeneous to social class rather than to ego strength. Because we were pioneers in implementing group therapy in this setting, we rigidly applied the standard group psychotherapy principles and selected patients more on the basis of ego strength than social class.

Mixing Black patients from different socioeconomic backgrounds worked well in groups if ego strengths did not differ greatly. After the initial resistance, which is manifested differently by different patients, the patients worked openly with their problems and seemed more concerned with their pain than with their social attitudes. In addition, we found that such mixing enabled the patients to change their initial perceptual distortions.

When patients are screened properly, the therapist can decide the modality of therapy that will be most helpful to each patient. The following case history illustrates this point:

C was a 29-year-old single Black woman whose surface symptoms in a screening interview led to a diagnosis of a hysterical personality with depressive features. She was placed in an insight-oriented uncovering group for treatment. After going through the initial resistive phase, she formed an intense transference with the male therapist who, with a female therapist, led the group. Although it appeared that the patient was attempting to resolve this issue in the group, she had an affair with a married man and became pregnant. All of her depressive symptoms disappeared; she became bright and cheerful and apparently had no other thoughts than to have the baby. When she returned to the group after delivery, she wanted to bring the baby to the meetings. The therapist explained that the group rules would be violated and interference with the group process would occur, and someone should keep the baby while she attended the group meeting. The patient didn't accept these suggestions, became involved in an intense struggle with the therapist and the other group members, and withdrew from the group. One week later, in a psychotic state, she had to be removed from the group and placed in another form of treatment.

Had this patient been properly screened, the diagnosis would have indicated a more severe illness beneath the surface symptoms. That the patient did not have the ego strength to be placed in an insight-oriented psychotherapy group would have been clearly determined.

Another issue often discussed is whether patients with different ethnic or racial backgrounds, especially Blacks and Whites, should be placed together in group psychotherapy. Experience suggests that patients with different racial backgrounds work very well together if the racial issue is not ignored and is recognized as a possible resistive phenomenon, and not exclusively an issue of social attitudes. Caution is necessary, however, when only one member of an ethnic group is placed in an insight-oriented group with others from a different ethnic group. Very often, in this situation, the majority tends to scapegoat the minority member, expecting him or her to have answers to ethnic issues and to solve the racial problems. In these circumstances, the therapist has to be especially protective of the minority patient and also fully aware of his or her own countertransferences.

CO-THERAPY

In group therapy there are two primary leadership models: (1) a trained therapist in a group with six to eight patients and (2) two trained therapists with a selected number of patients. When group therapists are fully trained and skilled, leadership style may be selected on the basis of preference or theoretical orientation. Some therapists prefer to work alone and feel that the group structure by itself is an effective stimulant. Others have proposed that the co-therapy model is most effective, especially when one therapist is female and the other is male, in stimulating issues relevant to the early family structure (Bardon, 1966). Male and female co-therapists are especially useful in working with nonpsychotic Black middle-class men and women who demonstrate difficulties in their intimate relationships as a significant part of their presenting problem. In such instances the male and female co-therapists provide actual behavior and interactions with each other that serve as a model for imitative behavior and identification, in addition to their clarifying the interpretive interventions. Our experience points to a greater tendency in the early phases of the group for Black middle-class men and women to see their co-therapists as models, as like them, and for lower-class patients to more readily see their therapists as authority, parental figures. If the group therapy continues for a long enough time, these early distinctions between lower and middle class disappear and what Yalom (1975) calls a "recapitulation of the early family experience" occurs, in which both lower- and middle-class patients develop transference to the co-therapists as significant parental and other figures from early life.

Most training programs utilize the co-therapy model, particularly when in the early phase a less experienced therapist is working for training purposes with a senior professional. The co-therapy model involves certain principles that should not be used exclusively for the training of group therapists or for convenience (e.g., one therapist can run the group while the other goes on vacation or is absent for other reasons). In the co-therapy model, it is held that patients form transferences and connection with both therapists. Frequent absences of a therapist stimulate feelings of neglect and rejection in the patients and can affect group cohesiveness.

The co-therapy model introduces an additional variable in the screening of patients for group psychotherapy. It is a common practice for therapists to see patients for five or six individual sessions prior to placing them in the therapy group, a practice that enables the patient to establish a relationship with the therapist. This feeling of connection to some significant person in the group serves as a buffer for the anxiety sometimes generated by initial interaction with the other group members. When patients see only one therapist in the pre-sessions, they tend to focus on that therapist later in treatment and exclude the other therapist. This situation often stimulates competitiveness between the therapists and can disrupt the group process. Preferably, the leadership responsibilities should be assumed equally by the therapists.

THE PROBLEMS PATIENTS BRING TO GROUP
THERAPY, AND HOW GROUP THERAPY HEALS

Do Black middle-class patients bring issues to group therapy that are significantly different from those brought by White middle-class patients? Black middle-class patients, like patients of other racial or ethnic groups, come to group therapy because they are malcontent. Though not totally dysfunctional, they are usually feeling unsettled with certain life issues related to their interpersonal relations (i.e., with family, friends, or co-workers) on an intimate or platonic basis. Patients' goals for therapy are often very vague. They express a certain tension level which remains despite numerous maladaptive attempts to reduce it, such as abuse of alcohol and other drugs, fights with loved ones, and sexual acting out of feelings.

Through group therapy, patients begin to find out more about themselves as things unfold. After the tensions are reduced, patients become eager to learn what type of people they are and how they are perceived by others. Often surprised to find that others perceive them altogether differently from the way they perceive themselves, patients start questioning the issues other members have raised about themselves.

Metaphorically, a thin cord that runs through all of the members enables them to form a cohesive unit with its own group personality. It provides a protective shelter for risk taking, and for exploring secrets and fleeting thoughts others have stimulated. For example:

M was a 22-year-old single Black woman with a college degree who presented with feelings of anxiety and lowered self-esteem. She experienced difficulties asserting herself at work. In the early phase of the group, this patient was extremely cautious about her participation and would respond only when called on by the therapist or one of the other group members. After several months of treatment, she observed another member, who was leaving the group, participate in a "go around" — a session in which she was to tell each member how she had experienced them during her stay in the group. Because this patient had worked through most of her issues and was an experienced group member, she was extremely frank, if not at times caustic. After she finished and had received positive feedback from the other members, the therapist asked Ms. M if she thought she could do something like that. After some hesitation, she agreed to try. At first she was somewhat timid and made only positive comments to the others. She repeatedly stated that she felt the other members wouldn't like her for her comments. However, after she had spoken to the second person, Ms. M's comments became more sharp, bristling, and at one point outright hostile.

When Ms. M was asked to explore her thoughts and feelings, she was able to express pent-up anger toward her parents and to recall childhood memories of how she was never allowed to express angry feelings at home. After this experience in the group, Ms. M became very assertive at work and participated in a rather daring maneuver with her co-workers to expose some of the inequities imposed by her employer.

Do Black middle-class patients hold racial prejudice primarily responsible for their maladjustment? The core conflicts that often contribute to the maladaptive behavior of middle-class Black patients differ very little from those reported by White patients. However, in group settings this issue of race frequently comes up. Sometimes there are very valid reasons for the topic to surface; then, it is explored fully. At other times, however, as a result of group interaction, race emerges in the form of projection or the patient's resistance to facing some painful issues about self. When patients are reporting conflicts experienced in their personal and intimate relationships, they say, with some degree of affect, "That is just how Black men are," or, "That is just how Black women are," rather than exploring aspects of their personality that could be contributing to the conflict. It then becomes the task of the group to help these patients overcome the resistive behavior and to explore further their intrapersonal issues.

On occasion, the patient can skillfully and emotionally present resistive issues in the form of racism and stimulate countertransference in the therapist. As a result, the therapist may process the racial content as the valid issue and ignore the resistive phenomenon. In such a situation the resistive behavior is reinforced and the patient misses the core conflicts.

Of additional interest is the variability with which the racial issue surfaces in short- and long-term groups composed of patients of different races and socioeconomic backgrounds. In short-term groups the racial issue seems to surface more rapidly with patients of both lower and higher socioeconomic level. With the lower-socioeconomic-level patient, the theme is usually "We are of different color, but that makes no difference; we should work together to overcome our common problem and love each other." With the middle-class patient in the racially mixed group, the racial issue seems to surface lightly but often, discussed as an insignificant variable. In long-term racially mixed groups, the racial issue tends to surface more slowly and often in the form of resistance; but by then cohesiveness is high, and the issue tends to be worked through rapidly if appropriately handled by the therapist. The patients at this level tend to concentrate more on working with intrapersonal issues through the interpersonal interaction with all patients than with the racial phenomenon.

EXPERIENCES WITH GROUP THERAPY
AS A TREATMENT MODEL FOR BLACK
PATIENTS IN A UNIVERSITY HOSPITAL SETTING

Group psychotherapy began in a formal sense as a treatment and training modality in the Howard University Hospital in 1971. Two psychiatrists and a psychologist were instrumental in planning and implementing the program.

The initial focus of these pioneers was with groups consisting of psychiatric inpatients in the acute phase of their illness. The groups were composed of university students and Black middle- and lower-class patients from the Washington, D.C., metropolitan area. The primary goals of the psychotherapy groups were to treat the patients and help them identify some of the issues that had resulted in their hospitalization. This experience allowed the patients to share their symptoms and issues and to interact with each other under the guidance of a trained therapist. As a result of this process and other therapeutic factors, their illness was stabilized and they were prepared for further treatment after discharge from the hospital. Later, the group program was expanded to the outpatient clinic, where supportive group psychotherapy was given to stabilize psychotic patients and insight-oriented group psychotherapy was used with patients with neurotic, character, and adjustment disorders.

The introduction of group therapy at this University Hospital had a mixed reception. With lukewarm administrative and professional staff support, it was often viewed as a lesser form of therapy. For example, some of the attending physicians would say, "My patients don't have to be involved in that sort of thing." Patients themselves offered resistance (e.g., they came to the hospital to relax; they didn't want to work in any group therapy; the group would stir things up; they didn't want to share their problems with others; they wanted to talk privately with their doctors; "My problems are different"). In some ways, the presenting problems were different. Since we had heterogeneous groups, the same group would often contain people with problems of alcoholism, schizophrenia, and depression. Also, the patients in the group would most likely be from different socioeconomic classes: they might have represented the unemployed, laborers, professionals, or the spouses of physicians. Basically, the resistance showed lack of understanding of how group psychotherapy works.

We were constantly faced with questions as to the relevance of group therapy and whether it works any differently with Black patients. Our answer is that despite resistance, group psychotherapy grew and persisted. When others began to understand that group therapy is a highly definitive modality of treatment with specific operations, principles, and techniques and not just a process of putting people in a room and letting them talk, it became accepted. The problems behind the distrust and fear of group therapy were clearly related to (a) lack of knowledge about the techniques of group therapy, (b) inability of the patient to use the self as a therapeutic agent for the recognition of inner fears, anxieties, and countertransferences, and (c) ignorance of the value of group therapy as a treatment modality. Resolution of these problems led to the development of an extensive group psychotherapy program in the Department of Psychiatry of the hospital.

GROUP PSYCHOTHERAPY AS A
TRAINING AND TREATMENT MODEL IN A
PREDOMINANTLY BLACK HOSPITAL SETTING

The group psychotherapy training program delineated here trains psychiatry residents and psychology interns to become practicing group therapists. The training program is divided into two related parts, dealing with inpatients and outpatients. The former consists of didactic orientation sessions, inpatient group observation, inpatient group participation and supervision, postgroup sensitivity sessions, a literature review seminar, and an experiential process group. The second half engages trainees in the observation of neurotic outpatients in groups and supervised outpatient therapy with neurotic and psychotic groups.

The training year begins with a lecture series about the basic concepts of group psychotherapy and the technical procedures employed in conducting therapy groups. Following the didactic series, trainees observe senior therapists treating inpatients who are acutely ill. After two weeks, the trainees conduct a therapy group with a trained therapist and shortly thereafter with one of their peers while the supervisor observes.

The inpatient psychotherapy groups provide the patients with an emotional reorientation through discussion. By coming into direct and meaningful verbal interaction with members of the group, the patient modifies feelings and habitual modes of responding.

The groups are open-ended, extremely heterogeneous, and, for the most part, represent a different composition at each meeting. Unless directed otherwise by their private physician, all patients on the psychiatric service, regardless of the nature of their problems, are expected to attend the group therapy sessions. Consequently, patients may be from many diagnostic psychiatric categories (e.g., psychotic, neurotic, alcoholic).

This type of group experience with inpatients is somewhat different from the traditional approach to treatment. However, the following goals, if achieved, aid patient recovery:

1. To provide an atmosphere where inpatients, often feeling socially isolated, can share current experiences, symptoms, fears, and feelings
2. To orient patients to examine some of the issues and conflicts that resulted in hospitalization
3. To give patients a treatment experience through interaction with other patients and the therapist, and, as a consequence, motivate them for more treatment
4. To give the therapist who has responsibility for the total treatment of patients an opportunity to observe maladaptive behavior in group interaction and to obtain further clarification of issues for diagnosis

Immediately following each session on the inpatient service, the observing supervisor conducts a session with other therapists, students, and ward staff who assumed a nonverbal participatory role at the group session. In this postgroup the members share the feelings they experienced as they observed patients interacting. This sharing enables the trainee to understand, through personal reactions, the patient's expressed affect, sometimes intense, and to develop a tool for comprehending the role of self in the dynamics of patient treatment procedures.

The following case example explains the importance of the first goal:

Ms. A was a 22-year-old college student who presented with an acute paranoid episode and complained of olfactory hallucinations. She was extremely withdrawn and frightened by this experience and isolated herself from the other patients. After the first group therapy session, this patient stopped the therapist in the hallway and thanked him for letting her into the group session. She explained how relieved she felt when she heard other patients describe similar symptoms and experiences. She had felt that she was the only one in the world who could have such an experience.

Although this patient was receiving other forms of treatment, she immediately became much more responsive to treatment and shortly thereafter was discharged from the inpatient service.

While the trainees are in the group training program, they meet regularly with their supervisors for technical supervision and attend a literature review seminar in which they discuss previously assigned articles on group psychotherapy. In addition, the trainees participate in a process group conducted by a trained therapist not associated with the teaching and administrative aspects of the program. The trainees therefore learn about group process through a threefold approach: (1) experiencing it individually in their group, (2) reading about and discussing professional issues in the literature review seminar, and (3) observing the process in action as they conduct groups.

The second part of the training program is housed in the outpatient mental health clinic. Here, the trainees observe (through a one-way mirror) an insight-oriented group being conducted by a trained therapist. They learn how to select patients to form a psychotherapy group with both stabilized psychotic (supportive) and neurotic/character disordered (insight-oriented) patients. The groups, conducted by a trained therapist, most often run for the course of the training period.

Since the mid-1970s, when this group program became fully developed, many trainees have successfully completed the program. Its far-reaching effects are apparent in the following example:

Dr. B, a former resident of Asian background, entered the group program with limited knowledge of group psychotherapy principles and techniques. He also had not been exposed to the cultural background of most of the patient population that he was expected to treat. Although Dr. B struggled with the English language and his emotional reactions to the patients, he mastered group psychotherapy concepts, became sensitized to his feelings in the therapy situation, and learned to use his feelings as a tool for understanding the dynamics of his patients. After completing the program and his residency training, he secured a position in a teaching hospital where the psychiatric orientation was predominantly biomedical. In the new setting, Dr. B secured permission to begin a group psychotherapy program on the inpatient service. As a result of a successful program, Dr. B has published articles describing the outcome of his patients treated with group psychotherapy.

CONCLUSIONS

In this chapter the aim has been to describe the authors' experiences over the past 15 years in using group psychotherapy as an effective treatment modality for Black patients in a university hospital setting with special emphasis on the Black middle class.

Because training and experience are critical in being able to accept and use this treatment method effectively, the chapter has included a section on training group psychotherapists who, for the most part, will be treating Black patients upon completion of their studies. The training approach outlined here not only teaches the basic didactic principles and techniques of group psychotherapy, but also gives the trainees multiple opportunities to experience and examine their own feelings, attitudes, and prejudices in a group setting. They also learn to make use of "the self" as a vital part of the diagnostic treatment process.

Although Black middle-class patients who live in a White-dominated society who present with mental health issues are strongly affected by the stress and pressures of such a society, it seems that the basic conflicts and the maladaptive coping mechanisms revealed by Black middle-class patients in group therapy situations vary only slightly from those reported by White middle-class patients. In addition, it appears that group psychotherapy is used more often by both Black and White therapists with Black middle-class patients than is reported in the literature.

REFERENCES

Bardon, E. J. (1966). Transference reactions to the relationship between male and female co-therapists in group therapy. *Journal of the American College Health Association, 14,* 287–289.

Kaplan, H. I., & Sadock, B. J. (1971a). *Modern synopsis of comprehensive textbook of psychiatry III* (3rd ed.). Baltimore: Williams & Wilkins.

Kaplan, H. I., & Sadock, B. J. (1971b). *Comprehensive group psychotherapy.* Baltimore: Williams & Wilkins.

Kaplan, H. I., & Sadock, B. J. (1983). Comprehensive group psychotherapy (2nd ed.). Baltimore: Williams & Wilkins.

Kolb, L. C. (1968). *Noyes' modern clinical psychiatry* (7th ed.). Philadelphia: Saunders.

Yalom, I. D. (1975). *The theory and practice of group psychotherapy.* New York: Basic Books.

23

Therapeutic Interventions with Troubled Children

Harry H. Wright

The specific rates of occurrence of most childhood mental disorders are not available (Gould, Wunsch-Hitzig, and Dohrenwend, 1981). Various studies have estimated the prevalence of such disorders as attention deficit disorder, childhood depression, and autism, but the range is considerable (Lotter, 1966; Walzer and Richmond, 1973; Carlson and Cantwell, 1980). In some cases, the reported prevalence rates varied from 1 to 50%, depending on the setting studied and the criteria used for diagnosis. A minimum overall rate of 12% has been estimated for childhood mental disorders (Gould et al., 1981). It has been recognized that the prevalence rate of developmental, emotional, and behavioral disorders in children varies with sex, age, ethnic group, social class, and geographic region (Langer, Gersten, and Eisenberg, 1974; Rutter et al., 1975, 1976; Rutter, 1977; Kellam, Ensminger, and Turner, 1977; Gould et al., 1981).

The literature indicates that children are at a greater risk for developmental, emotional, and behavioral disorders if they grow up in stressful environments (Brenner, 1979; Garmezy and Streitman, 1974). Racial prejudice has been and continues to be a major source of stress for Black children from all social classes (Willie, Kramer, and Brown, 1973). For Black children from lower socioeconomic classes, the effects of racism and poverty and the resultant poor opportunity to benefit from the various socioeconomic advantages have been considered to be a major factor in the increased risk of psychiatric disorders (Hallowitz, 1975).

Even when poverty is not a major issue, racism can have a devastating impact on the development of Black children. However, despite racial prejudice, most Black children and families make a healthy social and psychological adjustment to the environment they live in (Billingsley, 1968). Many Black children and families, however, do require therapeutic intervention and are referred for treatment. This chapter focuses on therapeutic interventions with troubled Black children from middle-class families.

SPECIFIC CHARACTERISTICS OF BLACK MIDDLE-CLASS FAMILIES

Black middle-class parents, defined as economically secure and upwardly mobile, bring their children for evaluation and treatment for the same reasons as do other families (Mishue, 1983; Rutter, Cox, and Tanting, 1975). However, there are difficulties that arise for Black middle-class children that are unique to their sociocultural situation. We will focus on some of these difficult issues.

Today most authors acknowledge that Black families are not so different from other ethnic families in structure and function (Gutman, 1970; Hall and King, 1982; Pinderhughes, 1982). Like other families, Black families struggle to provide for their needs. Although they are economically secure, middle- and upper-class Black families frequently face problems that stem from racism and systemic discrimination. All Black families must develop adaptive techniques to survive the life struggle and stress of the duality of existence in two or more subcultures (Devore, 1983). To understand this adaptive functioning, Black families must be viewed within the larger context of American society. This includes examining not only the values and attributes of the family, but its members' interactions with the neighborhood peer group, church, school, job, government, and economic institutions (Gutman, 1970).

Traditionally, some of the things that have helped Black families survive have been the kin-structure network, elastic households, steadfast optimism, resilient children, and egalitarian parental relationship, wherein both partners share equally in decision making and varying roles (Hall and King, 1982). Unfortunately, many of the traditional strengths of Black families gradually have been eroded after entrance into the middle class. The strong kinship bonds have been frequently lost or diluted by geographical distance.

Most Black middle-class children are placed in the position of having to conform to and understand the patterns of both Black and White middle-class society. This is often too much for any child to manage, even with appropriate preparation from parents or others. Many Black middle-class children, unfortunately, do not receive adequate preparation for what they will face in the broader society. Some are protected from the harsh realities of life and often grow up with a perception of the world that is quite different from that of other Black children who are continuously faced with the cold realities of poverty and stress. As a result, some of these children do not receive important information and may have serious identity problems. Others are able to balance their existence in a world of two different subcultures and with the advantage of economic security and motivation for achievement, go on to do very well.

Being a Black middle-class child is not a homogeneous experience. For example, the Black middle-class child living in a small town may be viewed as a prominent, very well known pace-setter who comes from one of the most economically secure families in the community. In contrast, the Black middle-class child living in a large urban area may be one of many, with no special status among his peers, and having no extraordinary family status in the community. Middle-class children living in small towns more often have very high expectations placed on them by their families and the community. However, they also have advantages derived from their parents' economic position, and privileges that come from the family's history and social status in the community.

Many middle-class Black children have the opportunity to travel with their families, and are exposed to a broad view of the world. They have more material things and more exposure to other cultural and ethnic groups than their peers from less well-off families. However, Black middle-class parents worry that their children are ill prepared to face the problems and conflicts of a society in which racism and discrimination still exist.

ASSESSMENT OF THE PRESENTING PROBLEM

One of the first tasks in assessing a child's problem is to determine whether there is a disorder for which treatment is needed. The fact that the child has been referred indicates that someone has a concern. The issue of concern may turn out to be a normal stage of development, a minor problem that does not require treatment, a problem that requires minimal therapeutic intervention, or a major individual or family problem that requires significant therapeutic interventions over a period of months to years.

An accurate assessment and diagnosis is most important, because the therapeutic intervention follows from this evaluation. An initial step is to obtain a developmental history and a history of current symptoms and behavior. If the child is determined to have a disorder, then the extent of impairment must be assessed.

Clearly, a comprehensive assessment requires a basic understanding of the sociocultural context from which the child comes as well as the individual assets and liabilities of the child. For the Black child, this is often problematic because of the numerous negative stereotypes that exist about Black children and families (Bender, 1939; Wilkinson and Spurlock, 1986; Ten Houten, 1970; Bennett, 1986; Bradshaw, 1978). Many of these stereotypes continue to drive the therapeutic intervention prescribed for Black children and their families.

Although there should be a recognition of the effects of racism on the development and functioning of Black children, the clinician should not view the child solely as a victim of a racist society and ignore the role of biological and intrapsychic factors in the etiology of the presenting problem.

One of the major problems, that of misdiagnosis of Black patients of all ages, has been well documented (Adebimpe, 1981; Mukherjee et al., 1983; Jones and Gray, 1986; Lawson, 1986). This issue of misdiagnosis is particularly problematic when Black children are involved, because the type of intervention, or lack of it, has much longer term consequences for these very malleable young patients. In addition, the biases, myths, and misconceptions about Black children last for decades and can continue to guide interventions long after they have been identified and refuted (Wilkinson and Spurlock, 1986). One of the major myths about Black children is that certain diagnoses, such as conduct disorder and psychosis, occur more frequently among them than in the dominant group. In fact, the prevalence of most psychiatric disorders do not differ in Blacks and Whites when standardized diagnostic protocols are used (Abramson and Wright, 1981; Adebimpe, 1981; Lawson, 1986).

Diagnostic accuracy has been reported to be related to the sociocultural distance between the patient and the diagnostician (Jackson, Berkowitz, and Farley, 1974; Abramson and Wright, 1981). Historically, Blacks have been referred for different types of interventions (Rosenthal and Frank, 1958) and to different settings (Wilder and Callhan, 1963; Lewis, Shanok, Cohen, Kligfeld, and Frisone, 1980; Sue, 1977) than Whites. These studies imply that the observed referral pattern may be due in part to misdiagnosis or misconception about Black patients. Appropriate and effective therapeutic interventions with Black children and their families follow from an accurate assessment of the referral situation.

THERAPEUTIC INTERVENTIONS
WITH BLACK CHILDREN AND
THEIR FAMILIES: LITERATURE REVIEW

There are several reports that indicate that the type of therapeutic intervention recommended by providers is associated with race (Lewis et al., 1980; Griffith, 1977). Black patients are more likely to be seen for diagnosis only (Jackson, Berkowitz, and Farley, 1974). Blacks are judged to be less suitable for insight therapy (Flaherty and Meagher, 1980). Black adolescents are more likely to be referred to non–mental health service settings (Lewis et al., 1980; Stehno, 1982). Additionally, studies indicate that Blacks are more likely to drop out of treatment settings, which have a predominantly White staff (Warren, 1972), and if they continue in treatment, there are many issues (e.g., anxiety about racial difference in the therapeutic relationship, the therapist's attitude toward Black culture) that must be addressed by the therapist (Ridley, 1984; Gardner, 1971; Griffith, 1977; Jones and Gray, 1983) if the outcome is to be positive. Most often, these issues are not addressed during treatment (Brantley, 1983).

It is important for clinicians to understand the diversity among Blacks in terms of educational attainment, socioeconomic status, and value orientation (Jones and Gray, 1983). However, for all Blacks the stresses of daily life are amplified by the oppressive nature of the common experience with covert and overt racism. It is equally important for the therapist to understand that ethnicity may play a major role in determining how a patient seeks help, and what he or she defines as a problem and views as a useful intervention. Unless ethnic variables are taken into account, therapeutic interventions are sure to fail (Sue, 1981; Acosta, Yamamoto, and Evans, 1982). Therapists' willingness and ability to examine their own attitudes and feelings about working with Black patients should lend success to the intervention (Wilkinson and Spurlock, 1986).

There are several reports that have focused on psychotherapy and Black patients (Carter, 1979; Gray and Jones, 1987; Jones and Gray, 1983), and a few that have focused on psychotherapeutic interventions with Black children (Spurlock, 1985; Heacock, 1980). However, most of the reports on therapeutic intervention with Black children have focused on children from poor families (Hallowitz, 1975). Very little has been written about therapeutic interventions with Black children of the middle class (Bagarozzi, 1980; Scanzoni, 1971; Frazier, 1966).

IDENTITY ISSUES FOR
BLACK MIDDLE-CLASS CHILDREN

Children from Black middle-class families are often viewed to be less resilient than same-race peers. They have been described as very easily frustrated and self-centered. Some have been labeled as shallow and as having little empathy when compared with less advantaged Blacks. Others have been described as indecisive and as having few interests outside of collection of material objects. On the other hand, others are known to be very sensitive to the fact that their family's moving ahead has left others behind. They feel guilty about their privileged position and are not able to participate fully in the community in a positive way. These are the children who may get involved in self-destructive behavior and delinquency. Furthermore, they may mistakenly associate Black identity with such behaviors. In doing so, they maintain some of the same stereotypes about Blacks that are held by many of the dominant group.

Although rarely a presenting problem, racial identity and self-concept are common issues for Black middle-class children in therapeutic settings. A case example will help illustrate some of the unique aspects of identity development that Black middle-class children bring to treatment.

T.W., a 13-year-old Black girl, was referred for evaluation because of poor school performance, social withdrawal, and increased oppositional behavior at home.

She was the second of three children (both siblings doing well). Father was a middle manager in a national company; the mother had worked part-time as a librarian for the past two years.

T.W. reported some difficulty in getting enough sleep for the last four months. She also had minor physical complaints (headaches and muscle pain). She had no close friends; she reported discomfort with both the Black and White children in her school, since she did not fit in with either group.

The father's promotion had led to the family's move (two years earlier) from another state to the current city of residence (the mother's childhood home). There were very few Black residents in the community from which the family had moved; their closest friends lived about 15 miles away in another city. Until the move, T.W. had attended a public school where there were fewer than 20 Black children enrolled.

Both parents grew up in middle-class families and attended predominantly Black primary and secondary schools. However, they attended an integrated college (with few Blacks) and moved to a sparsely integrated community when the father obtained a job offer after his graduation.

T.W. was having significant difficulty adjusting to her new community and school. For the first 10 years of her life, she had associated almost exclusively with children and families of the dominant group. Aside from her nuclear family and one other Black family, she was isolated from the Black community. Her knowledge of Blacks was gained primarily from television. Although T.W., like most children, became aware of racial differences during her preschool years, the issue of race was never discussed and, in fact, was ignored in her nuclear family. T.W. incorporated this attitude about race and quickly learned that race, like sex, was a very uncomfortable topic for parental discussion.

After the family's move, the parents frequently initiated visits with the children's maternal grandparents and other relatives. However, T.W. tried to spend as little time as possible with them, and admitted feeling uncomfortable with the relatives. The family remained somewhat isolated from the many positive Black role models in the larger community. Again, the family had settled in a sparsely integrated neighborhood and rarely attended the church of their extended family.

T.W.'s school did not provide an environment for positive Black identity development. Although the school was 40% Black, there were few Black teachers to serve as role models and counselors. Black students did not invite or encourage T.W.'s involvement with them because they viewed her as a shallow, materialistic adolescent with whom they had nothing in common. White students essentially ignored T.W.'s attempt to socialize with them.

Although it is generally accepted that the sociocultural context is of primary significance in the development of identity (Logan, 1981), T.W. has not had the benefits of situations in her family, school, or community that promoted her Black identity development. The therapeutic intervention with T.W. and her family involved enhancing her sociocultural context to promote positive identity development and working psychotherapeutically with T.W. on the issues of how she sees herself and how others see her.

Biracial Children: Complexity of Identity Development

For the biracial child, the issue of identity development is more complex. As the number of biracial children, currently estimated at one million (Gibbs, 1987), continues to increase, they may be expected to come to therapeutic settings more often, with issues primarily related to identity development.

The following case vignette will serve to illustrate the increased complexity that biracial children face in identity development.

> L.M., an 8-year-old biracial girl, was referred because of aggressive and oppositional behavior at home and school. There was a younger brother, aged 6. The father, who was Black, owned a small business. His extended family lived in the area. The mother, who was White, was enrolled in graduate school in nursing. Her family lived in a distant state, but she had frequent contact with them. The family lived in a mixed neighborhood with several biracial families within several blocks of its residence. After ten years of marriage, the mother still felt uncomfortable with her husband's family, who had not helped her feel at ease. Racial issues were not openly discussed in the family, but the mother admitted she did not consider her children to be Black, although they were clearly identified as Black children by the community. The brother had been more involved with the extended paternal family than L.M., who had been isolated and protected from intensive involvement by her mother.
>
> The parents had different opinions about events that daily had an impact on L.M. The most frequent discussion involved L.M.'s hair; the father liked it styled one way, the mother another. L.M. had difficulties with her interaction with schoolmates, Black and White; the former frequently made racial comments, such as calling her "Oreo." She had never told her parents about the racial slurs. She usually ended up in a fight with the children who called her names.

L.M. had conflicts about her racial identity that she could not talk about with her parents. In fact, her mother had not accepted the fact that others identified L.M. as a Black child, and was not able to talk about her daughter's dual racial and sociocultural heritage. These issues were not openly discussed by the parents, but fought out in arguments about other things, such as L.M.'s hairstyle. Whereas the

6-year-old brother had clearly identified with his Black relatives and viewed himself as Black, L.M. had not had the opportunity for such contacts with her paternal extended family. As a result, she was not able to cope with the racial slurs in school and this caused her significant difficulty, which was manifested in aggressive behavior at school and at home. Whereas some biracial children have difficulty in integrating their dual heritage and tend to overidentify with one parent's heritage and reject the other, most are able to adjust and are very comfortable with their biracial identity (Poussaint, 1984; Norment, 1985). L.M. was not able to integrate her dual heritage or identify with her father. Achieving a comfortable position with respect to dual heritage is nearly impossible without appropriate parental help. It is usually the responsibility of the Black parent to prepare the biracial child to deal with the racial slurs he or she will certainly encounter. Ideally, both parents should expose their children to their dual heritage and teach them to value both cultures. Parents should also acknowledge the reality of racism. To discount racism in the society is to ill prepare the children for what they will encounter. The major goal of therapy with L.M. was to help her value her dual roots and to point out ways to cope with the negative experiences she had with other children. The therapist did not relate each of her referral problems to race. Attention was also directed to conflicts within the family and herself.

Promotion of Positive Identity Development

In both of these cases involving conflicts with identity, the therapist worked with the child psychotherapeutically in ways that have been well described (Logan, 1981; Spurlock, 1985, 1986; Gibbs, 1987) and also helped the family to enhance the sociocultural context for the child. Identity development for Black middle-class children has been promoted by: (1) increasing the child's identification with the extended family, (2) increasing the child's socialization experiences with Black peers, and (3) assisting school personnel in promoting appropriate identity development (e.g., encouraging formal teaching about Black history and culture).

AUTONOMY ISSUES FOR
BLACK MIDDLE-CLASS CHILDREN

Middle-class Black children frequently come to therapeutic settings with issues of autonomy and high parental expectation. The autonomy issue is an exaggeration of the separation-individuation conflict seen in many adolescents. Black middle-class parents have frequently sheltered and overprotected their children from the prejudice and discriminating practices of the larger society. The children respond to the parental sheltering by either rebelling against the protection or becoming overly dependent and passive. Middle-class Black children are frequently conflicted about their inability to meet parental expectations. Some children react by putting all their energy into academics; others take a negative attitude toward achievement and lack the motivation to aspire to their best. The "battles" between a 17-year-old boy, C.S., and his father illustrate the struggle with autonomy and parental aspiration that many middle-class Black children face.

C.S., the youngest of three children and the only boy, was referred for evaluation because of poor school performance, fighting, and lying. C.S. had experienced academic problems throughout his school career. There was a very poor relationship with the father, who was very achievement oriented and expected his son to do well in school. Each of C.S.'s failures provoked both anger and disappointment in his father. C.S. felt that his father expected more of him than he could deliver. As a result, he had adopted an antiachievement orientation and developed a negative attitude toward school.

Black middle-class parents must realize that many of their children are not going to do as well as they expect. Some will not do as well as their parents. This is very difficult for Black middle-class parents, because the average parents believe that their children will do a lot better than they, in status, economic level, education, and other measures. Sometimes, parents do not see certain talents and creativity in their children because they have already decided on a career path for the child. First generation middle-class Black parents tend to have more investment in assuring that their children are outstanding.

PSYCHOPHARMACOLOGICAL INTERVENTIONS

A comprehensive therapeutic intervention with a troubled middle-class Black child includes consideration of psychosocial (primarily psychotherapy) and biological approaches to treatment. Some of the issues in the psychosocial treatment of children have been discussed.

The biological issues, primarily those concerning the use of psychoactive medications, are discussed in this section.

Although psychopharmacology is much less developed in children than in adults, increasing numbers of children are being prescribed medications (Fish, 1968; Kraft, 1968; Werry, 1977; Blau, 1978; Belfer, 1979; Absanuddin, Ivey, Schultzhauer, Hall, and Prosen, 1983; Werry and Aman, 1975).

The decision to place a child on a regimen of psychotropic medication is most frequently based on the presenting symptomatology or diagnosis. Three specific populations of children — those with thinking disorders, depression, and attention deficit disorders (Pfefferbaum and Overall, 1984) — are most frequently prescribed psychoactive medications. It has also been suggested that race plays a role in prescribing medication. For example, Black patients are more likely to be seen for prescribing of medication than for psychotherapy (Yamamoto, James, and Palley, 1968). Additional investigation is needed to determine if this pattern is primarily an issue of misdiagnosis or if other factors are involved. The role of demographic variables, including race, in prescribing psychotropic medication for children has not been extensively examined. One study reported no significant difference in the prescribing of psychoactive medications on the basis of gender in children (Ray, Schaffner, and Federspiel, 1986). There are no controlled studies on the effect of race in prescribing psychoactive medicine for children. Aside from the issue of misdiagnosis of disorders in Black children, the prescribing of psychoactive medication for these children is assumed not to significantly differ from that for children of the dominant group. The use of neuroleptics (Campbell, Anderson, and Green, 1983), antidepressants (Rancurello, 1985), and psychostimulants (Dulcan, 1985) in the childhood population has recently been reviewed and will not be discussed here. Because the field of child psychopharmacology is uncertain and unsettled (Gaultieri, Golden, and Fahs, 1983), psychoactive medication should be used only in the context of a comprehensive therapeutic intervention program for the child, including, of most importance, an accurate diagnosis of the psychiatric disorder, if present.

In therapeutic intervention with children, medications are adjunctive to the psychosocial treatments. The therapeutic effectiveness of psychotropic medication in children has been determined on an empirical basis in clinical settings. On the basis of clinical observation and some controlled studies (Conners and Taylor, 1980; Rapoport et al., 1980; Werry and Aman, 1975; Shapiro and Shapiro, 1982; Campbell, Anderson, and Green, 1983), several medications have been shown to play a major role in treating certain disorders and a possible role in other disorders.

Before starting a regimen of psychoactive medication, children should have a general medical and neurological examination and routine laboratory tests. For antidepressants, electrocardiograms at baseline and at dose elevation are useful to monitor cardiac side effects. For lithium, a thyroid screen and determination of blood creatinine and electrolyte levels at baseline are suggested. Other laboratory tests are advised for other medications and have been extensively described in the literature. The dosage of medication should be reevaluated every 6 to 12 months with consideration of a trial off medication if lower doses are tolerated well. When stopping medication, all (except perhaps lithium) should be tapered slowly while watching for recurrence of symptoms and withdrawal effects.

There is an emerging literature on the racial and ethnic differences in response to psychoactive medications (Overall et al., 1969; Ziegler and Briggs, 1982; Lin and Finder, 1983; Rudorfer et al., 1984). There has been little done with respect to the medication response of Black patients and nothing with Black children, because Black patients, including children, are often perceived to be more violent than Whites. Blacks are at high risk to receive more and higher doses of psychoactive medication (Flaherty and Meagher, 1980; Lawson, Yesavage, and Werner, 1984). This misconception about Black patients often leads to misuse of psychoactive medications.

Psychoactive medication may increase or decrease the effectiveness of other treatment interventions and educational programs for Black middle-class children. The expected effects and risk of use of psychoactive medication must be constantly reevaluated and a judgment made as to the benefit of continuing the drug treatment.

CONCLUSIONS

Although Black middle-class children have many of the problems experienced by other children, there are some that are unique to their situation. The issues of identity and autonomy frequently arise as problems with which Black middle-class children and their parents have to deal. Although racism is ever present, it does not explain all the issues of concern for Black middle-class families. A comprehensive assessment of the problems prior to intervention with troubled middle-class Black children requires a basic knowledge of Black middle-class families, and skills and comfort in dealing with them. It is important for providers to understand that there is considerable diversity among Black families, and to account for this diversity when planning intervention with them.

REFERENCES

Abramson, R. K., & Wright, H. H. (1981). Diagnosis of Black patients. *American Journal of Psychiatry, 138,* 1515.

Absanuddin, K. M., Ivey, J. A., Schultzhauer, D., Hall, K., & Prosen, H. (1983). Psychotropic medication prescription patterns in 100 hospitalized children and adolescents. *Journal of the American Academy of Child Psychiatry, 22,* 361–364.

Acosta, F. X., Yamamoto, J., & Evans, L. (1982). *Effective psychotherapy with low income and minority patients.* New York: Plenum.

Adebimpe, V. R. (1981). Overview: White norms and psychiatric diagnosis of Black patients. *American Journal of Psychiatry, 138,* 279–285.

Bagarozzi, D. A. (1980). Family therapy and the Black middle-class: A neglected area of study. *Journal of Marital and Family Therapy, 6,* 159–166.

Batey, S., and Wright, H. (1982). Psychoactive drug use before treatment in a child psychiatry clinic. *American Journal of Hospital Pharmacy, 39,* 1675–1678.

Belfer, M. L. (1979). Psychotropic medication in acute psychiatric disturbances in children. *Journal of Family Practice, 8,* 503–507.

Bender, L. (1939). Behavioral problems in Negro children. *Psychiatry, 2,* 213–228.

Bennett, L. (1986). The 10 biggest myths about the Black family. *Ebony, 41*(10), 123–133.

Billingsley, A. (1968). *Black families in White America.* Englewood Cliffs, NJ: Prentice-Hall.

Blau, S. (1978). A guide to the use of psychotropic medications in children and adolescents. *Journal of Clinical Psychiatry, 39,* 766–772.

Bradshaw, W. H. (1978). Training psychiatrists for working with Blacks in basic residency programs. *American Journal of Psychiatry, 135,* 1520–1524.

Brantley, T. (1983). Racism and its impact on psychotherapy. *American Journal of Psychiatry, 140,* 1605–1608.

Brenner, M. H. (1979). Influences of the social environment on psychopathology: The historical perspective. In J. E. Barrett (Ed.), *Stress and mental disorder.* New York: Raven Press.

Brown, J. A. (1987). Casework contacts with Black-White couples. *Social Casework, 68,* 24–29.

Campbell, M., Anderson, L. T., & Green, W. H. (1983). Behavioral disordered and aggressive children: New advances in pharmacology. *Journal of Developmental and Behavioral Pediatrics, 4,* 265–271.

Carlson, G. A., & Cantwell, D. P. (1980). A survey of depressive symptoms, syndrome, and disorders in a child psychiatric population. *Journal of Child Psychology and Psychiatry, 21,* 19–25.

Carter, J. H. (1979). Frequent mistakes made with Black patients in psychotherapy. *Journal of the National Medical Association, 71,* 1007–1009.

Conners, C. K., & Taylor, E. (1980). Pemoline, methylphenidate and placebo in children with minimal brain dysfunction. *Archives of General Psychiatry, 37,* 922–930.

Devore, W. (1983). Ethnic reality: The life model and work with Black families. *Social Casework, 64,* 525–531.

Dulcan, M. (1985). The psychopharmacologic treatment of children and adolescents with attention deficit disorder. *Psychiatry Annals, 15,* 69–86.

Erikson, E. H. (1956). The problem of ego identity. *Journal of the American Psychological Association, 4,* 56–121.

Fish, B. (1968). Drug use in psychiatric disorders in children. *American Journal of Psychiatry, 124,* 31–36.

Flaherty, J., & Meagher, R. (1980). Measuring racial bias in inpatient treatment. *American Journal of Psychiatry, 137,* 679–682.

Frazier, F. F. (1966). *The Negro family in the United States.* Chicago: University of Chicago Press.

Gardner, L. H. (1971). The therapeutic relationship under varying condition of race. *Psychotherapy Theory Research and Practice, 8,* 78–87.

Garmezy, N., & Streitman, S. (1974). Children at risk: The search for the antecedents of schizophrenia: Conceptual models and research method. *Schizophrenia Bulletin, 8,* 14–90.

Gaultieri, C. T., Golden, R. N., & Fahs, J. J. (1983). New developments in pediatric psychopharmacology. *Journal of Developmental and Behavioral Pediatrics, 4,* 202–209.

Gibbs, J. T. (1987). Identity and marginality: Issue in the treatment of biracial adolescents. *American Journal of Orthopsychiatry, 57,* 265–278.

Gould, M. S., Wunsch-Hitzig, R., & Dohrenwend, B. P. (1981). Estimating the prevalence of childhood psychopathy: A critical review. *Journal of the American Academy of Child Psychiatry, 20,* 462–476.

Gray, B. A., & Jones, B. E. (1987). Psychotherapy and Black women: A survey. *Journal of the National Medical Association, 79,* 177–181.

Griffith, M. S. (1977). The influence of race on the psychotherapeutic relationship. *Psychiatry, 40,* 27–39.

Gutman, H. G. (1970). *The Black family in slavery and freedom, 1925–1950.* New York: Pantheon Books.

Hall, E. H., & King, G. G. (1982). Working with the strengths of Black families. *Child Welfare, 61,* 536–544.

Hallowitz, D. (1975). Counseling and treatment of the poor Black family. *Social Casework, 56,* 451–459.

Heacock, D. R. (1980). The Black adolescent patient. In D. R. Heacock (Ed.), *A psychodynamic approach to adolescent psychiatry: The Mount Sinai experience.* New York: Marcel Dekker.

Jackson, A., Berkowitz, H., & Farley, G. (1974). Race as a variable affecting the treatment involvement of children. *Journal of the American Academy of Child Psychiatry, 13,* 20–31.

Jones, B. E., & Gray, B. A. (1983). Black males and psychotherapy: Theoretical issues. *American Journal of Psychotherapy, 37,* 77–85.

Jones, B. E., & Gray, B. A. (1986). Problems in diagnosing schizophrenic and affective disorder among Blacks. *Hospital and Community Psychiatry, 37,* 61–65.

Kellam, S., Ensminger, M. E., & Turner, R. J. (1977). Family structure and the mental health of children. *Archives of General Psychiatry, 34,* 1012–1022.

Kraft, I. A. (1968). The use of psychoactive drugs in the outpatient treatment of psychiatric disorders of children. *American Journal of Psychiatry, 124,* 1401–1407.

Langer, T. S., Gersten, J. C., & Eisenberg, J. G. (1974). Approaches to measurement and definition in the epidemiology of behavior disorders: Ethnic background and child behavior. *International Journal of Health Services, 4,* 483–501.

Lawson, W. B. (1986). Racial and ethnic factors in psychiatric research. *Hospital and Community Psychiatry, 37,* 50–54.

Lawson, W. B., Yesavage, J. A., & Werner, P. D. (1984). Race, violence, psychopathology. *Journal of Clinical Psychiatry, 45,* 294–297.

Leckman, J. F., Cohen, D. J., Detlor, J., Young, J. G., Harcherik, D., & Shaywitz, B. A. (1982). Clonidine in the treatment of Tourette syndrome. *Advances in Neurology, 35,* 391–401.

Lewis, D. O., Shanok, S. S., Cohen, R. J., Kligfeld, M., & Frisone, G. (1980). Race bias in the diagnosis and disposition of violent adolescents. *American Journal of Psychiatry, 137,* 1211–1216.

Lin, K. M., & Finder, E. (1983). Neuroleptic dosage for Asians. *American Journal of Psychiatry, 140,* 490–491.

Logan, S. L. (1981). Race identity and Black children: A developmental perspective. *Social Casework, 62,* 47–56.

Lotter, V. (1966). Epidemiology of autistic condition in young children. *Social Psychiatry, 1,* 124–137.

Lyles, M. R., Yancey, A., Grace, C., & Carter, J. H. (1985). Racial identity and self esteem: Problems peculiar to biracial children. *Journal of the American Academy of Child Psychiatry, 24,* 150–153.

Mishue, J. M. (1983). *Clinical work with children.* New York: Free Press.

Moynihan, D. P. (1965). *The Negro family: The case for national action.* Washington: Department of Labor.

Mukherjee, S., Shukla, S. S., Woodle, K., Rosen, A. M., & Olarte, S. (1983). Misdiagnosis of schizophrenia in bipolar patients: A multi-ethnic comparison. *American Journal of Psychiatry, 140,* 1571–1574.

Norment, L. (1985). A probing look at children of interracial marriages. *Ebony, 40*(10), 156–162.

Overall, J. E., Hollister, L. E., Kimball, I., & Shelton, J. (1969). Extrinsic factors influencing responses to psychotherapeutic drugs. *Archives of General Psychiatry, 21,* 89–94.

Parson, E. R. (1985). Ethnicity and traumatic stress. In C. Figley (Ed.), *The study and treatment of post-traumatic stress disorder.* New York: Brunner/Mazel.

Pfefferbaum, B., & Overall, J. E. (1984). Decisions about drug treatment in children. *Journal of the American Academy of Child Psychiatry, 23,* 209–214.

Pinderhughes, E. B. (1982). Family functions of Afro-Americans. *Social Work, 27,* 91–96.

Poussaint, A. (1984). Study of interracial children present positive picture. *Interracial Books for Children Bulletin, 15,* 9–10.

Powell, G., & Fuller, M. (1972). The variables for positive self concept among young southern Black adolescents. *Journal of the National Medical Association, 43,* 72–79.

Rainwater, L. (1966). Crucible of identity: The Negro lower class family. *Daedalus, 95,* 172–216.

Rancurello, M. D. (1985). Clinical applications of antidepressant drugs in childhood behavioral and emotional disorders. *Psychiatry Annals, 15,* 88–100.

Rapoport, J. L., Buchsbaum, M. S., Weingartner, H., Zahn, T. P., Ludlow, C., & Mikkelsen, E. J. (1980). Dextroamphetamine: Its cognitive and behavioral effects in normal and hyperactive boys and men. *Archives of General Psychiatry, 37,* 933–943.

Ray, W. A., Schaffner, W., & Federspiel, C. F. (1986). Differences between female and male children in the receipt of the prescribed psychotropic and controlled analgesic drugs. *Medical Care, 24,* 801–813.

Ridley, C. R. (1984). Clinical treatment of the non-disclosing Black client. *American Psychologist, 39,* 1234–1244.

Rosenthal, D., & Frank, S. (1958). Fate of psychiatric clinic outpatients assigned to psychotherapy. *Journal of Nervous and Mental Disorders, 127,* 330–343.

Rudorfer, M. V., Lane, E. A., Chaney, W. H., Zhang, M. D., & Potter, W. F. (1984). Desipramine pharmacokinetics in Chinese and Caucasian volunteers. *British Journal of Clinical Pharmacology, 17,* 433–440.

Rutter, M. (1977). Classification. In M. Rutter & L. Hersov (Eds.), *Child psychiatry: Modern approaches.* Oxford: Blackwell Scientific.

Rutter, M. (1985). *Helping troubled children.* New York: Plenum Press.

Rutter, M., Chadwick, O., & Tule, W. (1976). Adolescent turmoil, fact or fiction. *Journal of Child Psychology and Psychiatry, 17,* 35–56.

Rutter, M., Cox, A., & Tanting, C. (1975). Attainment and adjustment in two geographical areas. *British Journal of Psychiatry, 126,* 493–509.

Scanzoni, J. H. (1971). *The Black family in modern society.* Boston: Allyn & Bacon.

Shapiro, A. K., & Shapiro, E. (1982). Clinical efficacy of haloperidol pimozide, penfluridol, and clonidine in the treatment of Tourette syndrome. *Advances in Neurology, 35,* 383–386.

Spurlock, J. (1985). Assessment and therapeutic intervention of Black children. *Journal of the American Academy of Child Psychiatry, 24,* 168–174.

Spurlock, J. (1986). Development of self concept in Afro-American children. *Hospital and Community Psychiatry, 37,* 66–70.

Spurlock, J., & Lawrence, L. E. (1979). The Black child. In J. Noshpitz (Ed.), *Basic handbook of child psychiatry, Vol. 1.* New York: Basic Books.

Stehno, S. M. (1982). Differential treatment of minority children in service systems. *Social Work, 27,* 39–45.

Sue, D. W. (1981). *Counseling the culturally different.* New York: Wiley.

Sue, S. (1977). Community health services to minority groups: Some optimism, some pessimism. *American Psychologist, 32,* 616–624.

Takahashi, R. (1979). Lithium treatment in affective disorders: Therapeutic plasma level. *Psychopharmacology Bulletin, 15,* 32–35.

Ten Houten, W. D. (1970). The Black family: Myth and reality. *Psychiatry, 33,* 145–173.

Walzer, S. W., & Richmond, J. B. (1973). The epidemiology of learning disorders. *Pediatric Clinics of North America, 20,* 549–565.

Warren, R. (1972). Different attitudes of Black and White patients toward psychiatric treatment in a child guidance clinic. *American Journal of Orthopsychiatry, 42,* 301–302.

Werry, J. S. (1977). The use of psychotropic drugs in children. *Journal of the Academy of Child Psychiatry, 16,* 446–468.

Werry, J. S. (1982). An overview of pediatric psychopharmacology. *Journal of the American Academy of Child Psychiatry, 21,* 3–9.

Werry, J. S., & Aman, M. G. (1975). Methylphenidate and haloperidol in children: Effects on attention, memory, and activity. *Archives of General Psychiatry, 32,* 790–795.

Wilder, J., & Callhan, M. (1963). The walk-in psychiatric clinic: Some observations and follow-up. *International Journal of Social Psychiatry, 9,* 192–199.

Wilkinson, C. B., & Spurlock, J. (1986). The mental health of Black Americans. In C. Wilkinson (Ed.), *Ethnic psychiatry.* New York: Plenum.

Willie, C. V., Kramer, B. M., & Brown, B. S. (Eds.). (1973). *Racism and mental health.* Pittsburgh: University of Pittsburgh Press.

Wilson, J. (1978). Growing up "White": The crisis of the Black middle-class child. *Black Enterprise, 9*(4), 28–34.

Wood, W. D., & Sherrets, S. D. (1983). Race as a factor in the perceived importance of the use of psychotropic medication. *Journal of Psychiatric Research, 17,* 297–301.

Yamamoto, J., Fung, D., Lo, S., & Reece, S. (1979). Psychopharmacology for Asian Americans and Pacific Islanders. *Psychopharmacology Bulletin, 15,* 29–31.

Yamamoto, J., James, Q. C., & Palley, N. (1968). Cultural problems in psychiatric therapy. *Archives of General Psychiatry, 19,* 45–49.

Ziegler, V. E., & Briggs, J. (1982). Tricyclic plasma levels: Effect of age, race, sex, and smoking. *Journal of the American Medical Association, 238,* 457–460.

Afterword

Of particular significance in this volume are the references that point to the heterogeneity of the Black middle class (C. Pinderhughes, Coner-Edwards and Edwards), and the race-related stresses referred to by each contributor. We are aware that more questions have been raised than answers or solutions given. It is our hope that the questions will stimulate further study and explorations.

We are also aware that a number of significant issues have not been addressed, or have been mentioned only briefly. In the preliminary conceptualization of the volume, it was recognized that time and space constraints would not permit the inclusion of every important issue. Several contributors have touched upon significant topics that were not dealt with in depth. For example, only passing references have been made to the significance of religion.

It has been noted that religion and religious institutions have served Black Americans well, even though religion has not served consistently or in all situations operated to foster the advancement of Black people (Wilmore, 1983). Yet, historically, religious institutions have been the mainstay for Black Americans.

Biracial/bicultural families constitute another topic that warrants further attention in any discussion about Black families. Spurlock and Booth refer to the topic in a case vignette through the comments of the parents of an adolescent girl. The parents "wondered about their reactions (and the responses of the extended family) should one of their children choose to marry across racial lines." Historically, miscegenation has been a controversial issue even though the practice has existed in this country since the early 1600s. Black Americans have not responded to our complex heritage with one voice. Some associate their White ancestry with the sexual exploitation of the slavery era, and view their mixed heritage with shame or anger. Others have publicly acclaimed their White heritage (e.g., the Black descendants of Thomas Jefferson). The long history of the biracial/

bicultural background of Black Americans, and how this history has influenced our coping styles, warrants further study.

Coner-Edwards called attention to same-sex gender preference as one of the factors in the increased separation and divorce rates, but the topic has not been dealt with in depth in this volume. The intensity of homophobia and racist practices in large pockets of the country places Black homosexuals in positions of double jeopardy. A gay person "coming out of the closet" has been known to generate considerable discord for some families; for others, conflict is of minimal significance or absent. Homosexuality is but one of the subjects related to sexuality and Black Americans that warrants further exploration.

We recognized that we are not free of biases and that we needed to guard against the "tyranny of experts" as we reviewed the manuscripts we received. Accordingly, we requested some input from individuals who were not trained as health service providers. Their reviews of several original manuscripts and of our critiques were helpful in identifying significant blind spots and unsubstantiated conclusions.

We challenge our colleagues to search for answers to the questions that have been raised in this volume. Each of us might well add to the body of knowledge about Black American families, a body of knowledge that could increase our understanding of the functioning of other families and their individual members.

REFERENCE

Wilmore, G. S. (1983). *Black religion and Black radicalism.* Maryknoll, New York: Orbis Books.

Alice F. Coner-Edwards
Jeanne Spurlock

Name Index

Abramson, R. K., 273
Absanuddin, K. M., 280
Acosta, F. X., 274
Adebimpe, V. R., 273
Adler, A., 257
Akbar, N., 207
Alderfer, C. P., 23
Allen, J., 174, 176, 181
Allen, W., 239
Alleyen, S. I., 181
Altman, J., 44
Aman, M. G., 280
American Psychiatric Association, 197
Anderson, J., 172, 173
Anderson, L. T., 280
Anonwu, E., 176
Antley, R. M., 173
Arling, G., 106
Ashe, A., 165–166

Babor, T. F., 199–200, 208
Bacon, F., 150
Bacon, S., 200
Bagarozzi, D. A., 220, 275
Baker, E., 51, 188
Baldwin, W., 91
Bales, R. F., 40, 43
Balir, S., 280
Ball, R., 39
Ballard, J., 142
Bardon, E. J., 261
Barrett, L., 150
Battle, S. F., 170, 171, 174, 175, 178, 181
Beattie, A., 176
Belfer, M. L., 280
Bell, C. C., 207
Bender, L., 273
Bennett, L., 84, 101, 273
Benoit, M. B., x, xiii, 114, 139–146, 147, 149–155
Bergman, A. B., 172, 173

Bergum, K., 163
Berkowitz, H., 273, 274
Bernard, V. W., 246
Berne, E., 234
Betts, J., 190
Billingsley, A., 1, 38, 39, 107, 116, 271
Bion, W., 257
Bird, B., 245
Birren, J. E., 99
Blood, R., 38
Bloom, B. S., 129
Blumstein, P., 62
Booth, M. B., x, xiii, 77, 79–88
Bowen, M., 215
Boyd-Franklin, N., 220, 222
Boykin, A. W., 129
Bradshaw, W. H., Jr., v, x, xiii, 213–214, 240–241, 250, 273
Braithwaite, P., 224
Braithwaite, R. L., 61
Brantley, T., 274
Brenner, C., 64–65, 69, 72
Brenner, M. H., 270
Briggs, J., 281
Brisbane, F. L., 206
Broady, E., 102
Brown, W. E., 180
Brubaker, T. H., 100
Buchsbaum, M. S., 280
Butler, A., 100

Caldwell, F. J., 207
Callhan, M., 273
Calnek, M., 247, 249, 250
Campbell, B. M., 56
Campbell, M., 280
Cantwell, D. P., 270
Carlson, G. A., 270
Carter, J. H., 245, 250, 274
Castelli, W. P., 166
Cazenave, N. A., 61, 62, 63
Census Bureau, 2

291

Thomas, A., 240
Thomas, J. F., 172
Thompson, C., 53
Thompson, J. D., 191
Thompson, Y., 190
Treas, J., 99
Tropouer, A., 175
Tule, W., 270
Turner, R. J., 270

U.S. Department of Health and Human
  Services, 164, 199, 201, 203

Vaughn, W. M., 177
Vaughn family, 216
Vavasseur, J., 174
Viorst, J., 232
Vogelson, E., 44

Wackman, D. B., 44
Walker, K., 154
Wallach, E. E., 192
Walzer, S. W., 270
Waring, E. M., 182
Warren, R., 274
Watson, C., 81
Watson, G., 17
Watson, J., 18
Watson, W. H., 104
Webster's Seventh New Collegiate
  Dictionary, 16
Weiner, M. F., 160
Weingartner, H., 280
Weintraub, F. J., 142
Weisman, C. S., 119

Werner, P. D., 281
Werry, J. S., 280
Wesley, C., 29
White, I., x, xiii
White, R. W., 117
Whitten, C. F., 171, 172, 174, 176,
  177, 178, 182
Wilder, J., 273
Wilkinson, C. B., 273, 274
Williams, I., 170, 171, 174, 176–177,
  178
Williams, J., 18, 200
Willie, C. V., 270
Wilmore, G. S., 289
Winch, R. F., 40
Wint, E., 181
Wolfe, D., 38
Womble, M., 206
Woodle, K., 273
Woodridge, E. Q., 173
Wright, H. H., 147, 170–183, 213,
  270–282
Wunsch-Hitzig, R., 270

Yalom, I. D., 257, 258, 261
Yamamoto, J., 274, 280
Yesavage, J. A., 281
Yohalem, D., 142

Zabin, L. S., 91
Zahn, T. P., 280
Zelnik, M., 92
Zetzel, E. R., 244
Zhang, M. D., 281
Ziegler, V. E., 281

Subject Index